Sport Psychiatry

Theory and Practice

A NORTON PROFESSIONAL BOOK

Sport Psychiatry

Theory and Practice

Daniel Begel
and Robert W. Burton
Editors

W. W. NORTON & COMPANY
New York • London

Printed in the United States of America
First Edition

Composition by Bytheway Publishing Services
Manufacturing by Haddon Craftsmen

Library of Congress Cataloging-in-Publication Data
Sport psychiatry : theory and practice / Daniel Begel and Robert
Burton, editors.
p. cm. — ("Norton professional book.")
Includes bibliographical references and index.
ISBN 0-393-70295-2
1. Athletes—Mental health. 2. Sports—Psychological aspects.
3. Sports—Social aspects. I. Begel, Daniel. II. Burton,
Robert,
1941– . III. Series.
RC451.4.A83S65 1999
616.89′0088′796—dc21 99-35444 CIP

W. W. Norton & Company, Inc., 500 Fifth Avenue, New York, N.Y. 10110
www.wwnorton.com
W. W. Norton & Company Ltd., 10 Coptic Street, London WC1A 1PU

1 2 3 4 5 6 7 8 9 0

For Milt and Bob,
our fathers and first coaches.

Contents

II
Clinical Issues

III
Therapeutics

Acknowledgments

WITH TWO EDITORS there are twice as many people to acknowledge, and therefore twice as much reason to be brief

This work would have been impossible without the loving support of our families. Bob thanks his wife, Julie, his children, Evan and Sarah, and his parents, Bob and Nella. Dan thanks his wife, Kym, his twins Carter and Cole, his parents, Carol and Milton, and Amy, Dave, Donny, Justin, Vanessa, Brandon, Star, Kita, and Rhonda.

Ernst Jokl, Haskell Bernstein, Bruce Ogilvie, Bill Bliss, and Arnie Beisser, we hope the consummation of this project pleases you, as you have inspired us.

Thanks Dan Kirschenbaum, Peter Jokl, Rudy Gittens, and Shane Murphy for taking us seriously from the start.

To our mentors, Bob Arnstein, Steve Fleck, Stan Jackson, George Mahl, Gideon Nachumi, Ernst Prelinger, and Marshall Edelson, we hope that our work reflects your wise teaching.

There was no reason for members of the athletic community to welcome us, and yet you did so Evelyn Lewis, Bill Lewis, Carm Cozza, Greg Lehman, Steve Bartold, Mark Young, Mark Rieff, Bill Sutherland, Brady Greathouse, John Boles, Eamonn Coughlin, Al Oerter, Roger Kingdom, Jackie Joyner Kersee, Joe Douglas, Bob Lanier, Jane Frederick, Dick Fosbury, Kay Tellez, Tom Hall, the Yale vaulters, Jamaris, Kamitra, and so many others.

Carl Hampton and Katie Lyons, thanks for being such good professional teammates.

Thank you Anna Green for your research, Harry Prosen for the support of your department, and Carolyn Washburne for your help with our writing.

To our contributors, thanks for some outstanding chapters.

Susan Munro, thank you for being our gentle but firm literary midwife.

Finally, we wish to acknowledge our collaboration with each other. Sharing the vision as well as the labor made this arduous task pleasant and satisfying.

Contributors

Murray Allen, M.D., formerly an Associate Professor of Kinesiology at Simon Fraser University, has published widely in the areas of sports medicine, musculoskeletal medicine, and spinal injury and rehabilitation. He is a Fellow of the American Academy of Sports Medicine, lead author of that organization's competency exam in sports medicine, and a Fellow of the North American Spine Society.

Antonia L. Baum, M.D., is an Assistant Professor of Psychiatry at George Washington University. She is the psychiatric consultant to the George Washington University Athletic Department, a member of the U.S.A. Gymnastics Health Care Referral Network, and chairperson of the committee for special projects of the International Society for Sport Psychiatry.

Daniel Begel, M.D., is Founder and Past-President of the International Society for Sport Psychiatry and a Fellow of the American Academy of

Sports Physicians. His research and clinical work in sport psychiatry, initiated at Yale University, spans nearly twenty years, and he is frequently regarded as the father of modern sport psychiatry. He is currently an Assistant Professor of Clinical Psychiatry at the Medical College of Wisconsin.

Robert W. Burton, M.D., is President of the International Society for Sport Psychiatry and Assistant Professor of Clinical Psychiatry at Northwestern University Medical School. He has worked with professional and amateur athletes in a wide variety of sports over many years, and has been Consultant to the Chicago Bears Football Club.

Gregory B. Collins, M.D., is Founder and Section Head of the Alcohol and Drug Recovery Center of the Cleveland Clinic Foundation. He has been Consulting Psychiatrist to both the old and the new Cleveland Browns Football Teams, as well as the Cleveland Indians Baseball Club.

Jon C. Hellstedt, Ph.D., is Professor of Psychology at the University of Massachusetts Lowell and consultant to the Athletic Department there. He is a family therapist and has published extensively in the area of families and sports. He is the author of *On the Sidelines*, a parent's guide to parenting a young athlete.

Todd Hendrickson, M.D., is Professor of Psychiatry and Director of Residency Education at Creighton University. He is a Director and Officer of the International Society for Sport Psychiatry and has authored a comprehensive curriculum in sport psychiatry for residents and medical students.

Ronald L. Kamm, M.D., is Vice-President of the International Society for Sport Psychiatry and Assistant Clinical Professor of Psychiatry at the MCP Hahnemann School of Medicine. He consults and publishes frequently in the area of youth sports and has chaired numerous symposia designed to educate psychiatrists and the general public on issues in sport psychiatry.

Introduction: The Origins and Aims of Sport Psychiatry

Daniel Begel

TO ANYONE TRAINED in the field of psychiatry or in the related fields of psychology, sociology, and neurobiology, the world of athletics offers a vast and wonderful geography to explore. The mysteries of competitive success and failure, the tension between healthy training and pathological obsession, and the universality of the athletic instinct itself are but three of the many phenomena that invite the eager attention of the human sciences. Although, for various reasons that will be addressed, psychiatry has been slow to turn its gaze toward sport, now that it has done so we can sketch the outlines of this fascinating terrain, along with many of its details.

Three kinds of observations, made over the course of many years by different people in various specialties, point to the value of a psychiatric perspective on sport. The first observation is that an athlete's state of mind has a significant impact on performance. What appears to be a purely physical action depends on a complex psychic calculus of motives, fears, and ideas. To paraphrase the apocryphal expression of Yogi Berra, 90 percent of sports is 90 percent mental.

The second observation is that participation in sports affects the mood, thinking, personality, and health of the participant. In childhood, the discovery of athletic talent may determine a person's role within the family and identity within society in significant, if not always salutary, ways. The role of professional athlete may increase the risk of suffering a specific narcissistic vulnerability, and retirement from sports at any level carries with it an increased risk of clinical depression, especially if that retirement is enforced by injury or waning abilities, as it usually is.

The third observation is that the psychiatric care of athletes must be adapted to the athletic context in specific ways in order to be effective. What may constitute a relatively minor occupational dysfunction for anyone else, for example, may represent a significant crisis for an athlete facing competition. Tricky ethical questions arise when a psychiatrist is consulting to an athletic team and his clinical outlook is buffeted by the organization's preoccupation with winning. Countertransference issues frequently become problematic because the psychiatrist may be just as inclined as the public at large to idealize those athletes who play especially well.

Together these observations add up to the fact that for an athlete, as for anyone else, there is a continuous interaction between who the person is and what he does. The athlete's innate ability and instinct propel him into the arena in the first place. His performance there, and the choices he makes, help to define his goals and his sense of identity. In the course of his career he faces many obstacles, some of which are thrust upon him and some of which are of his own creation. It is the sport psychiatrist's job to ease the journey by caring for the athlete when he is confused, uncertain, and fighting with himself. To do this we need to know as much as possible about his world and our appropriate role within it.

The first book-length study of athletes by a psychiatrist was *The Madness in Sports*, by Arnold Beisser, published in 1967. This book is a collection of clinical studies of athletes who had either retired from sports or were about to retire, and Beisser's focus was on the development of psychiatric symptoms in people deprived of athletics as an "integrating personality force." *Madness* is a kind of book we do not come across very often any more. It is unusually rich in clinical detail, while drawing informatively on the ideas of the classic writers of behavioral science, among them Parsons, Reismann, Erikson, Freud, and Kohut.

As a young man, Beisser was a highly ranked tennis player for whom "sports were the single most important thing" in his life (Beisser, 1989). Shortly after completing his internship in surgery, however, he was stricken with polio. "In a matter of hours," he wrote, "I went from feeling strong and agile to being barely able to stand, unable to stand at all, eventually unable to move, and finally not able to move at all." Although he survived 18 harrowing months in an iron lung, he was permanently confined to a wheelchair and dependent on caregivers for assistance with all of the basic tasks of living. Beisser wrote poignantly about his loss of physical capacities. Of his stint as a tennis jounalist he said, "I was a spurned lover who hated the love I could no longer possess. I was still in the process of mourning and neither the winners nor the losers escaped my acidulous comments." His memorable observation about the difficulty of doing psychotherapy with athletes, that "anyone whose primary satisfaction comes from action will find words a weak substitute," could easily have applied to himself.

In spite of his disability, Beisser returned to medicine and completed a residency in psychiatry. He married Rita, the physical therapist who had cared for him in the hospital. He became a pioneer of public psychiatry in Los Angeles and authored six books. He is glowingly described by those who knew him as a "gentle, compassionate person of good humor" (G. Jampolsky, personal communication, April, 1998). He had a "wonderful attitude, a winning personality," and was usually the "center of attention" at social gatherings (M. Miller, personal communication, May, 1998). His aim in personal relations was to "create a spirit of kinship" (Beissser, 1989).

Today it strikes us as strange that a book as fine as *Madness* and a person as vigorous as Arnold Beisser did not immediately spawn a school of sport psychiatry. Beisser consulted with professional baseball briefly and saw a few athletes in therapy, but his work in sport psychiatry "just stopped," according to Rita (R. Beisser, personal communication, April, 1998). Having died in 1991, Beisser is unable to tell us how and why. Until quite recently, studies in the field of sport psychiatry have been few, and we can only speculate on the reasons for this. It may be that even with all evidence to the contrary, psychiatrists have succumbed to the widespread tendency to idealize athletics in such a way as to blind them to instances of pathology. We may have inadvertenly shared the view of the philosopher Paul Weiss, who, in his neo-Platonic study of sport, defined athletes as "excellence in the guise of human beings" (Weiss, 1969).

The stubborn reluctance of the athletic community to perceive psychiatry as a beneficial resource may also have played a role in retarding the development of sport psychiatry. If there is any character trait that is anathema to an athlete it is that of weakness. Being unable to handle one's feelings, and confessing that inability to another human being in intimate conversation, is not ususally concordant with an athlete's sense of mastery. Even today, after all the publicity given to the psychological troubles of athletes, professional sports organizations call upon psychiatry primarily for the narrow purpose of solving problems with substance abuse. Other problems are dismissed in pejorative terms, such as "brain-lock" and "head case." As the general manager of one professional football team put it, "We draft character, not characters."

It must be admitted that psychiatry has not always put its best foot forward. A psychiatrist writing about his work with a professional football team described how the team members became dependent on him for their supply of amphetamines (Mandell, 1976). Other psychiatrists have publically elucidated in great detail the pathology and treatment of their athletic patients ("Gooden returns," 1987) and later regretted having done so. Although it is doubtful that many people in the athletic community read the *International Journal of Psychoanalysis*, a work by Helene Deutsch published there in 1926, in which she explained her analysand's talent for "ball games" as the result of an unresolved Oedipus complex, might give some justification for the suspicion that psychiatry will reduce athletic performance to pathology, much like early studies of artists tended to do.

Whatever reasons there may have been for the delayed entry of psychiatry into sports, they did not apply to sport psychology, which launched a vigorous and successful effort. In 1966, Bruce Ogilvie and Tom Tutko brought a psychodynamic perspective to the understanding of athletes. Although their book, *Problem Athletes and How to Handle Them*, was primarily a manual for coaches rather than clinicians, it nevertheless called explicit attention to the athlete's feelings, personality style, and object relations. Many books were subsequently published by sport psychologists, but, surprisingly, the authors of these books deliberately retreated from the psychodynamic perspective taken by Ogilvie and Tutko.

It is difficult to summarize briefly the huge body of work in sport psychology, but the three areas in which it has been strongest are performance enhancement, experimental sport science, and the organizing of the profession itself. In 1928, the educational psychologist Coleman Griffith, working at the University of Illinois, published *Psychology and Athletics*. In this work, Griffith noted, among other things, that people learning to hit a golf ball for the first time learned better if they were blindfolded than if they could see the ball. He attributed this to a heightened kinesthetic sense and the enforced formation of a mental image of the stroke. This idea was elaborated extensively by sport psychologists in the 1970s and 1980s into a systematic approach to imaging techniques, enhanced by techniques for relaxation.

The scientific underpinnings of these performance-enhancement techniques were provided by the experiments of Bill Morgan, Richard Suinn, and others. Morgan, Raven, Drinkwater, and Horvath (1973) found that hypnotized subjects recorded lower pulse rates when they believed that they were pedaling a cycle ergometer downhill than when they believed they were pedaling uphill, although the amount of work was the same in each case. Suinn (1980), examining the electromyographic recordings of the quadriceps of downhill skiers while they were mentally rehearsing their run, observed spikes that corresponded to the tasks of the event, such as changing direction at the gates and stopping at the bottom of the run, even though there were no observable muscle contractions during the imaging exercise, which was carried out with the skiers at rest. Because the strength of sport psychology has been in the area of performance enhancement, it has been well received by the athletic community. Many colleges, athletic clubs, and individuals employ a sport psychologist to improve the performance of athletes. The field of sport psychology itself has become highly organized, with graduate programs and lively professional bodies and journals to its credit.

Quite naturally, athletes consulting sport psychologists for assistance with performance also began to confide their personal problems, even though many of the professionals they spoke with were not trained as therapists. To the consternation of some people in the sport psychology community, numerous individuals of dubious credentials and methods began to call themselves sport psychologists, creating a dangerous circumstance for athletes. For this reason, such organizations as the United States Olympic Committee and the Association for the Advancement of Applied Sport Psychology have instituted credentialing and certification procedures in an effort to define a practitioner's capacities in the areas of education, basic sport science, and clinical competence.

While it is fair to say that these efforts have had some success, it is also fair to say that with few exceptions, most notably in the subsequent work of Ogilvie, the voice of clinical knowledge and competence in sport psychology has been faint. Shane Murphy's *Sport Psychology Interventions* (1995), for example, offers an excellent and comprehensive introduction to the methods of sport psychology while intentionally adopting a nonclinical stance. Thus, the treatment recommended in a vignette of a drug-abusing athlete is "career-planning assistance," while "attribution retraining" is recommended for an adolescent gymnast with complex concerns about her body and her emotions. The developmental and clinical perspectives we have come to take for granted in psychiatry appear to be quite neglected in sport psychology, even where they would seem essential.

As a result of this clinical void in the practice and literature of sport psychology, sport psychiatrists were left with little but their own experience and the inspiration of Arnold Beisser as a guide. Occasional papers appeared in the literature, such as Bob Arnstein's discussion of the problems of adolescent athletes, published in 1976; Michael Sacks's discussion of the psychodynamics of running, published in 1985; and J. H. Massamino's paper on sport psychiatry, published in 1987. For a time, during the running craze of the 1970s, psychiatry studied the therapeutic effects of exercise, echoing the practices of exercise therapy employed in hospitals as long ago as the mid-nineteenth century. But psychiatrists who worked with athletes and consulted to athletic teams worked largely in isolation from one another, modifying their techniques to the context of their work, and modifying the techniques of sport psychology to the biopsychosocial circumstances of individual patients.

This isolation of sport psychiatrists from one another diminished somewhat after the publication in 1992 of a paper entitled "An overview of sport psychiatry" in the *American Journal of Psychiatry* (Begel, 1992). Readers of this article corresponded with one another and soon formed a professional society, The International Society for Sport Psychiatry, to share their findings and debate their ideas. Later, groups of sport psychiatrists coalesced within such organizations as the American Psychoanalytic Association and the American Academy of Child and Adolescent Psychiatry. The latter organization has a formal sport psychiatry committee, whose chair, Ian Tofler, edited a groundbreaking volume of papers on psychiatric issues in youth sports (Tofler, 1998). Although the possible historical reasons for the development of sport psychiatry in the 1990s are quite unclear, it seems that the field is finally evolving at a brisk pace thirty years after Beisser. This book is a step in that evolution.

Part I of this book presents a few basic ideas about the athlete's mind, body, and social role. The psychological process of becoming an athlete, the complex interactions of endocrine systems during training and competition, and the perils for the psyche of an athletic career are discussed. In part II some of the fundamental clinical phenomena of sport psychiatry are described, including the variety of mental illnesses among athletes, the abuse of drugs (including performance-enhancing ones), and the problems endemic to youth sports. Part III explains how the basic evaluation and treatment modalities of psychiatry, including psychotherapy, pharmacotherapy, family therapy, and group therapy, are adapted to the athletic context in sport psychiatry. This survey of the theory and practice of sport psychiatry, while comprehensive, is admittedly incomplete. Some areas that deserve independent consideration, such as the fascinating world of coaching and the use of athletics itself as a therapeutic modality, are hardly mentioned. Other areas that are the object of intensive study may look different tomorrow than they do today. For the new visitor to sport psychiatry, however, this book should function as a reasonably accurate map, whose precise distances and landmarks can be debated by its various inhabitants.

It is the hope of all contributors to this book that sport psychiatry will enhance the experience of being an athlete by unambiguously endorsing the healthy aspects of training and competition. The presence of the psychiatrist in sports, far from constituting a "negative," helps to ensure, we think, that what happens on the field will not be easily disconnected from what happens in the soul.

We also hope that sport psychiatry will benefit the field of psychiatry itself. Consider the work of Coen (1989), for example, who found that losing wrestlers have higher endorphin levels than winning ones. Did their endogenous opiates induce a "calmness" antithetical to aggressive performance? Or is the secretion a response to the psychic pain of losing, "nature's way of consoling the loser," in Murray Allen's fine phrase (see chapter 2)? Sports offer an intriguing array of "experiments of nature" like this one, through which psychiatry can study the familiar puzzles of mind-brain interactions.

In the intensely commercial environment in which psychiatric services are now delivered, there is increasing pressure on psychiatry to confine itself to the prescription of drugs. In this climate, interviewing skills, interpretive methods, and personal attention to the private suffering of our patients is eroding fast. The athletic community, however, is inherently suspicious of drugs, at least those that do not build muscle. This appears to be one group that still values insight and, contrary to the prediction of Beisser, is increasingly willing to explore whatever emotional obstacles stand in the way of inspiration and success. Thus, it may very well be that sport psychiatry, in addition to its other functions, has a crucial role to play as a guardian of psychotherapy.

Our final hope in compiling this volume is that it will be useful to members of the athletic community, including members of the sports medicine community, who may be unfamiliar with some of the psychiatric terminology that is necesssary in a work of this type. It is not easy to preserve the freshness of an experience while trying to explain it, and so the athletes, coaches, and families whose life experience has shaped our perspective may not instantly recognize themselves in these pages. Nevertheless, we hope that we have kept in sight the humanistic origins of sport psychiatry that were established by Arnie Beisser.

REFERENCES

Arnstein, R. L. (1976). Emotional problems of adolescent athletes. In J. R. Gallagher, F. P. Heald, & D. C. Gavell (Eds.), *Medical care of the adolescent* (pp. 272–278). New York: Appleton-Century-Crofts.

Begel, D. (1992). An overview of sport pychiatry. *American Journal of Psychiatry, 149*(5), 606–614.

Beisser, A. (1967). *The madness in sports*. New York: Appleton-Century-Crofts.

Beisser, A. (1989). *Flying without wings*. New York: Doubleday.

Coen, D. (1989). *Endorphin's role in a win-lose paradigm*. Unpublished doctoral thesis (psychology), Simon Fraser University, Burnaby, BC, Canada.

Deutsch, H. (1926). Contribution to the psychology of sport. *International Journal of Psychoanalysis, 7*, 223–227.

Gooden returns to Shea but says little. (1987, May 1). *The New York Times*, p. D2.

Griffith, C. R. (1928). *Psychology and athletics*. New York: Charles Scribner's Sons.

Mandell, A. J. (1976). *The nightmare season*. New York: Random House.

Massamino, J. H. (1987). Sport psychiatry. *Annals of Sports Medicine, 3*, 55–58.

Morgan, W. P., Raven, P. B., Drinkwater, B. L., & Horvath, S. M. (1973). Perceptual and metabolic responsivity to standard bicycle ergometry following various hypnotic suggerstions. *International Journal of Clinical and Experimental Hypnosis, 21*(2), 86–101.

Murphy, S. (Ed.). (1995). *Sport psychology interventions*. Champaign, IL: Human Kinetics.

Ogilvie, B., & Tutko, T. (1966). *Problem athletes and how to handle them*. London: Pelham.

Sacks, M. (1985). A psychodynamic overview of sport. *Psychiatric Annals, 9*(3), 3–7.

Suinn, R. M. (1980). *Psychology in sports: Methods and applications*. Minneapolis: Burgess.

Tofler, I. R. (Guest Ed.). (1998). *Child and adolescent clinics of North America: Child psychiatry* (Vol. 7, No. 4). Philadelphia: Saunders.

Weiss, P. (1969). *Sport: A philosophic inquiry*. Carbondale, IL: Southern Illinois University.

Sport Psychiatry

Theory and Practice

I

THE BIOPSYCHOSOCIAL MATRIX

1

The Psychologic Development of the Athlete

Daniel Begel

A DOZEN OR SO ASPIRING DECATHLETES attended an intensive two-week camp for study and training. At this camp, visiting coaches analyzed the athletes' techniques for high jumping, shot putting, pole vaulting, and the other seven events of their grueling sport, the decathlon. Each athlete's capacity for sustained physical effort, required especially for the final 1500-meter run, was quantified by sport scientists using the most sophisticated equipment. Each was assessed for psychological strengths and weaknesses in order to assist them in achieving an attitude, say, of peaceful intensity for the javelin or controlled recklessness for the pole vault. They experienced the camp as exhilarating, challenging, and, in the view of the organizers, exhausting. On the last day of camp, a picnic was held at a park with a panoramic view of the city, so that athletes and staff, along with the families of staff who lived nearby, could unwind in relaxing, scenic surroundings.

As they lounged in the grass and on benches, waiting for the charcoal to become hot, a certain restlessness, apparent in the unconscious shifting of positions and stretching of muscles, was noticeable. Two or three of them picked up a frisbee they found among bags of hot dog buns and potato chips and tossed it between them in huge, soaring arcs. Soon others joined in and there was some discussion and experimentation on the most effective method of throwing the plastic disc far. They settled fairly quickly on a forearmed throw with a flat trajectory as the best technique. By the time the hot dogs and hamburgers were placed on the grills, an impromptu competition had been set up, with a foul line defined by two empty soda cans placed a few meters apart. The throws, while quite long, landed remarkably close together, just short of the edge of the bluff. When at last the food was done the winner of the frisbee throw was awarded first choice of victuals.

Watching these athletes play, I was impressed by the nearly instinctual progress of their activity. A restless physicality seemed to guide them imperceptibly from casual warm-up to technical analysis to structured competition. It is said that when decathletes get together they often invent games and competitions in this way, throwing an old tire, for example, that may have been discarded near the track, or setting up hurdles to be jumped backwards. They possess a special mental quality that makes them athletic in some essential way, displaying an intrinsic tendency to play sports and the knowledge of how to go about it. Athletes in other sports possess this same quality, making it easy for us to identify them, too, as essentially athletic people.

This special quality itself is not easy to define. Judging by the complexity of most athletic actions, it is something more than an instinct. Even the simple act of playing catch with a ball is an amalgam of motive, technique, and social relations. Similarly, it is more than the sum of a person's experience, since genuinely athletic people feel comfortable in any athletic setting, not only in that which they are trained. Competition and movement are important elements, but these elements are probably also involved in the performing arts, for example, or police work. Although we know it when we see it, a definition of athletic consciousness is elusive.

Often the behavioral sciences study a thing by studying how that thing came to be. In this way, ambiguities of current human behavior become clarified. In Freudian theory, for example, psychosexual concerns of the oedipal-aged child are thought to explain the unconsciously eroticized rivalries of the adult (Freud, 1910). In Piagetian psychology, the mental operations performed with imaged symbols in the middle years of childhood provide the basis for formal operations with abstract signs later on (Piaget, 1945). Kohlberg (1981) for morality, Erikson (1950) for ego strength, and Gilligan (1982) for female gender identity, all trace the origins of behavior to capacities that emerge during various stages of life.

To understand the athletic frame of mind it is helpful to observe athletes in their psychologic development, and when we do so we can quickly see trends that are not apparent by observing mature athletes alone. For example, athletes of any given age display capacities that have not been displayed at earlier ages. Ten-year-olds generally know enough to organize their own athletic contests, whereas four-year-olds, in spite of their enjoyment of physical play, do not yet understand how to do so. It also seems that the capacities that emerge at various ages persist and evolve in later years. The stubbornness of the preathletic toddler, for example, looks like an early version of the mature athlete's perseverance. Similarly, debates over rules among children on the playground form the basis for a mature sense of sportsmanship. When we attempt to view as a whole the mental accomplishments of athletes at various ages of life, we observe a continuously evolving development of the athletic frame of mind.

This chapter will outline a model of how that development proceeds, suggesting that at each stage of life an athletic person adds some essential ingredient to his or her developing consciousness. The timing of this process appears to be linked to the passage of cognitive, emotional, and motor milestones, and, beyond a certain point, variability from the norm becomes pathological (see chapter 6).

THE STAGES OF ATHLETIC DEVELOPMENT

Infancy and the Love of Movement

The sine qua non of athletics is movement. Without it, there is no sport. Other elements that we usually think of as essential to sport are dispensable. One can swim without competing. One can throw a ball with a friend without establishing rules. One can play golf without training for it, and take a morning run without enthusiasm. But one cannot perform any athletic activity at all without physical movement, and the love of movement is the most prominent feature of the athlete's consciousness.

In this respect, the athlete is like the average infant, who delights in exercising an expanding repertoire of actions. For the infant, such actions as stretching, squirming, turning, crawling, reaching, sucking, and grasping are complemented by such passive movements as being fed, changed, lifted, inverted, and thrown in the air. The coordination of the infant's activity with the activity and circumstances of the environment constitutes an essential aspect of what Piaget termed "sensory-motor intelligence." For the infant, the body is the primary source of knowledge of reality, and the mature athlete is similar in this regard. During competition, an athlete tries not to "think too much," allowing his body to tell him what movements to make and to discern the flow of events. Between competitions, athletes let their bodies tell them when to accelerate their training and when to back off.

Years ago, a mediocre high-school high jumper discovered a new technique by allowing his body to think for him. While growing up, this athlete played many sports, and though he was not overly gifted, he was competitive and worked hard. For some reason, he was especially attracted to the high jump, and fashioned a landing pit in his yard with wood chips from a nearby lumber mill. Hours of practice resulted in the achievement of some proficiency for his age, using the old-fashioned "scissors" technique. This technique, in which a jumper leaped over the bar sideways, sitting up, one leg at a time, was outmoded by the time the boy reached high school. His coach told him that he would be at a disadvantage unless he converted to the more efficient "straddle," in which the jumper rolled over the bar belly down. Alas, although he didn't do any worse with the straddle, he failed to improve, and for the first two years of high school was consistently "one of the first guys to go out in every meet," as he later remembered.

As his frustration deepened, he longed to return to his old scissors style in which he had more confidence, and his coach, figuring there was nothing to lose, allowed him to do so in the second-to-last meet of his sophomore year. What then happened is simply that in trying to jump high he lifted his hips up and as a result his shoulders went back. His sitting posture, in other words, became a back layout, and this transformation was accomplished with "no analysis and no preconception." His personal best improved six inches in that one meet, from five feet, four inches to five, ten, and he placed fourth, "a small miracle in itself."

He didn't think of himself as inventing a new style at the time, but the next week, when he and his coach reviewed old training films in search of pertinent instruction, they could find none. It wasn't, in fact, until Dick Fosbury won a gold medal at the Olympics six years later that the "Fosbury Flop," as it was dubbed, caught on. Today, jumpers take a longer run and arch their back, losing visual contact with the bar, but otherwise use the same technique as the one Fosbury, with an infant's trust in the movements of his body, discovered at a small high-school meet in Medford, Oregon.

The Will of the Toddler

When locomotion is established, in the toddler period, the child becomes capable of acting on his or her own, as the parents of any toddler know only too well. This autonomy is dependent on the achievement of locomotion, on the establishment of a sense of self (Mahler & Furer, 1968), and on the ability to think with symbols that are independent of direct action (Piaget, 1945).

In exercising this new capacity for autonomy, the toddler often willfully defies the wishes and commands of his or her beleaguered parent. The toddler will have in mind the intention, say, of turning a full plate upside down on the kitchen table, or remaining in pajamas when it is time to dress for church, and such autonomous intentions can often be thwarted only with physical force. The toddler may struggle with the parent over bowel training, going to sleep, running in the street, and generally getting into things that are not supposed to be gotten into. The toddler will usually learn to say "no" before he learns to say "yes."

The enjoyment of the willful exercise of autonomy is evident in the preathletic behavior of children of this age. For example, the ability to project a ball or similar object, an activity under the child's control, is learned before the ability to receive an object, which requires the child to conform to external actions. The two-year-old does not enjoy passing a ball back and forth half as much as clutching the ball and challenging a bigger and stronger person to catch him and take it away. Preathletic defiance may be revealed in situations that are not obviously athletic, such as social occasions and, even, medical procedures.

According to his mother, Justin required a "papoose" to restrain him for his last DPT immunization as a child. Justin's pediatrician recalled that the restraint was required not because of any unusually intense panic, but because of Justin's deft defiance of the combined efforts of his mother, his doctor, and his nurse to hold him still. Squirming free an arm, then a leg, Justin countered each move of his captors with a move of his own. The medical chart revealed that this episode occurred at Justin's vaccination at 18 months of age, and that when he was finally jabbed, "the patient did not cry." In a sense, Justin engaged in a primitive form of wrestling, instinctively inventing a repertoire of "escapes" to avoid, if you will, the "pin." He displayed a defiant but playful unwillingness to be dominated, characteristic of his age and essential to what would become for him a relatively successful career as an athlete.

The true athlete's enjoyment of a good challenge recapitulates the attitude of the toddler. The challenges will come from many sources, including the drudgery of training, the disappointments of injury and loss, direct punishment by a strong opponent, and internal wishes to surrender. Endurance, perseverance, willpower, drive, and "heart" (Bell, 1998) are related terms that describe an essential psychologic quality of the athlete, one that originates when an athlete is still a toddler.

Competitive Strivings in the Preschool Years

The next phase of development, between the ages of approximately three and six, corresponds to the Freudian "oedipal period," during which the child customarily will compete with the same-sex parent for the affection of the other parent. The concept of the Oedipus complex has been chanted overinclusively by psychoanalytic writers over the years, and it has practically become a symbol of sterile orthodoxy. This has resulted in the renaming of the oedipal period of child development as the "preschool years," which is thought to be a more neutral term. Nevertheless, the concept of an oedipal period seems to fit well the process by which quasi-romantic competition at home finds a parallel in the developing athlete's behavior. During this period, children will become interested in athletic competitions of various kinds. Though they may not understand the rules or carry out the techniques in a very effective way, they will throw themselves wholeheartedly into the competition, as the following example illustrates.

A group of four- and five-year-olds ran a 50-meter race. One child, running faster than the others, looked behind her for a rival. She slowed down to allow the rival to catch up to her, whereupon she resumed running fast and pulled ahead. She then looked for another opponent, slowed down, ran ahead, and then looked for a third. In this way, moving side to side on the track as well as forward and back, she achieved several competitive victories in the span of a single race. Although she came in second by standard measures, this did not dampen her enjoyment or detract from the establishment of her superiority.

While oedipal strivings may provide a concurrent motive for athletic competition, a competitive attitude is also facilitated by progress in cognition. One of the trends of the preconceptual period of cognition involves an increasing ability of the child to take the point of view of another person (Piaget, 1945). For the two-year-old, the parent who opposes his will is perceived as an obstacle whose intention is defined by that will. The parental rival to the oedipal child's romantic interest, on the other hand, is perceived as having intentions of his or her own. This notion, that the other person is not merely resisting one's will, but has similar intentions of his own, is essential to the idea of competition.

It should not be surprising that a competitive attitude, which is often experienced as something instinctual, should require a degree of cognitive maturation for its existence. But athletes will not generally remember very much about their early stages of development, even, perhaps, after years of psychoanalysis. They will say that as far as they can remember they have always loved competition, and will give examples from when they were somewhat beyond the preschool years. Whether this limitation of memory is due to a global repression thought to occur at the close of the oedipal years, or to cognitive transformations of some other kind, it means that the best, and perhaps only, way to study the origins of competitive strivings is to do so directly, at the time they are born. When we do so, we find that the physicality and willful autonomy of very young children evolve into competitiveness between the ages of approximately three and six. At that time, and forever after, competitive strivings become an essential ingredient of the athlete's psychology.

The Middle Years of Playground Conditioning

Between the ages of approximately six and the onset of puberty, participation in true sports blossoms. This is the period when organized teams and leagues become important, and playground games are carried on spontaneously. Although adults may attempt to organize athletic contests for children younger than six, and appear to succeed to a degree, the children themselves do not really "get it," as shown by the fact that they do not organize athletic games on their own, without the intervention of older people. The middle, or playground years, of childhood is the period of youth sports that is most studied (Martens, 1978; Tofler, 1998; Weiss & Gould, 1986).

The transition from preathletic behaviors to participation in true sports is of interest for its clear connection to progress in motor, emotional, and cognitive development. Seefeldt and Haubenstricker (1982), for example, have described in detail the progress in hip rotation, weight shift, and contralateral movement required for a minimally adequate throwing motion, such as a motion that would be required to join a game of softball on the playground. Similarly, the resolution of the Oedipus complex temporarily solves a domestic dilemma that frees the child for participation in a new world of peers. The cognitive capacity to carry out "concrete intellectual operations," to use the terminology of Piaget, and to disencumber oneself from the limitations of egocentric thinking makes it possible for the child to understand a great deal about sports that he did not know before.

For example, when preoperational children run a short footrace, they tend to stop just at the finish line, rather than running through it, as they should. It is not uncommon in the races of young children to see an enthusiastic parent crouched beyond the line exhorting their child to "run to me."

The cognitive limitation is an absence of what Piaget calls "reversibility." This means that the child is not yet able to grasp the counterintuitive notion that what he or she does after the race is over, beyond the finish line, affects the outcome of what has gone before, the race itself. Establishment of the capacity for concrete operations, after approximately the age of six, enables the child to understand this idea as well as related ones. Soccer players, for example, will soon be able to run the field while maintaining their relative positions, in contrast to preoperational children who will swarm to the ball.

Because concrete operations enable a person to generalize about what is true in all situations of a given type, athletes in the middle years of childhood are also able to understand a host of other facts about athletic life. Interest in movement now extends beyond an immediate result, and so one sees children of playground age practicing their "moves" for the first time, moves that are generalizable to an unlimited number of situations. Also, the capacity for understanding the general rules of a game becomes established, and this is reflected in the habit of school gym teachers for inventing a seemingly endless variety of contests to keep the interest of their young students.

Athletic rules are concrete, because they apply to actions, and conceptual, because they are general. Practice in the understanding of athletic rules is a significant part of what is healthy about participation in sports, and becomes possible in the middle years of childhood.

A group of children gather at a park in a residential neighborhood in order to play football. They fling their jackets to the ground and throw the ball around casually, warming up and determining the likely candidates for the "good arm" that day. They pick sides and a game begins.

All is well for a while, but in the course of the action, a dispute arises when a defender hits a receiver who is trying to catch a ball.

"That's interference. First down," the intended receiver says.

"No way!" says the defender.

"Yes, it was. You hit me in the back."

"I can do that. I was going for the ball."

"You hit me before the ball got to me."

"You ran into me. I couldn't help it."

One of the bigger athletes tries to enforce a decision. The debate keeps going. Another athlete says he doesn't care what the ruling is, he will quit unless they start playing again. Two others bide their time by throwing the ball around. Somehow agreement is eventually reached that "you can't hit a guy before the ball gets there, no matter what," and that is the way it will be "from now on."

This debate is not only about the contact itself, but also about how to interpret the contact. In debating the rule governing interference, these athletes are defining their sense of what is right and what is wrong, and how to tell the difference. Piaget (1932), in his study of children playing marbles, identified this process as a construction of a system of morality superior to a system that depends on the imposition of a ruling by an authority. In the terminology of Kohlberg (1981), this process prepares for morality based upon "self-accepted moral principles." Practice in creating, defining, and obeying rules is a hallmark of the middle years of an athlete's childhood, and at no time is the coaching truism that "sports are preparation for the game of life" more true.

Along with an understanding of the rules of play, an understanding of the cultural rules of athletics grows during this time. The young athlete learns how to deal with winning and losing, how to adapt to a change in status, and how to react to the decisions of the athletic authorities, such as coaches and referees. During the playground years the athlete develops a savoir-faire about the athletic scene in general and a feeling of comfort within that scene. The athlete learns the right gestures, the right attire, the right slang, and the right attitude. Because all of this progress in understanding the rules of athletic life may occur without the interference of adults in the games that kids spontaneously play among themselves, this period is sometimes called the era of "playground conditioning" (Begel, 1985). Its overall psychological result is an appreciation of sportsmanship.

Although the opportunities for playground conditioning may be lessening in the current era of adult-organized athletic leagues, pick-up games and other forms of spontaneous athletic play among children are far from becoming extinct. In their survey of over 8,000 young athletes, Ewing and Seefeldt (1996) found that significant numbers participated in sports outside of structured programs during their free time. Thirty percent, for example, played basketball on their own, while 20 percent bowled and 29 percent swam. Data from the Sporting Goods Manufacturers Association (1997) indicates that between 1992 and 1996 the three fastest growing sports for kids were ones in which organized leagues are minimal: in-line skating, mountain biking, and weight lifting. Even in organized youth sports, enlightened coaches often create opportunities for impromptu play to ensure age-appropriate development.

Desire, Idealism, and Specialization in Adolescence

By the end of the middle years of childhood the athlete will be comfortable with the demands and intricacies of participating in a good athletic contest. He or she will enjoy the competition, persist in attempting to win, and live with the outcome. But an important ingredient that is almost automatically associated with sports will be missing from the athlete's play, and that ingredient is passion.

Many studies have indicated that children of latency age play sports primarily for fun, rather than to satisfy a lust for competition. The outward emotions connected with their games are so muted that it is often not easy to distinguish the winners from the losers without knowing the final score. With the onset of puberty, however, athletic passions come to the fore as part of a generalized emergence of new emotion.

Although Offer and Schonert-Reichl (1992) have pointed out that extreme turmoil is not the norm for adolescence, great changes occur simultaneously in various realms, including cognition (Piaget, 1945), defensive structure (Valliant, 1977), and gender identity (Gilligan, 1982). Anna Freud described, in psychoanalytic terms, the juxtaposition of a weak ego and a strong id (Freud, 1936), an imbalance ushered in by pubertal activation of the hypothalamic-pituitary-gonadal axis. In addition, Blos (1962) described profound transformations in the adolescent's love life and Erikson (1950) described the adolescent "identity crisis," which he considered normal.

One familiar result of these complex developments is that the adolescent will experience a variety of fluctuating, strongly felt emotions that are, to some degree, new. Such feelings may include those of triumph and loneliness, awe and disdain, conviction and confusion. The adolescent athlete, like others of the same age, will be wrestling with new emotions, and suddenly victory becomes an object of desire.

The spirit of the adolescent athlete soars when performing before his or her romantic interest, and adolescent athletes "live or die" with the fortunes of their team. Coaches find that the "pep talk" has an effect on adolescent athletes that is entirely absent in younger athletes. The excitement generated by the contests of adolescents are capable of altering the mood of an entire community (Bissinger, 1990), while the contests of latency-aged athletes have no such potential.

With sports now the scene of intense desire, symptomatic behavior may develop. The sports-related syndromes, such as "choking" and "slump," often first appear in adolescence. These syndromes are discussed in chapter 5, but one example is of a high-school basketball player who was promoted to the starting lineup only to "freeze" in a state of extreme anxiety shortly after the tipoff of her first start. More extreme reactions, some even involving suicidal intentions, have also been known to occur. Arnstein (1976) pointed out that failure of an adolescent athlete to achieve may have "serious emotional consequences" on mood, self-confidence, and gender identity. Success, he added, can "buoy self-esteem, ability to cope, and general outlook on life" (p. 273).

In addition to desire, the quality of idealism makes its appearance in adolescence. This is reflected in new entries to the athletic lexicon, such as "destiny" and "school spirit," along with a range of exhortational aphorisms, for example, "when the going gets tough the tough get going." Idealistic thinking now pervades the process of identity-formation, as Erikson (1950) has discussed, and so the athlete may specialize in a particular sport or aspect of a sport. Reflecting on his or her essential nature, the athlete will become, for example, "a skater," instead of simply a person who skates. The athlete will perceive a direct bond between him- or herself and some famous and wonderful person who is imagined to possess the same essential nature. Although athletes in the middle years of childhood will specialize with parental assistance, adolescent athletes will specialize on their own. Latency-aged athletes will have favorite athletes whom they admire; adolescent athletes will worship heroes.

True Training in Young Adulthood

It is universally acknowledged that talent and desire do not guarantee athletic success, and that a solid "work ethic" is essential for it. To be effective, a work ethic requires more than simply working hard in practice, showing up to the game on time, and trying hard to win. It requires comprehensive and systematic training of the mind and body—true training—in which every activity has a purpose. The single, most intensely desired goal, whatever that might be, is conceptualized as the result of an interwoven fabric of actions carried out within a complex hierarchy of temporal segments that include the practice, the cycle of the season, and the span of a career. Work ethic is not the same thing as working hard. Work ethic is the mental outlook that sustains hard work and gives each action its immediate and long-range purpose.

Although the latency-aged athlete will work hard, and the adolescent one intensely desire success, only a mature athlete will carry out systematic training on his or her own. Up to and including the years of adolescence, the training schedule and routines of athletes are normally prepared for them and often enforced by a parent or coach. Sometime during the course of adolescence, and increasingly during the years that follow, the athlete becomes a collaborator in creating a training regimen, and eventually subordinates the input of the coach to what he or she has decided will be the training plan. Even in team sports, where the coach determines the role an athlete is to play, effective performance depends on the athlete's assimilating coaching instructions to a well-defined, personal plan over which the athlete is final arbiter. This development is linked to the identity-forming processes of late adolescence and is the athlete's way of taking responsibility for his or her identity.

The difference in perspective of an adolescent and mature athlete can be seen in the response to injury. Adolescent athletes are shocked and often outraged at the occurrence of such an unfair event as an injury, while mature athletes understand that injury is a risk of training and competition and yet another occasion for hard work. It is not surprising, perhaps, that the emergence of a full work ethic within the athlete's consciousness occurs at an age when apprenticeships of all kinds are often initiated.

The decathletes who we last observed as they were picking hot dogs off the grill exemplify the systematic approach of true training. When they return home they will put into practice what they learned at camp. Their plan will be based on the fact that in their sport, a final score is determined by the sum of points earned in each of the ten events, and each decathlete will sit down with coach, paper and pen, and his *Little Blue Book* of scoring tables. One athlete may pick a figure, a total number of points, that he feels will ensure him a spot on the next Olympic team. He computes the difference between that score and his previous best, which was not quite good enough. He will need about 300 additional points at the next Olympic trials.

His strong events are the "speed" events, like the hurdles, long jump, and hundred meters, while two of his three "throws," the discus and javelin, are relatively weaker. If he can improve his javelin mark by four meters, he has 60 quick points. A two-meter improvement in the discus will yield another 40. His pole vaulting, which is quite good in practice, has never been right during competition, and the psychologist at training camp thinks that this is because the vault immediately follows the troubling discus. A good 100 points are ripe for plucking from the vault if he can keep his composure after the discus. He scans the other events, picking up points here and there, and discovers that reasonable improvements in the various areas will yield 500 points, which will put him right where he wants to be.

This calculation of performance goals will be assimilated into the decathlete's ongoing self-assessment and guide the creation of his training plan. This plan will take into account the unique physical demands of each event as well as demands that overlap between events. A complex balance will be established between training oriented toward technique and training oriented toward strength and endurance, and this balance will evolve in the course of a season. The necessity to perform certain drills and exercises consistently must be measured against the dangers of diminishing utility and boredom. Although the complexity of a decathlete's training probably defies description by anyone one who has not done it himself, like mature training in other sports it requires the athlete to coordinate both psychological and physical parameters. As the decathlete mentioned above improves his discus, for example, there will be frustrating days when he will revert to his old ways and throw poorly. On those days, especially, he will follow his discus work with vaulting, in order to practice the mental transition that has held him back in the past. An observer who is not familiar with his analysis would be impressed by his hard work. His coach will be impressed by his work ethic.

The Wisdom of Age

We may call the final era of an athlete's life "old age" even though the athlete may not be particularly old in absolute terms. Because physical abilities wane before mental ones, an athlete's self-awareness, knowledge of his sport, and perspective on the role of sport in society will be growing at the time when abilities are shrinking. His expanding knowledge will help to prolong his career by compensating for and retarding the gradual loss of speed and strength. If, as so often happens, retirement is forced upon an athlete prematurely, as a result of injury or of being replaced by someone better, his athletic wisdom may continue to develop and find expression in coaching and in family and community life.

The attainment of athletic wisdom is an essential component of an athlete's capacity for leadership. Without wisdom, athletic leadership is primarily a consequence of prowess and is not fully developed, a fact that should not be neglected by coaches as they attempt to mold their teams.

The coach and general manager of a professional sports organization that was suffering a prolonged losing streak, for example, asked their consulting psychiatrist to identify the team's leaders. Although the consultant was puzzled by the fact that two people so closely connected to the team could not identify its leaders, he dutifully observed the team at their next practice. It was quite obvious by the way that many of the athletes on the team, especially the younger ones, sidled up to two of the older and better athletes for a few moments of desultory conversation, that these two athletes were the undisputed team leaders.

When given the news, the general manager's response was "we're in trouble." Instead of improving his relationship with these leaders, as the psychiatrist suggested, he attempted to undermine them and prop up leaders of his own choosing. But since leadership is not an artificial quality, but one that crowns a long development with wisdom, the players were nonplussed. Though they continued to lose, they were pleased that the stubborn GM was dumped immediately after the season.

THE ATHLETE'S REPERTOIRE OF PSYCHOLOGIC CAPACITIES

In passing through the stages of athletic development successfully, an athlete acquires a repertoire of psychologic capacities. Table 1.1 summarizes the hypothetical stages of athletic development and the contributions of each stage to this repertoire.

1. *Physicality.* An athlete loves movement, trusts and delights in the activity of the body, and relies on the actions and reactions of the body as a source of knowledge and experiment. This attitude is established in infancy.
2. *Willpower.* An athlete enjoys a challenge, the opportunity to test

TABLE 1.1
The Psychologic Development of the Athlete

AGE (approx.)	*DEVELOPMENTAL LEVEL*	*ATHLETIC FOCUS*	*ATHLETIC CAPACITY*
0–1	Infancy	Movement, sensorimotor knowledge	Physicality
1–3	Toddler	Autonomy, will, defiance	Willpower
3–6	Preschool, Oedipal	Competition	Competitiveness
6–12	Middle years, latency	Techniques, rules, playground conditioning	Sportsmanship
12–18	Adolescence	Passion, idealism, specialization	Desire
18–25	Young adulthood	True training	Work ethic
	Old age	Wisdom	Leadership

his or her will and persevere against a dominating force. This capacity grows out of the willfulness of the toddler.

3. *Competitiveness.* An athlete loves to compete against others who also love to compete. An athlete prefers the pressure of competition to the safety of practice. This preference derives from the Oedipal years.
4. *Sportsmanship.* An athlete prefers that competition be fair, and respects the formal and informal rules of sport. He or she is comfortable in a variety of athletic settings, familiar with athletic culture, and at home as a member of a team. Sportsmanship grows out of the playground conditioning of the middle years of childhood.
5. *Desire.* An athlete is passionate and is able to tap that passion and channel it in the service of performance. An athlete is also idealistic, seeking a level of purity and perfection in performance that may exist only as an abstraction. Desire is the emotional charge of motivation and it emerges in adolescence.
6. *Work ethic.* An athlete takes personal responsibility for his or her role and identity. In true training, the work is tailored to the complex demands of the sport, specific personal abilities and shortcomings, and the accidents of injury and luck. Specific goals are set and a coherent strategy devised for achieving them. A mature work ethic is established in the athlete's young adulthood.
7. *Leadership.* Athletes grow in wisdom, gaining knowledge of them-

selves, their sport, and the meaning of sport. The wise athlete is a leader, conveying his or her wisdom to other athletes, helping them to improve and to discover greater enjoyment in sports. An athlete also conveys this wisdom to that portion of the public that wishes to hear it, tempering hero-worship with an understanding of sports as but one meaningful human endeavor.

THE VARIABLE PATH OF A UNIVERSAL INSTINCT

This account of the athlete's development is not exactly a prescription, on the one hand, nor a natural law, on the other. The descriptive notions chosen here to emphasize certain aspects of an athlete's development may be replaced by better ones, the timing of various achievements of athletic development may vary, and the development of specific capacities are not entirely confined to specific ages. It would certainly be unwise to discourage manifestations of leadership in a ten-year-old athlete because an expert on sport psychiatry says that it is too soon for such manifestations to occur.

Athletic development appears to be especially influenced by social expectations and the role that others require an athlete to play. In the United States, where social circumstances dictate that school-aged athletes are highly likely to participate in sports that are organized by adults, systematic training and specialization begin at an earlier age than they otherwise might. In adolescence, the star athlete is prematurely thrust onto the social stage, with the result that he or she is often denied the normal adolescent "moratorium," the opportunity to lose one's individuality in collective behavior of one's peer group. For professional athletes, the dependence of a career on physical abilities that decline more rapidly than mental ones forces athletes into retirement at an age when persons in other fields have not yet reached their prime. In general, an athletic role often introduces a "developmental skew" (Begel, 1992) in the direction of prematurity.

But if the timing of athletic development is variable, and its shape determined both by individual choices and social expectations, the basic psychological path taken by an athlete seems to follow a normal sequence. In this sequence athletic development is inherently linked to the development of cognitive and emotional functions.

Occasions where children are trained as if they are adults, or, as sometimes happens in professional sports, where adults are treated like children, may be understood as socially derived distortions of normal athletic development. A coach, for example, who attempts to instill "killer instinct" in eight-year-olds is mistaken not just on ethical grounds, but on empirical ones as well, since passion is not a crucial element in the unfolding athletic consciousness of an eight-year-old. In addition to the distorting effects of "too much, too soon," whereby young athletes who are subjected to prematurely intense training have their love of sport tarnished (chapter 6), there is also the phenomenon of "too little, too late," whereby children are denied opportunities to develop their athletic capacities fully. Girls, especially, historically have been limited in their access to both playground sports and organized youth sports, although this appears to be changing (chapter 3).

The wonder of athletic development, however, is not in the distortion of it, but in the fact that it occurs at all. For some reason athletic people, at every stage of their lives, blend their emerging physical, intellectual, and emotional abilities with their love of sports. They display from birth a greater interest in athletic activities than other children, even other children who eventually can be seen to possess superior physical endowment. There seems to be some sort of "x-factor," an unknown element inherent in the human psyche, that drives the whole process. This factor seems to have an existence of its own, independent of talent or opportunity, and it may best be considered as another instinct, like the instinct to draw, speak, or make music.

The postulation of an athletic instinct that exists independently of upbringing is compatible with the observation of athletic universality. Athletic behavior occurs in widely divergent epochs and cultures. Sports metaphors were used even in biblical times (Hebrews 12, Judges 17), and anthropologists have reported athletic activity among nations throughout the world, activity that is sometimes connected with religious observance. Everywhere, it seems, children display an interest in ball games, footraces, and games that use implements such as marbles and sticks.

The idea of an athletic instinct is also consistent with the observation of athletic behavior arising de novo. Adults who have had little previous athletic experience may decide to take up a sport and do so with moderate success. Similarly, children with little demonstrable talent may suddenly display an unexpected athleticism. An example of this occurred in the childhood of a friend of mine named Steve, who claims to be totally devoid of any interest in athletics. Although Steve showed a serious a lack of athletic talent at an early age, and was discouraged from participating in sports by his father, neither of these circumstances prevented him from expressing his athletic instinct on one particular occasion when it was called for.

At the summer camp Steve went to as a child, they played an unusual brand of softball. The entire population of 50 or 60 campers was divided into two teams, and they played as many innings as it took for each player to bat once, much like cricket. As the worst player in camp, Steve was not only picked last, but batted last as well, with the ironic result that the outcome of a close game would inevitably hinge on his performance.

One day, in a tie game, Steve's bat miraculously made contact with the ball, which rolled between the pitcher's legs. The second baseman threw to first, beating Steve, who was not exactly fast, but the throw hit the dirt and skipped off the first baseman's glove. Young Steve, propelled by some instinct he did not know he had, rounded the bag toward second. Then, a succession of throwing errors by the fielders, along with this reckless impulse on Steve's part to run, enabled him to round second and third and to score, winning the game for his team. This sudden display of athletic spirit, surprising even to Steve, was a sign of the athletic instinct working even in a relative vacuum.

The idea of an athletic instinct is more speculative than the model of the athlete's psychologic development proposed in this chapter. Mention of it here serves the purpose, however, of assuring coaches and parents that the motive to play sports does not need to be supplied to a person from without. Nor does the path of athletic development need to be charted anew in each instance.

REFERENCES

Arnstein, R. L. (1976). Emotional problems of adolescent athletes. In J. R. Gallagher, F. P. Heald, & D. C. Gavell (Eds.), *Medical care of the adolescent.* New York: Appleton-Century-Crofts.

Begel, D. (1985). Concepts of sport psychology. *Annals of Sports Medicine, 2,* 133–135.

Begel, D. (1992). An overview of sport psychiatry. *American Journal of Psychiatry, 149*(5), 606–614.

Bell, C. (1998, May). *Training heart.* Paper presented at the sixth annual meeting of the International Society for Sport Psychiatry, Toronto.

Bissinger, H. G. (1990). *Friday night lights.* Reading, MA: Addison-Wesley.

Blos, P. (1962). *On adolescence.* New York: Free.

Erikson, E. (1950). *Childhood and society.* New York: Norton.

Ewing, M. E., & Seefeldt, V. (1996). Patterns of participation and attrition in American agency-sponsored youth sports. In F. L. Smoll & R. E. Smith (Eds.), *Children and youth in sport: A biopsychosocial perspective* (pp. 31–46). Madison, WI: Brown & Benchmark.

Freud, A. (1936). *The ego and the mechanisms of defense.* London: Hogarth.

Freud, S. (1910) A special type of choice of object made by men (contributions to the psychology of love I). In J. Strachey (Ed. & Trans.), *The standard edition of the complete psychological works of Sigmund Freud* (Vol. XI, pp. 163–175). New York: Norton.
Gilligan, C. (1982). *In a different voice*. Cambridge, MA: Harvard University.
Kohlberg, L. (1981). *Essays on moral development*. San Francisco: Harper & Row.
Mahler, M. S., & Furer, M. (1968). *On human symbiosis and the vicissitudes of individuation*. New York: International Universities.
Martens, R. (1978). *Joy and sadness in children's sports*. Champaign, IL: Human Kinetics.
Offer, D., & Schonert-Reichl, K. A. (1992). Debunking the myths of adolescence: Findings from recent research. *Journal of the American Academy of Child and Adolescent Psychiatry, 31*, 1003–1014.
Piaget, J. (1932). *The moral judgement of the child* (M. Cook, Trans.). New York: Norton.
Piaget, J. (1945). *Play, dreams, and imitation in childhood* (C. Gattegno & F. M. Hodgson, Trans.). New York: Norton.
Seefeldt, V., & Haubenstricker, J. (1982). Patterns, phases, or stages: An analytical model for the study of developmental movement. In J. A. S. Kelso & J. E. Clark (Eds.), *The development of movement, control, and co-ordination*. New York: Wiley.
Sporting Goods Manufacturers Association. (1997, September 3). *Youth movement in sports*. [Press release]. North Palm Beach, FL: Author.
Tofler, I. R. (Guest Ed.). (1998). *Child and adolescent psychiatric clinics of North America: Sport psychiatry* (Vol. 7, No. 4). Philadelphia: Saunders.
Valliant, G. E. (1977). *Adaptation to life*. Boston: Little, Brown.
Weiss, M. R., & Gould, D. (Eds.). (1986). *Sport for children and youth*. Champaign, IL: Human Kinetics.

2

The Psychobiology of Athletic Training

Murray Allen

ATHLETES ARE OFTEN LOOKING for that special nutrient or magical program that will somehow help them to configure their minds and bodies into some purpose-fulfilling mold. While some of these so-called juices may be externally derived, there now appears to be an abundance of complex intertwining neurohormonal substrates that both influence athletic behavior and, in turn, are influenced by that same behavior. This chapter will discuss some of the endogenous neurochemicals that may be part and parcel of the athlete's psychiatric status.

The catecholamines were perhaps the first recognized endogenous agents that might be part of athletic psychobiology—an adrenergic driver of performance. The early work on the stressor effects of the hypothalamic-pituitary-adrenal axis (HPA) and the general adaptation syndrome was an important first link with the body's endogenous chemicals and emotional status. In 1975 the endorphins were discovered, and were intuitively considered to influence mood—first thought of as the "runner's high." This was not confirmed until 1987 (Allen & Coen). Although the endogenous morphines have been found to activate a calm neuroinhibitory mood state, it has also been noted that certain moods could independently influence endorphin's mood-state effect, a sort of feedback loop between moods and chemicals. The example modeled by the endorphins is probably mimicked by countless other neural-acting substrates, the actions of which have yet to be uncovered.

What is the source of these potential mood-modifying neuropsychological markers? A simple overview starts with 26 chromosomes, which contain about 80,000 genes, which in turn are composed of about 3 billion chemical bases within the DNA chains. DNA sits as a paired RNA helix within the cell nucleus, dictating what that particular cell will do and when it will do it. With endless permutations and combinations, it is utterly amazing that anything works at all. Yet it does—but not without flaws. Some are obvious, like cystic fibrosis or schizophrenia; others are not, like excessive serotonin reuptake. The development of our chemical basis was probably predicated upon a background of natural selection that favored those genes that governed the most favorable combination of physical and mood states.

Among some cellular duties are the production of neurochemicals, or some response to the perception of neurochemicals at receptors. Neurochemicals are usually secondary or tertiary messengers, either to activate or suppress something. The primary messenger within a particular neurochemical sequence is usually some external cue. For example, darkness is a primary messenger (zeitgeber) that sets the biologic clock, which then sets in motion a whole series of fluctuations within the humoral systems. These rhythms within the neurochemical brew sets forth a background hippus, or ebb and flow, of chemical levels that peak at specific times, then subside to their baseline level, which in some cases is near or at zero. Cortisol levels, for example, reach their highest just prior to the morning wake. The clinical effects of these chemicals can generally be felt on both sides of the peak. When thyroid hormone rises, we feel energized; when it drops we feel lethargic.

In many circumstances, if we know the effect of an elevated neurochemical, then we can roughly predict the effect of its low level—the abstinence or opposite. For the stimulator chemicals like cortisol or thyroxin, abstinence is expressed as an inhibitory-type function. For the inhibitory chemicals like endorphin, abstinence becomes an excitatory-type function. This excitation or inhibition is primarily measured at the cellular level, but as the affect influences several million cells, the effect is felt macroscopically, that is, at the human behavior level. The malfunction scenario for each neurochemical may be expressed as either excessive or deficient amounts; that is, the rise—or the fall.

Each neurochemical has a unique functional life span, which for the most part is determined by the speed and amount of its formation, its degradation, and the level of opposing chemicals. Thus, the measurement of a particularly high level of a neurochemical may mean an overabundant production, lack of proper degradation, or the presence of opposing chemicals which have forced an adaptive rise of the first chemical in order for it to fulfill its normal role. The mere presence of high levels of a chemical tells you little about the most important questions: Why? and Does it matter?

Withdrawal reactions have a life of their own beyond the simple cessation of the drug. Let's look at an obvious but normally unthought of example. When the body lacks circulating nutrients, we call it "hunger." It has a predictable onset lag of about 4 to 6 hours from the last dosage, reaches a withdrawal peak over 12 to 24 hours, then the abstinence feelings subside, even if not satisfied. Another example: Nicotine withdrawal is felt in 30 minutes, peaks by 60, and lingers for up to 2 weeks. It was once thought that nicotine directly caused people to be agitated; however, the agitation does not come from nicotine, but from its abstinence—the withdrawal. It would thus appear that for some agents, the so-called clinically interesting phase may not come from its action, but from its inaction. Each agent (the list is endless) has its own profile.

ENDORPHIN

Perhaps it all started with Morphia, the Greek goddess of dreams. Morphine was developed in the 1920s as a substitute for heroin (*papaver somniforum*); its advent immediately set off the search for an endogenous ligand. This was discovered in 1975 and named "endorphin" for *endo*genous mo*rphine*. The current short list shows five major endogenous opiates recognized in mammals, and four major opiate receptors; the most clinically interesting opioid is beta (β)-endorphin (Henry, 1986; Yaksh, 1987), but the receptors are so intertwined as to make it impossible to ascertain any predominance of any one receptor type for any one physiological sphere.

Endorphin is the word given to a group of endogenous opioid polypeptides that exhibit inhibitory effects upon vast segments of human physiology. Exercise can be one of the physiological inducers for elevating endorphin in the circulation. This closely ties athleticism to some of our most basic neuroendocrine systems, some seemingly far removed from sport.

Phylogenetically, the roots of endorphin dig deep into our animal past; even primitive protozoa have been found with opiate-like substances. According to Darwin, survival was associated with fitness, and since endorphin was present from the beginning, it is expected to be part of that evolution. Our ancestors did not have sport in mind—they were more interested in survival.

β-endorphin is a 31-chain polypeptide derived from a much larger peptide called pro-opiomelanocortin, which is released from the hypothalamus following input to the thalamus of physical stress signals. β-endorphin is cleaved from its precursor and transported from the hypothalamus to the pituitary, where it is then released into the general circulation. Pro-opiomelanocortin is also cleaved into other hormones, such as corticotrophin-releasing hormone (CRH), and β-melanocyte stimulating hormone (β-MSH) (Allen, 1983).

Other similar pathways within the central nervous system subserve the enkephalins and dynorphin, the other major neuroinhibitor peptides. All opiates have the common function of inhibition, the differences being site and duration of action. All have specific peptidases, which break them down after release, checking the rise of endorphin.

Once a cell with an opiate receptor accepts the endorphin at that site, that cell or cell extension (axon, synapse) will inhibit the ability of adenylate cyclase from converting adenosine triphosphate (ATP) to adenosine 3′,5′ cyclic monophosphate (c-AMP). C-AMP is a second messenger that helps regulate cellular activity, something like a thermostat. When c-AMP action is suppressed, an adaptive rise in adenylate cyclase follows, bringing c-AMP's action back to its previous baseline. If there are no further endorphin pulses, that is, no further exercise, then c-AMP is no longer suppressed and the full brunt of the excess adenylate cyclase is felt with a rebound c-AMP overactivity, which is felt as a state of cellular excitability (Allen, 1983; Sharma, Klee, & Nirenberg, 1975) (see figure 2.1).

The opiate model of dependency-tolerance is one that is probably widely duplicated throughout various neurochemical substrates, each having its own time profile and list of activators, facilitators, inhibitors, etc. One cell is not enough to effect a significant change, but when all the trillions of cells within the 100-plus cell lines that are within the endogenous opioid system are inhibited by the endorphin, then some outward

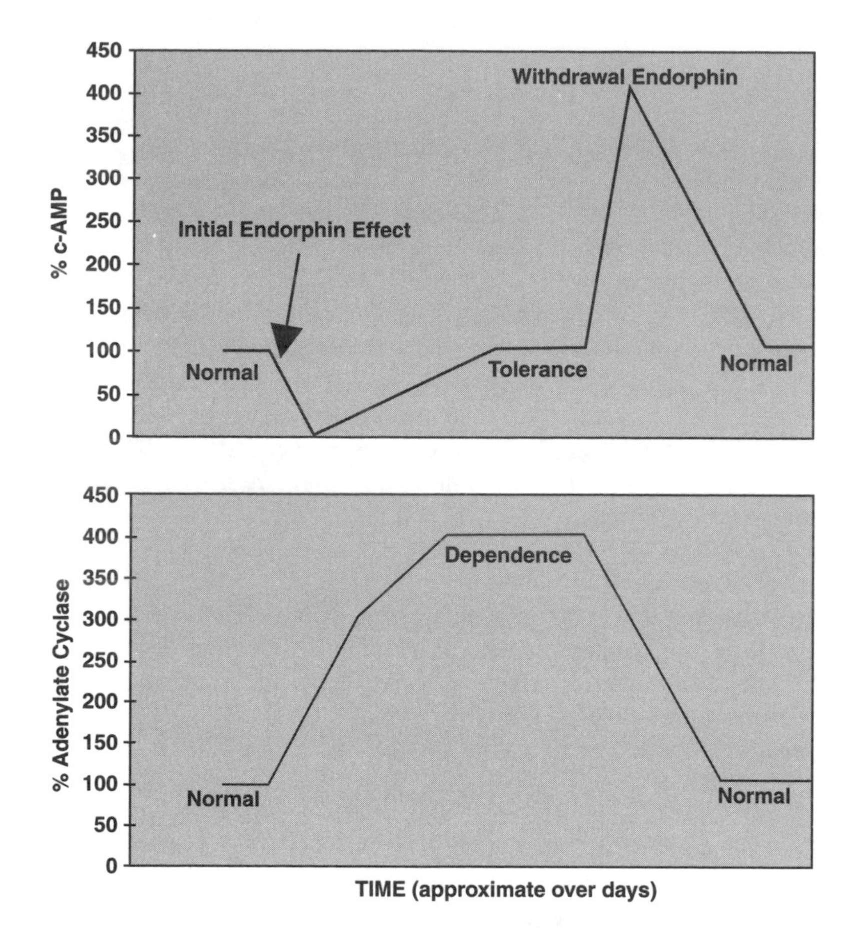

Figure 2.1 Cellular model of endogenous opiate dependency/tolerance (data from Allen, 1983; Sharma, Klee, & Nirenberg, 1975). Adenosine-3′5′-cyclic monophosphate (c-AMP) is a basic cellular controller which directs specific functions. Opioids inhibit the activity of adenylate cyclase in converting adenosine triphosphate (ATP) to c-AMP, but an adaptive rise of adenylate cyclase occurs in the presence of opiates in order to return c-AMP to its original level. Upon withdrawal of the endorphin inhibition, cellular hyperactivity ensues until readaption to normal occurs.

affect will most certainly be observed. The widespread role of endorphin can be compared to morphine: Whereas endorphin has a subtle physiologic affect, morphine will have the same effect only at an exaggerated pharmacologic intensity (Henry, 1986; McNicholas & Martin, 1984; Yaksh, 1987).

Endorphin, for example, has a pulsatile pattern that shows a base level near zero, with a rapid rise after being triggered by an exercise stressor that reaches a peak over 30 minutes, and then drops back to near zero over the next 60 minutes, even in the presence of continued exercise. A sort of one-shot stressor starts it off, and then lies back and waits for the reaction. Once endorphin fills a receptor, it will inhibit the action of that cell for the next 24 to 48 hours. By 72 hours, the same cells will show evidence of hyperexcitability, that is, a withdrawal reaction that will linger for the next 2 to 3 days before resetting to the original baseline. An illustration of this endorphin-mediated inhibition with rebound hyperexcitability is shown in figure 2.2.

The very act of neurochemical secretion depletes the storage. Thus, a too-early stimulation that attempts to resecrete the chemical again may

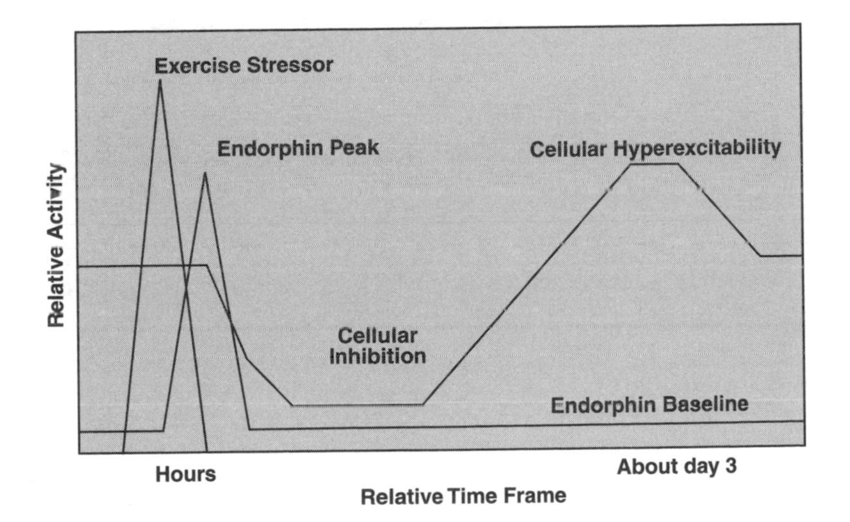

Figure 2.2 Model of dose response of β-endorphin induced by exercise-stress, and subsequent cellular inhibition effect and later rebound hyperexcitability. About day 3 of exercise withdrawal may be felt as an abstinence syndrome.

result in a somewhat lesser or inadequate secretion to fulfill its intended task. For example, β-endorphin is secreted with a pain signal, but a second independent pain signal within a few hours of the first will not cause as robust a release of β-endorphin as did the first pain signal (Allen, 1983). The same process occurs with panic or phobic reactions. The first phobic-environmental stimulation can cause a massive release of noradrenaline from the locus coeruleus with a subsequent profound adrenergic fear-type reaction. However, if a similar phobic-environmental stimulation should follow within the half-hour, only a meager noradrenaline release follows, and the adrenergic fear-type reaction is much blunted. Basically, there is not an endless supply-flow of neurochemicals, and it takes time for the cells to replenish the stores.

Once a cell has responded to a message at its receptor, the cell will usually proceed with its task regardless of what else happens at that receptor site. In the case of endorphin, once the receptor has been activated as the first message, the second message of cellular inhibition takes over and continues autonomously without the need for a repeated first message. This inhibition will persist even if the receptor is then filled with naloxone—an opiate-receptor blocker. In this case, the naloxone can block the receptor, but cannot reverse its effect once started. Figure 2.3 illustrates this process.

A major site of endorphin activity is the brain stem. Here we find that endorphin inhibits somatostatin, dopamine, noradrenergic effects from the locus coeruleus, luteinizing hormone releasing hormone (LHRH), vasopressin, substance P, and has secondary effects on serotonin and thyroid-stimulating hormone (Allen, 1983; Henry, 1986; Yaksh, 1987). Although it may appear that endorphin plays a pivotal role in the modulation of some of our most important basic physiologic processes, it must be remembered that there are other equally important influences over the control of these other hormones. The overall clinical effect of endorphin may in fact be quite trivial; its robustness has not been established. For example, although endorphin has an inhibitory affect at the cellular and synapse level, this role may be totally drowned in a sea of hyperactivity within other systems such that the inhibitory affect is not appreciated. The clinical relevance of elevated endorphin may be more complicated than simply extrapolating the cellular-synaptic level affects (micro environment) to the whole body (macro environment). Nonetheless, it is likely that the most clinically significant aspect of endorphin relates in some manner either to its cellular inhibition or the withdrawal of that inhibition. Clinically, this may be reflected as a sense of calm after an invigorating

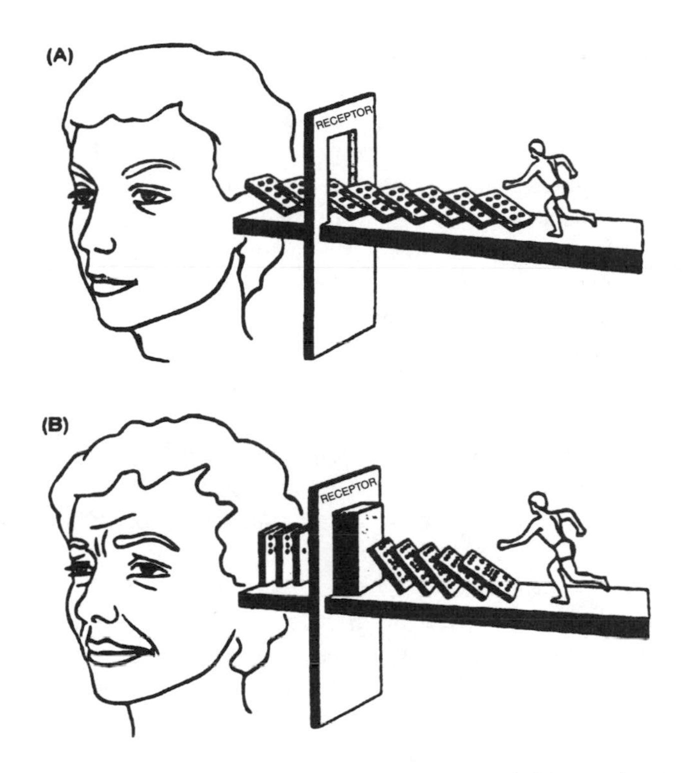

Figure 2.3 Pictorial perspective of how running may initiate a domino effect (endorphin release) which leads to receptor activity that causes a "calm" state (A). If the receptors are pre-blocked, activity-generated endorphins do not appear to initiate cellular inhibition within neurons that might subserve emotions (B). Once a stressor activity has activated the receptor, as in A where the dominos are down, subsequent attempts at receptor blocking do not appear to reverse the cellular calm (not shown).

exercise, and a sense of agitation if one has not had a good workout in the last three days (Allen, 1983; Allen, McKay, Hamilton, & Eaves, 1986).

The elevation of endorphin is a clonic, not tonic, event. Baseline serum levels are generally very low, and only after some stressor event do they rise above the baseline—as much as 400 percent. In a study by Fraioli and colleagues (1980), β-endorphin reached its zenith in just over 10 minutes of intense running, then dropped to the pre-exercise level over the next 30 minutes. An unpublished study by this author found that radioimmune assays of β-lipotropic substances were noted to rise after the mid-break of a recreational jog at about 46 minutes, but then fall to below baseline levels despite another 20 minutes of additional running (Allen, Banister, & Singh, 1987). This study tried to link endorphin to mood changes by administering naloxone 0.8 mg at the mid-break, but there were no significant mood changes on visual analogue scales between the pre-, mid-, or post-run testing for the naloxone or placebo conditions. This was probably due to the fact that the second messenger "calm" from the receptors had already been activated, and could not be reversed. Figure 2.4 illustrates the time sequence of endorphin-like rise and fall in this study. Note that some subjects showed no change in their endorphin levels.

Since exercise appears to be a major stimulator of tonic endorphin elevation, would gender or a difference in exercise type, duration, or intensity influence its rise? In rats, a sprint stimulus would elevate serum endorphin, and with repeated sprint conditioning the levels would rise higher with each sprint stimulus, whereas between stimuli, baseline levels dropped (Lobstein & Ismail, 1989; Metzger & Stein, 1984). Similar exercise conditioning affects on endorphin substances have been noted in both men (Colt, Wardlaw, & Frantz, 1981; Fraioli et al., 1980) and women (Carr et al., 1981). This suggests that either the production and release of endorphin is increased with each stimulus—a neural learning process—or that its degradation is delayed. Adaptation within the endorphin receptor-cell milieu, which could lead to a desensitization of the mechanism, would be expected in order to handle the increased absolute volume of endorphin in the circulation.

The rise of endorphin has been noted with most physically stressful events: pain, surgery, pregnancy, starvation, acupuncture, motion stress, scuba diving, sexual activity. However, which type of activity leads to the greatest rise of endorphin is not known. A sports comparison study showed significant rise in endorphin between cycling and running of comparable intensity in the same subjects (Langenfeld, Hart, & Kao, 1987). Assuming that we feel good from our endorphin pulse, it is probable that different sports at the same intensity-duration will lead to similar endorphin elevation profiles, but different sports have different stressor magnitudes and thus probably different endorphin profiles. It might be possible that we choose our personal sports participation based on how our endorphin responds.

Perhaps a certain threshold of activity is necessary to trigger the release of systemic endorphin. Running or cycling under 50% VO_2 max showed

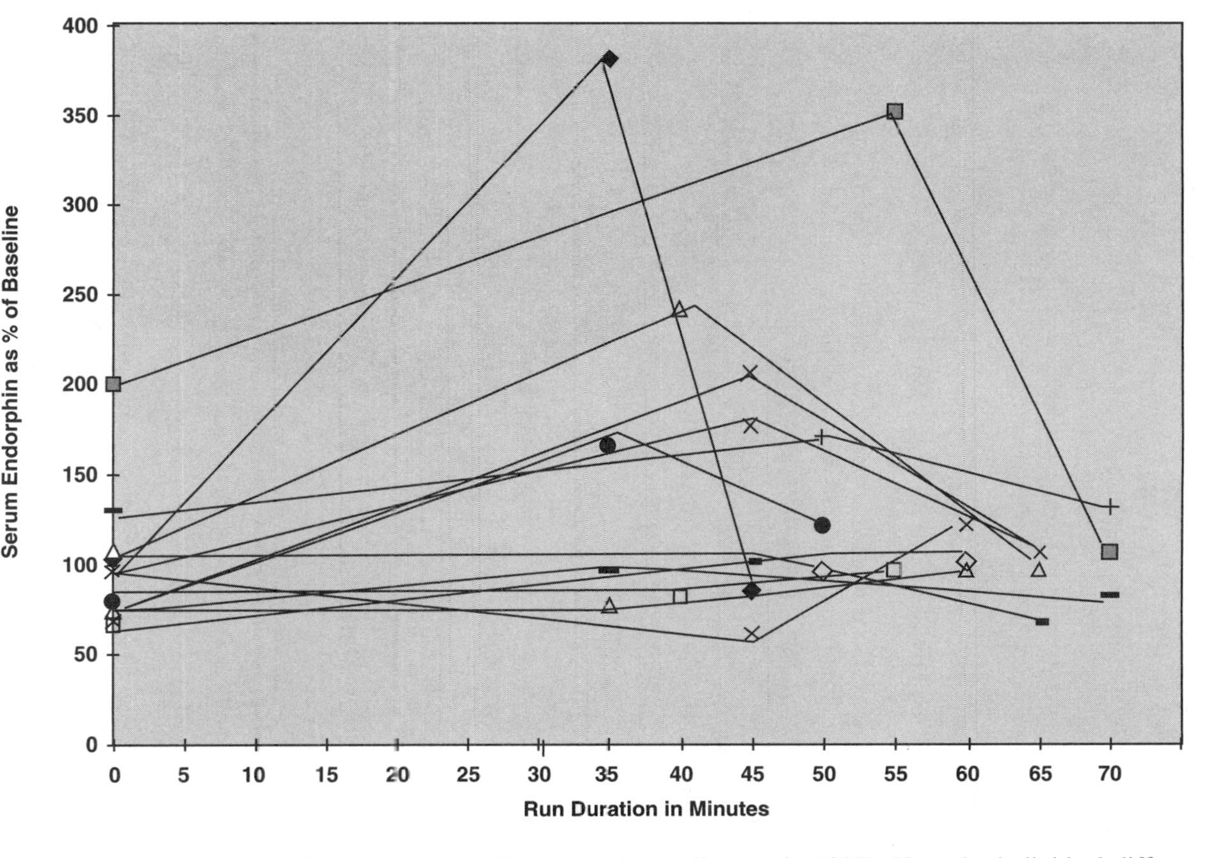

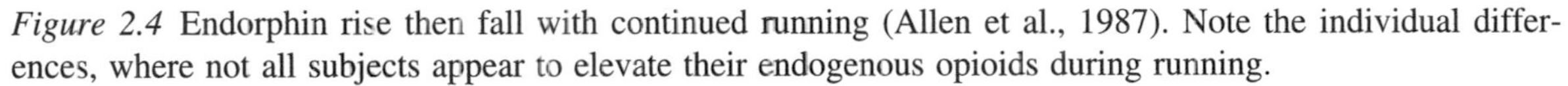

Figure 2.4 Endorphin rise then fall with continued running (Allen et al., 1987). Note the individual differences, where not all subjects appear to elevate their endogenous opioids during running.

little rise of endorphin, but when the intensity was over 60%, quite significant elevations of endorphin were noted (Donevan & Andrew, 1987; Farrell, Gates, Maksud, & Morgan, 1982; Farrel, Gustafson, Morgan, & Pert, 1987; Goldfarb, Hatfield, Sforzo, & Glynn, 1987; Rahkila, Hakala, Salminen, & Laatikainen, 1987). The quality of that stress may also be critical, but the nature of that quality is unknown. For example, scuba divers who merely languished in the water without any exertion were noted to elevate their endorphin somewhat (Adams, Eastman, Tobin, Morris, & Dewey, 1987). These were experienced divers, so novelty was not likely a factor in their response.

Does age affect the robustness of our endorphin response to exercise? One study failed to find any difference in endorphin response from running between younger men and those of more mature years—about 66 (Hatfield, Goldfarb, Sforzo, & Flynn, 1987). This is encouraging; it may mean that we can continue being active at any age and still elevate our endorphin in order to gain some of its presumptive benefits. It might also be assumed (wishful thinking!) that many other of our neurochemicals also do not suffer proportionately to the ravages of age as do the other frail parts of our bodies.

There is little doubt that overall, exercise is good for the human soul, both physically and psychologically. Morgan (1985) argued the virtues of three possible candidates to fill the role of "affective beneficence" of vigorous physical activity. The hypotheses are based upon:

1. distraction (Are we so busy being fit that we don't feel the pain?)
2. monoamine metabolism (We enjoy our adrenaline rushes?)
3. endorphin release (It makes us feel "calm"?)

Maybe it's all three—or more!

Exercise causes a concomitant rise of a great many other neurochemicals with which endorphin interacts, particularly adrenocorticotropic hormone (ACTH), prolactin, growth hormone, epinephrine, and norepinephrine. Endorphins may exert a profound suppressive effect upon the two principal stress axes, the hypothalamic-pituitary-adrenal axis, and the sympatho-adrenomedullary system (Grossman, 1988). This suggests an important role for endorphin in modulating the potential excesses of the general stress adaptation system. Yet it should be strongly emphasized that despite the significant reduction of ACTH and catecholamine elevations due to endorphin, ACTH and catecholamines still rise very high with exercise. It is probable that under high stress levels, endorphin has little modulating effect upon ACTH or the hypothalamic-pituitary axis, but after the stress is reduced the endorphins many play a pivotal role in ameliorating the stress response.

Endorphin's Role as a Mood Modifier

Despite the failure of early studies to find a positive link between endorphin and mood states in athletes, most researchers continued the search. The first of the serious studies failed to link endorphin to a "high" mood state in runners (Markoff, Ryan, & Young, 1982). This study used a low 0.8 mg dose of naloxone in an attempt to reverse endorphin affects, but failed to demonstrate any link between moods and naloxone use over placebo. Cohen, Cohen, Pickar, Murphy, and Bunney (1982) found that high (10 mg) doses of naloxone were necessary to block sympathetic activity in resting inactive subjects. Conventional wisdom has shown that only 0.4 mg of naloxone will reverse the stupor of morphine overdose; here we probably invoke a reversal of the "*mu*" receptor, one that is also integrally involved in the transmission of pain. If mood states were activated by endorphin occupation of the common *mu* receptor, then low-dose naloxone might reverse the mood. Markoff's study (1982) did not show this.

Markoff's study (1982) also served as an example of the need to tightly control the intensity and reason for running. The volunteers in that study were runners in a competitive 10-mile race. Most competitive athletes would not consider a serious race as an ideal scene in which to test their moods. Mood research should choose runners for their dedication to a research protocol, not a race. As well, they should be tested in a milieu that is devoid of social cues, competition, or environmentally pleasant surroundings. Although the moods of runners may be quite profound, the testing of these psychologic states should try to exclude other cues that might influence human feelings.

Other studies used various controlled protocols in field and laboratory environments with different levels of physical activity or sport and with various doses of opiate antagonists. Although noting subtle mood changes, there was no significant difference between the blocked and placebo conditions. However, most researchers had been looking for a "high" or "euphoric" mood, something akin to a psychedelic drug state, and their opiate antagonist drugs were administered at a time intended to "reverse" a mood, not block or prevent it. Yet if endorphin is at the root of a mood, its effect would be one of "calm" inhibition, not euphoria

(Allen, 1982; Farrell et al., 1986; Goldfarb et al., 1987; Grossman et al., 1984; Janal, Colt, Crawford-Clark, & Glusman, 1984; McMurray, Berry, Hardy, & Sheps, 1988).

Allen and Coen (1987) conducted the first study that showed a positive link between endorphin and mood. Noting previously that not all athletes appeared to elevate their endorphin with exercise, and not all admitted to mood changes when running (Allen et al., 1987), Allen selected subjects who declared they could recognize a sense of calm after they ran; these were not randomly selected athletes. The workload was individualized and increased in a step-wise fashion during the run, up to 75 percent predicted VO_2 max on a treadmill in an isolated environment devoid of the normally pleasant social or outdoor cues. Subjects were trained in the use of the Profile of Mood States (POMS) and Visual Analogue Mood Scale (VAS). The POMS vigor scale was reversed in order to have all sub-scales directed equally in regards to positive or negative mood states. High-dose naloxone in a 5 mg bolus (or equivalent volume placebo) plus 5 mg continuous IV drip (or placebo) was used prior to each run. There were four treadmill runs, in a random order double-blind crossover protocol, two each with naloxone and placebo, plus a pretraining run. This allowed the protocol to use a powerful repeated measure mixed model analysis of variance statistical design. The results showed a consistently significant "calmness" for every index in the VAS or POMS ($P < 0.05$ or $P < 0.10$) for the unblocked endorphin state during placebo conditions, but a flat "no change" response when naloxone was used. Figure 2.5 illustrates the mood state changes before and after running, with and without naloxone. This data strongly suggested that activity-generated endorphin produces a calm mood. This is probably the proverbial "runner's high."

If we can claim a link between endorphin and positive moods in athletes, what are some of the consequences? If we can presume that some of the cellular physiology of morphine and endorphin is similar, then it should be expected that the endogenous opiates, like their exogenous ligands, could have an addictive/dependency role. Regular exercisers claim to experience irritability, frustration, and increased nervousness if prevented from exercising, and many runners claim to experience discomfort if they miss a run (Carmack & Martens, 1979). Are they missing their post-run endorphin "inhibition," which reduces the excitability of their nervous system? Was this the anticipated calm, the inner reward they expect for their efforts? Physiologic inhibition should not be considered a negative attribute. Opioids are an important part of the central nervous

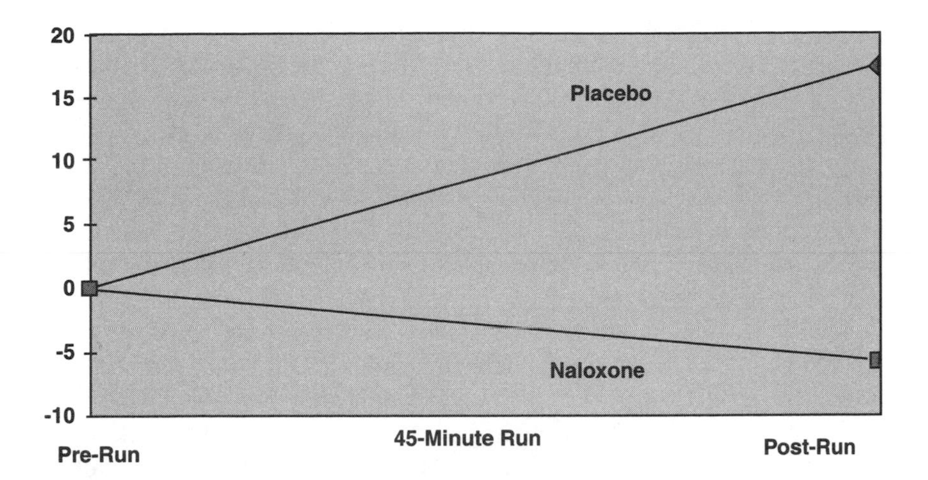

Figure 2.5 Combined global Visual Analogue Mood Scale (VAS) and Profile of Mood States (POMS) taken before and after running ($P > 0.05$) with naloxone or placebo in a repeated measures double blind protocol (Allen & Coen, 1987).

reward system. For example, rats would appear to enjoy electrically self-stimulating their pontine central gray matter, and monkeys enjoyed self-injecting met-enkephalin analogues into their brain stem region; these are endorphin-associated events (Stolerman, 1985). Are athletes, too, self-regulating their humors?

Activity-generated endorphin may play a role in the management of exogenous dependencies. During pregnancy, for example, women have reported being able to smoke only one or two cigarettes per day with minimal abstinence syndrome. Elevated endorphin has been reported during pregnancy (Gintzler, 1980). In a single-blind controlled study, acupuncture in naive subjects was successful in a stop-smoking program with 66% continued cessation at 3 months, whereas in the placebo acupuncture group the success was only 17% (Allen & Reznik, 1986). The hypothesis stated that endorphin was responsible for a diminished withdrawal syndrome, which facilitated the success. In a study of runners, smoking cessation was successful at 92% long-term (Morgan, Gildner, & Wright, 1976). If running and acupuncture both have endorphin release as a common ingredient, then running would appear to be a more natural method through which to elevate endorphin. It's too bad that not all smokers are capable of committing themselves to a running program.

Problems with travel or motion sickness may be obviated in people who keep fit. In a double-blind crossover study of motion sickness, subjects who were stressed with rotation motion became very sick when they had been given naloxone prior to the motion stress (Allen et al., 1986). During the placebo condition, it took significantly more rotations to make them sick, and the severity of their malaise did not last as long. This strongly implies that endorphin has an inhibitory effect on the nausea centers, and suggests that exercise may be a useful modality for preventing motion sickness.

Endogenous opioids are now considered the prime candidate in the regulation of the hypothalamic-pituitary-luteinizing hormone axis and testosterone's negative feedback control of luteinizing hormone (Cicero, Schainker, & Meyer, 1979). Activity-generated endorphin will block luteinizing hormone releasing hormone (LHRH), leading to an absence of the normal mid-cycle LH surge (Cicero et al., 1979). Increased intensities of this scenario may lead to a long follicular phase and/or an absent luteal phase—both with normal length periodicity. Oligomenorrhea or amenorrhea—both with lengthened periodicity—may also occur (Prior, 1982, 1985). Fortunately, activity-related infertility does not appear to be permanent or harmful. This series of events is related in part to certain unrecognized preconditions of the female hormone system, for it does not occur to all athletic women. The question of "percent body fat" per se is no longer an issue in athletic amenorrhea or infertility.

We've now seen that activity can alter neurochemicals, which in turn can alter our moods. What about the reverse? Can moods alter our neurochemicals? In the endorphin field again, the same researchers ran an unusual paradigm (Coen, 1989). Within a team of competitive university wrestlers, each match will have a winner and loser—there is no tie. Usually the matches are set such that the competition is fair and close—each has a near equal chance of winning, or losing as the case may be. Winners and losers have predictable mood states, or so it was thought. However, with repeated psychological testing before and after competition, it was found that in evenly matched wrestlers, the loser usually had a mood change towards calmness, and the winner became more agitated—sometimes viewed as being ecstatic. Only the loser's change in mood state could be blocked by naloxone. This was a statistically very robust finding, except for one loser whose calming mood failed to be blocked or altered by naloxone; it was later realized that he had been vastly mismatched but nonetheless scored very close to his much superior competitor. In this case, the principle actually held up; the loser actually felt like a winner for scoring so high, and his agitated-euphoric mood state was unaltered by naloxone, and the winner behaved like the loser for letting such in inferior wrestler get so close to winning. His mood state was calm—the endorphinergic consolation prize of a loser.

It would appear that winners have other mood state activators that probably override any endorphinergic calming affect. This hypothetical "winning" chemical has not been identified. But the athletic loser, like the jungle beast that is about to be pummeled, downtrodden, or eaten, might benefit from the calming and analgesic effects of endorphin—nature's way of consoling the loser.

Endorphin Summary

Exercise can elevate endorphin, a collection of endogenous opiates with inhibitory effects on vast segments of human physiology. Endorphins may help us adapt to travel sickness. In addition, they are probably the principal agent involved with exercise-related infertility and amenorrhea. They may play a useful role in the management of exogenous dependency-withdrawal states, such as smoking.

The psychological benefits of exercise are well documented. Public interest has centered on the role endorphin plays in mood-state changes (Hopson, 1988) and lately there is some scientific evidence to support such a link. Perhaps the reason we continue to pump up our endorphin with exercise is because it makes us feel calm—an inner reward for being fit. This was previously called the "runner's high," but should likely be renamed "athletic calm." This supports the concept "healthy body = healthy mind." However, endorphins may act similarly to the exogenous opioids; the obligatory athlete may have learned to self-titrate his or her endorphins, and thus mood states, and that discontinuing pulsatile activity could lead to an endogenous dysphoric withdrawal state that could only be alleviated by the hedonistic pleasures of exercise-induced endorphin. Endorphin may have been an important modulator of human evolution—the human species functioned best when physically fit—a state that endorphin may have helped facilitate.

There are probably many other neurochemicals that effect moods and human performance; it just so happens that endorphin is one of the few for which such information is known. The profile of endorphin physiology may form the basis for how we research and reconcile other potential neurochemical markers of mood and sport.

STRESS AND THE HPA

The hypothalamic-pituitary-adrenal axis—stress axis—is the classic example of a stimulatory system, with its myriad actions, reactions, and feedback loops (Herman, Prewitt, & Cullinan, 1996). It is also an example of a system that can be overactivated with maladaptive outcomes. Normally, the HPA axis functions as a pulsatile system for management of stress and control of energy production. Glucocorticoids (cortisol) are the end result, which have widespread multifunction catabolic stimulatory effects, including the release of glucose from the liver for energy availability.

The physiology of the HPA stress response is the outcome of sequential and parallel processing of relevant stimulus attributes of both positive and negative effect, which, upon reaching a certain threshold at the hypothalamic paraventricular nucleus (PVN), then activates the HPA system. There would appear to be two overall approaches to activating this system. The primary "systemic" high-priority system demands immediate response via unimpeded input to the PVN region—such as from major blood loss or serious respiratory distress. When this happens, all the stops are pulled, and the body instantly goes into a profound stress-response mode (Herman et al., 1996).

The second "processive or neurogenic" stress-response system requires a series of active processing by the brain to determine if the stress has enough relevance to cause activation of the PVN. This requires indirect routing of the stimulatory message, such as pain or stress, via the cortex, prefrontal cortex, hippocampus, amygdala, and septum (among probable other regions as well). The locus coeruleus can release massive amounts of catecholamines, mostly noradrenaline, which can give the effect of a full-blown panic-phobic reaction, and subsequently indirectly activate the PVN. Stressor stimulation mediated through the dorsal raphe nucleus (serotonin) is also a modest excitator to the PVN-HPA. In addition, various fluid and electrolyte shifts and blood-pressure changes can cause a sudden release of various peptides, one being angiotensin II, which has indirect effects upon the PVN-HPA. This multisystem modulation of stress-filtering is a variable requirement prior to activating the PVN. There may be an additional final screening within the limbic system before final loading of the PVN. But once loaded, the PVN activates the HPA, and the systemic stress response is irrevocably on its way (Herman et al., 1996).

The HPA system is but one aspect of the limbic system's role in stress integration. Limbic outflow goes to many regions of the brain, the PVN to HPA system being but one. The final relays insure proper control of the degree of the HPA response, and in part is prone to habituation by repeated exposures—cellular learning. Athletes, by their repeated training, are exposing their PVN-HVA to stress-management learning, even at the cellular level. The closer the training can simulate the true stress of competition, the more optimum the adaptation should be to stress.

Normally, the levels of cortisol fluctuate over 24 hours, part of the day-night circadian rhythm, reaching a 40-fold peak up to 150 ng/mL in the morning, and dropping to near zero by late afternoon. Under circumstances of stress, cortisols may rise to 400 ng/mL. Therefore, depending on the timing of the stressor, the effect may be more or less magnified. However, due to the fact that the stress-response levels are so much greater than the normal fluctuations, the stressor-outcomes are probably not much blunted by the time of day. If enough stress is placed on a person, time of day becomes mostly irrelevant.

However, after a major stressor event, the body tries to return to its baseline. Initially, part of the stressor signal will cause a somewhat delayed release of β-endorphin. This in turn has an inhibitory effect on the HPA axis. The athlete with robust (cellular training) release of endorphin probably has an advantage in managing this stressor-modulating counter-response. Secondly, the very presence of elevated cortisol will have a negative feedback effect upon further activation within the hypothalamus. Thus, the body is stressed, it responds, and then it calms itself down—a pulsatile event.

This nicely designed clonic stimulatory system starts to maladapt if the stress is continuous. Prolonged activation of the hypothalamus will, in time, lead to a failure of the negative feedback systems such that the HPA axis becomes tonically stimulated, resulting in continuous high levels of glucocorticoids. This in turn can lean to multiple end-organ disorders, some of which can be fatal (see figure 2.6).

For the athlete, controlling PVN and HPA responses is tricky. Insufficient stressor activation might lead to a poor competitive response. Yet an overactivity of the stressor-response system may also lead to a poor athletic response—or worse. Unfortunately, there are no simple tests that can be used to titrate on-line the stressor responses, nor are there any guidelines as to what response levels are optimum. In addition, some athletic activities, such as a biathlon, require a calm mental-physical state, but others, such as weight-lifting, may best be served by being in a state of near explosive stress. Many athletes have unwittingly learned how to gauge or titrate their stress levels in order to facilitate their personal best

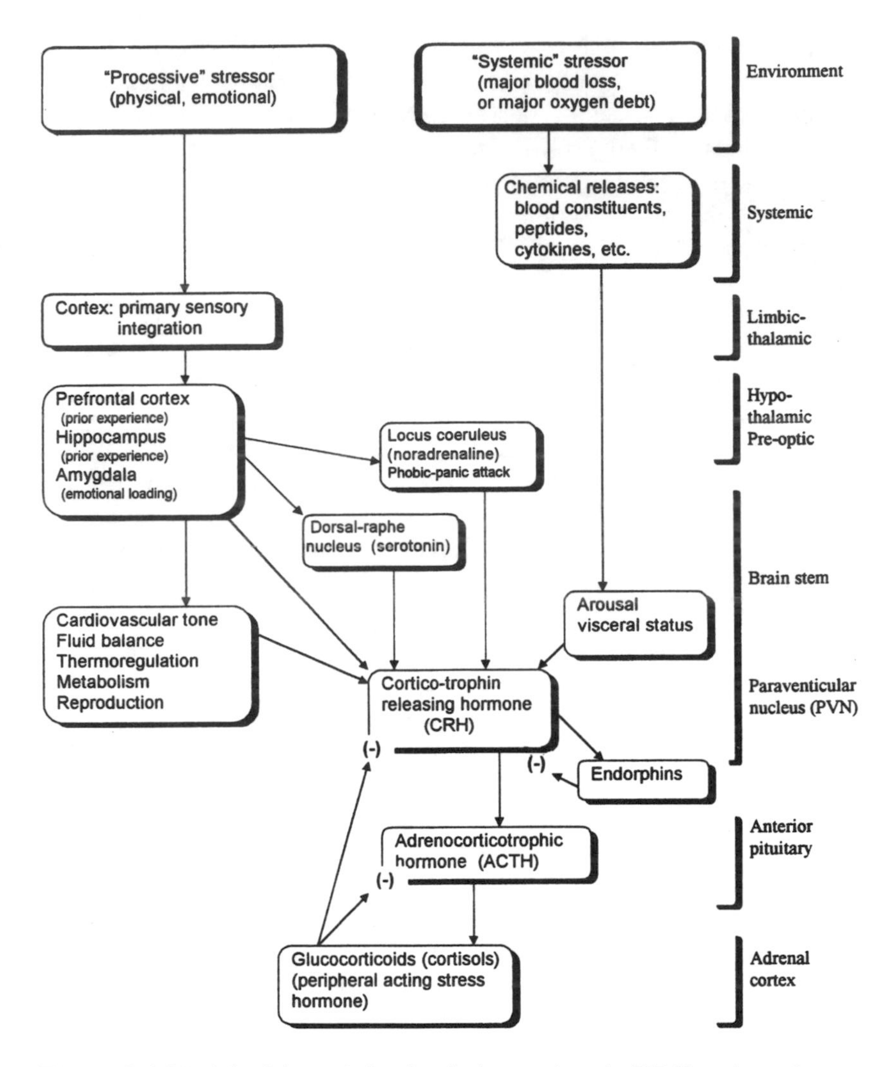

Figure 2.6 Model of hypothalamic-pituitary-adrenal (HPA) axis pathways that influence stressor responses (data from Allen, 1983; Herman et al., 1996).

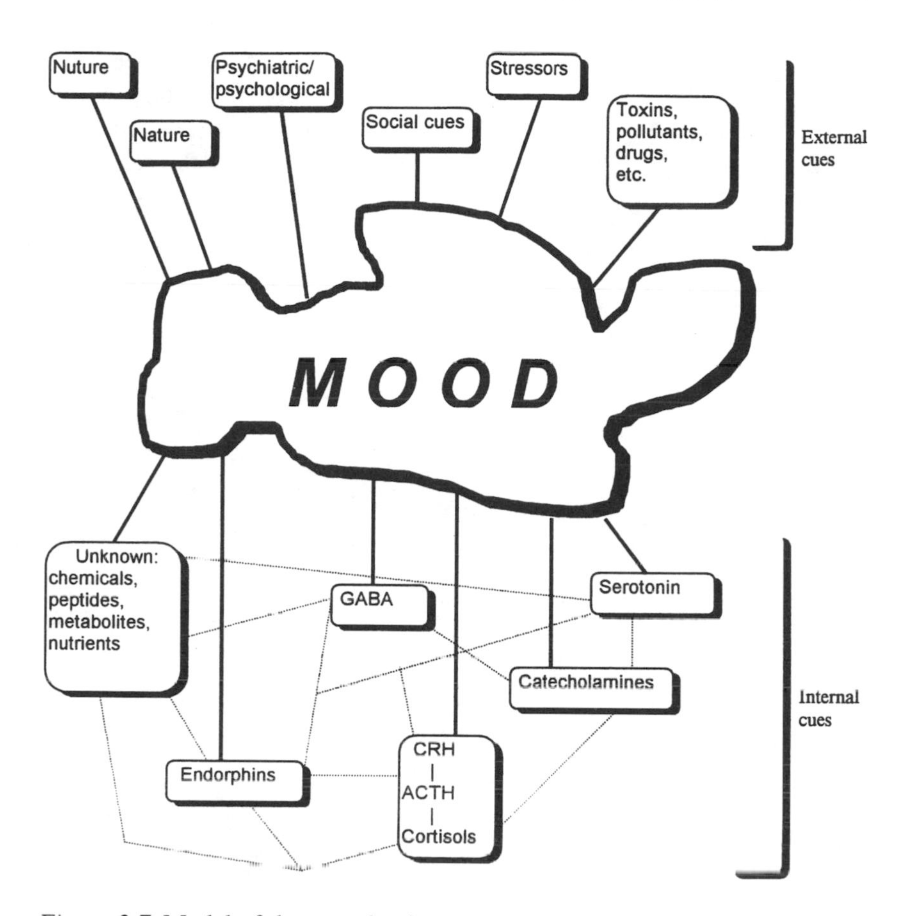

Figure 2.7 Model of the complex interconnections of influencing factors that could modify mood states in athletes. This model is not to scale, nor does it reflect the significance of each factor, nor is it intended to be complete. It is a reflection of our current understanding of the overall influences of internal and external cues that influence mood.

performance. This usually takes many practice sessions at their particular sport and at various levels of competition in order to know how hard to push the stress, or when to back off and foster a calmer mood.

Recent studies have suggested that a host of other neurochemicals, such as serotonin and gamma-amino-butyric-acid (GABA), are felt to have a profound influence on moods, and thus presumably on athletic behavior. However, the details are currently not known. All these neurochemicals affect each other; action on the part of one will affect another. It would appear that the neuropsychobiologic soup that influences our behavior is somewhat like a child's mobile, a ripple at one end can send repercussions rattling all through the system. To compound the confusion, it is likely that we are currently only looking at a very small portion of the mobile. We have much to learn about ourselves (see figure 2.7).

REFERENCES

Adams, M. L., Eastman, N. W., Tobin, R. P., Morris, D. L., & Dewey, W. L. (1987). Increased plasma β-endorphin immunoreactivity in scuba divers after submersion. *Medicine and Science in Sports and Exercise, 19*(2), 87–90.

Allen, M. E., & Banister, E. W., & Singh, A. (1987). *β-endorphin–like substances rise then fall with continued running, but show no psychological state changes* (Technical Report). School of Kinesiology, Simon Fraser University, Burnaby, B. C., Canada.

Allen, M. E., & Coen, D. (1987). Naloxone-blocking of running-induced mood changes. *Annals of Sports Medicine, 3*, 190–195.

Allen, M. E., McKay, C. Hamilton, D., & Eaves, D. M. (1986). Naloxone enhances motion sickness: Endorphins implicated. *Journal of Aviation Space and Environmental Medicine, 57*, 647–53.

Allen, M. E., & Reznik, S. (1986). *Long-term benefit of acupuncture for smoking dependency in a single-blind control study* (Technical Report). School of Kinesiology, Simon Fraser University, Burnaby, B. C., Canada.

Allen, M. E. (1983). Activity-generated endorphins: A review. *Canadian Journal of Applied Sports Science, 8*(3), 115–133.

Allen, M. E. (1982). Runner's calm. *Journal of the American Medical Association, 248*(23), 20.

Carmack, M. A., & Martens, R. (1979). Measuring commitment to running: A survey of runners' attitudes and mental status. *Journal of Sport Psychology, 1*, 25–42.

Carr, D. B., Bullen, B. A., Skrinar, G. S., Arnold, M. A., Rosenblatt, M., & Beitins, I. Z. (1981). Physical conditioning facilitates the exercise-induced secretion of beta-endorphin and beta-lipotropin in women. *New England Journal of Medicine, 305*, 560–563.

Cicero, T. J., Schainker, B. A., & Meyer, E. R. (1979). Endogenous opioids participate in the regulation of the hypothalamic-pituitary-luteinizing hormone axis and testosterone's negative feedback control of luteinizing hormone. *Endocrinology, 104*, 1286–1291.

Coen, D. (1989). *Endorphin's role in a win-lose paradigm*. Unpublished doctoral thesis, (psychology). Simon Fraser University, Burnaby, B. C. Canada.

Cohen, M. R., Cohen, R. M., Pickar, D., Murphy, D. L., & Bunney, W. E. (1982). Physiological effects of high-dose naloxone administration to normal adults. *Life Science, 30*, 2025–2031.

Colt, E. W. D., Wardlaw, S. L., & Frantz, A. G. (1981). The effect of running on plasma β-endorphin. *Life Science, 28*, 1637–1640.

Donevan, R. H., & Andrew, G.M. (1987). Plasma β-endorphin immunoreactivity during graded ergometry. *Medicine and Science in Sports and Exercise, 19*(3), 229–233.

Farrell, P. A., Gates, W. K., Maksud, M. G., & Morgan, W. P. (1982). Increases in plasma β-endorphin/β-lipotropin immunoreactivity after treadmill running in humans. *Journal of Applied Physiology, 52*, 1245–1249.

Farrell, P. A., Gustafson, A. B., Garthwaite, T. L., Kalkhoff, R. K., Cowley, A. W., &

Morgan, W. P. (1986). Influence of endogenous opioids on the response of selected hormones to exercise in humans. *Journal of Applied Physiology, 61*, 1051–1057.

Farrell, P. A., Gustafson, A. B., Morgan, W. P., & Pert, C. B. (1987). Enkephalins, catecholamines, and psychological mood alterations: Effects of prolonged exercise. *Medicine and Science in Sports and Exercise, 19*(4), 347–353.

Fraioli, F., Moretti, C., Paolucci, D., Alicicco, E., Grescenzi, F., & Fortunio, G. (1980). Physical exercise stimulates marked concomitant increase of β-endorphin and adrenocorticotropic hormone (ACTH) in peripheral blood in man. *Experientia, 36*, 987–989.

Gintzler, A. R. (1980). Endorphin-mediated increases in pain threshold during pregnancy. *Science, 23*, 1197–1207.

Goldfarb, A. H., Hatfield, D., Sforzo, F. A., & Glynn, G. (1987). Serum β-endorphin levels during a graded exercise test to exhaustion. *Medicine and Science in Sports and Exercise, 19*, 78–82.

Grossman, A., Bouloux, P., Price, P., Drury, P. L., Lam, K. S. L., & Turner, T. (1984). The role of opioid peptides in the hormonal responses to acute exercise in man. *Clinical Science, 67*, 483–491.

Grossman, A. (1988). Opioids and stress in man. *Journal of Endocrinology, 119*, 377–381.

Hatfield, B. D., Goldfarb, A. H., Sforzo, F. A., & Flynn, M. G. (1987). Serum beta-endorphin and affective responses to graded exercise in young and elderly men. *Journal of Gerontology, 42*(4), 429–431.

Henry, J. L. (1986). Role of circulating opioids in the modulation of pain. *Annals of New York Academy of Science, 467*, 169–181.

Herman, J. P., Prewitt, C. M.-F., & Cullinan, W. E. (1996). Neuronal circuit regulation of the hypothalamo-pituitary-adrenocortical stress axis. *Critical Reviews in Neurobiology, 10*(3&4), 371–394.

Hopson, J. L. (1988). A pleasurable chemistry. *Psychology Today, 22*(7), 28–33.

Janal, M. N., Colt, E. W. D., Crawford-Clark, W. C., & Glusman, M. (1984). Pain sensitivity, mood and plasma endocrine levels in man following long-distance running: Effects of naloxone. *Pain, 19*, 13–25.

Langenfeld, M. E., Hart, L. S., & Kao, P.C. (1987). Plasma β-endorphin responses to one-hour bicycling and running at 60% VO_2 max. *Medicine and Science in Sports and Exercise, 19*(2), 83–86.

Lobstein, D. D., & Ismail, A. H. (1989). Decreases in resting plasma beta-endorphin/lipotropin after endurance training. *Medicine and Science in Sports and Exercise, 21*(2), 161–166.

Markoff, R. A., Ryan, P., & Young, T. (1982). Endorphins and mood changes in long-distance running. *Medicine and Science in Sports and Exercise, 14*, 11–15.

McMurray, R. G., Berry, M. J., Hardy, C. J., & Sheps, D. S. (1988). Physiologic and psychologic responses to a low dose of naloxone administered during prolonged running. *Annals of Sports Medicine, 4*, 21–25.

McNicholas, L. F., & Martin, W. R. (1984). New and experimental therapeutic roles for naloxone and related opioid antagonists. *Drugs, 27*, 81–93.

Metzger, J. M., & Stein, E. A. (1984). β-endorphin and sprint training. *Life Science, 34*, 1541–1547.

Morgan, P., Gildner, M., & Wright, G. (1976). Smoking reduction in adults who take up exercises: A survey of a running club for adults. *Canadian Association of Health, Physical Education & Recreation Journal, 30*, 39–43.

Morgan, W. P. (1985). Affective beneficence of vigorous physical activity. *Medicine and Science in Sports and Exercise, 17*(1), 94–100.

Prior, J. C. (1982). Endocrine "conditioning" with endurance training, a preliminary review. *Canadian Journal of Applied Sport Science, 7*(3), 148–157.

Prior, J. C. (1985). Luteal phase defects and anovulation: Adaptive alterations occurring with conditioning exercise. *Seminars Reproductive Endocrinology, 3*(1), 27–33.

Rahkila, P., Hakala, E., Salminen, K., & Laatikainen, T. (1987). Response of plasma endorphins to running exercises in male and female endurance athletes. *Medicine & Science in Sports & Exercise, 19*(5), 451–455.

Sharma, S. K., Klee, W. A., & Nirenberg, M. (1975). Dual regulation of adenylate cyclase accounts for narcotic dependence and tolerance. *Proceedings of the National Academy of Science USA, 72*, 3092–3096.

Stolerman, I. P. (1985). Motivational effects of opioids: Evidence on the role of endorphins in mediating reward or aversion. *Pharmacology & Biochemistry of Behavior, 23*, 877–881.

Yaksh, T. L. (1987). Opioid receptor systems and the endorphins: A review of their spinal organization. *Journal of Neurosurgery, 67*, 157–176.

3

The Athlete's Role

Daniel Begel   Antonia L. Baum

AMONG THE ROLES AN ATHLETE MAY PLAY in the course of a lifetime is that of hero. In the role of hero, the athlete fulfills the hopes and embodies the virtues of whatever groups claim him or her as their own. Athletic heroes are a source of pride for nations, cities, and neighborhoods. They are symbols of liberation to oppressed races, genders, and social classes. Athletic children cast in the role of hero provide families lost in the complexities of modern life with a sense of purpose. Paul Weiss (1969), giving philosophical voice to the heroic status of athletes, defined them as "excellence in the guise of human beings" (p. 17), and a journalist described them as "living symbols of the ultimate" (Leonard, 1988, p. 74).

Although the status of hero has many potential rewards, including wealth, fame, romantic opportunity, and the adulation of others, athletes themselves often point out that it has an inherent drawback. The person worshiped one moment as a hero may in the next be condemned as a villain. A Colombian soccer player who accidentally scored a goal for an opposing team in the World Cup matches was subsequently murdered for his crime. The fickle attitude of fans toward their athletic heroes was illustrated by Bill Bradley (1976), the senator and former professional basketball player, in his book, *Life on the Run*. While pausing briefly to tighten his shoelaces during a pregame warm-up in Madison Square Garden, Bradley heard two young fans call him to look up for a picture, saying that he was their "favorite Knick." Bradley looked up, but when the young photographers did not take the picture he returned to his shoes, lowering his head. He next heard his two fans commanding him to look up again. "Look up!" they said. "Look up, you jerk!" (p. 82).

The casting of athletes in the role of hero, and of jerk, goat, loser, traitor, and other varieties of villain, is said to derive from the importance of the institution of sports itself within modern culture. Beisser (1967) suggested that sports are a "last outpost" for the acceptable expression of physical aggression, and a "seasonal masculinity rite" that provides assurance to American men that "their biology is not obsolete." Singer (1994), in his discussion of "baseball fever," points out that "the performance of the team becomes a direct incarnation of the fate of the individual and the tribe," and so "elaborate mythologies begin to build around players and teams of destiny" (p. 59). Hoch (1972), adopting a Marxist view, discussed sports as a kind of narcotic, analogous to religion in its capacity for distracting people from an awareness of unfair economic circumstances. The connection of the institution of sports with various other social institutions, cultural assumptions, and political tensions has led many authors to regard sports as a "reflection of society" (Lapchik, 1986), and the athletic hero, therefore, as a vehicle for social triumph and defeat.

According to this view, an athlete is often seen not only as a sports hero, but also as a black hero, a female hero, a child hero, a rich hero, a white hero, and so on, along with the fallen versions thereof. Society's battles over money, gender, and ethnicity and its concerns with eroding values, drug use, violence, bad manners, and other ills are dramatized in the athletic arena, where athletes are cast as protagonists. Thus, the superstar basketball player is a product not only of his athletic virtuosity, but also of the economic needs of the National Basketball Association and of footwear companies. The trial of an athlete accused of murdering his former wife proceeds not only according to the rules governing adversary procedures in court, but according to conflicting social agendas about race and gender as well. The expectation for an athlete to fulfill the twin role of hero and representative of a particular class of people is likely to have an impact on that athlete's thinking and conduct, an effect that may become of clinical interest in sport psychiatry.

RACE AND GENDER

Two areas that have drawn particular interest among social scientists and historians are those of race and gender. The available roles for both women athletes and black athletes have been profoundly influenced by exclusionary practices of various kinds. In the case of both race and gender, the evidence for unfair discrimination is overwhelming. A number of historical illustrations of this are provided by Art and Edna Rust, in their history of the black athlete (Rust & Rust, 1985). They describe, for example, how African American jockeys dominated horseracing at the turn of the last century much the way black basketball players dominate today, only to be systematically excluded from their sport when *Plessey v. Ferguson* (1896), which established the "separate but equal" doctrine, made it possible to do so.

Racism in contemporary sport has been documented in numerous ways by Richard Lapchik, as part of his ongoing attack on the problem. Among other facts, Lapchik has documented the higher standards that must be met by black baseball players in order to work. In major league baseball in 1983, for example, 10 percent of blacks hit better than 300, while only 2 percent of whites did so. Twenty-nine percent of black pitchers had greater than 100 career victories against 17 percent of white pitchers. Thirty-one percent of white pitchers had earned run averages greater than 4.01 while only 11 percent of black pitchers did. Among home-run leaders, 5 of 11 were black, as were 6 of 10 leaders in runs batted in and 8 of 10 leaders in base hits, even though only 23 percent of all ballplayers were black (Lapchik, 1984).

In the case of exclusionary practices aimed at women, the history of the Olympic Games provides an illustrative story. As Wilson (1996) has explained, the founder of the modern Olympics, Pierre de Coubertin, was a lifelong opponent of women's participation, and only men were allowed to compete in the first modern Olympics of 1896. Women participated in the games of 1900, 1904, and 1908, but only in a few sports and primarily as a result of the efforts of local organizers. In 1912 there were three women's events—swimming, diving, and tennis—and with the the exception of the controversial 800 meter run of 1928, women were not permitted to compete in a running event longer than 200 meters until 1960. The governing administrative body of the Olympics, the International Olympic Committee (IOC), did not elect a woman to membership until 1981.

Dubious claims about the delicacy and inherent weakness of the female constitution were used to buttress exclusionary practices. A journalist commenting on the 800 meter run of 1928 Games is quoted by Wilson (1996) as having said, "Below us on the cinder path were 11 wretched women, 5 of whom dropped out before the finish, while 5 collapsed after reaching the tape." The fact that there were nine runners, all of whom finished and displayed no unusual distress, did not prevent the IOC from using exaggerated journalistic accounts to justify eliminating the 800 meter race from the Games.

More recently, claims that women lack sufficient upper body strength to compete in the pole vault have been used to discourage and prevent women from participating in this track and field event. That the ability to pole vault is not limited to one gender has been known since the 1920s, when girls were taught to pole vault at the progressive Shady Hill School in Massachusetts (L. Cunningham, personal communication, 1983; Yoemans, 1979). Yet pole vaulting for women is still not a part of the Olympic Games, and has only recently been added to the World Championships, Millrose Games, and other prominent track and field meets (Rhoden, 1998).

Since exclusionary practices do not sit well with athletes who are affected by them, periodic efforts are made to overcome such practices. Some of these efforts are made by individuals, as when the parents of a female high-school pole-vaulter retained a lawyer to help establish their daughter's right to compete. Often these efforts seem to be related to politics of the times, as when racial integration in American sports paralleled the Civil Rights movement.

An intriguing study of the tension between exclusionary and progressive efforts in women's sports during an era of social change is contained in Kathleen McCrone's account of the rise of women's field hockey in Victorian England. According to McCrone (1988), the value for women of participating in sports was pointed out as early as 1792 by Mary Wollstonecraft, who warned that "bodily dependence produced mental dependence and weak mothers, with weak children." McCrone (1988) also pointed out that the progressive educators of the Taunton Commission of 1868 decried the lack of programs for girls and judged "the want of systematic and well-directed physical education as one of the main impediments to good health and academic success for women."

Although other British commentators made similar points over the years, the notion of a constitutional incapacity for vigorous exercise by women was the prevailing one at the onset of the Victorian era. McCrone (1988) reports that as women's field hockey, which was initially an upper-class enterprise, gained momentum in the 1890s, attempts were made to prohibit hooking, checking with sticks, and other practices that were considered too dangerous for women. These restrictive attempts, however, were outweighed by growing public interest in the sport. By 1914 there were approximately 100 field hockey programs for women in schools and colleges, and field hockey clubs that held competitions for prize money and charged admission to spectators were popular. According to McCrone, this progress was an element of the broader movement for women's emancipation occurring at the time.

Steps toward greater equality in sports often seem to be followed by efforts to reimpose inequality. Although the tacit prohibition to hiring a black head coach in professional football was broken in 1989, no blacks were hired for 15 head coaching jobs that became available in 1997 and 1998 (Rhoden, 1998). The increasing participation of African American athletes in university-sponsored programs that resulted from civil rights legislation was followed by the establishment of eligibility rules that reduced such participation. Greene (1984) examined the legal aspects of Proposition 48, which established new academic requirements for athletic eligibility for schools affiliated with the National Collegiate Athletic Association. She found evidence for racism on both procedural and subtantive grounds, the former by the exclusion of blacks from the process of formulating the requirements, and the latter by the differential impact of such requirements on blacks and whites.

Similarly, Title IX of the Educational Amendments Act of 1972, which required gender equality in educational programs, was partially undone by the Supreme Court ruling in *Grove City College v. Bell* of 1984, which effectively exempted from Title IX the athletic programs of schools that do not receive federal funding for these programs. And in the Olympic movement, the flurry of women added to the governing body in the mid-1980s died down quickly, so that by 1995 only 7 of the 107 members of the IOC were women.

Some of the retrenchment is apparently a paradoxical result of progess. The rapid increase in the number of athletic programs for college women resulted in a significant decrease in the the percentage of women's teams coached by women, from 81 percent in 1974 to 51 percent in 1986 (Birrell, 1988). And, according to Hoberman (1997), the great success of black athletes in the course of the twentieth century has given "the biological racism of the last century a new lease on life" (p. xxvi).

In Hoberman's view, the representations of the black athlete in print and video "sustain the traditional view of blacks as essentially physical and thus primitive people." Media images suggest, Hoberman says, that black men are essentially aggressive, and that the stereotypically violent black male is the "dangerous twin" of the star athlete. Because of the possibility that menacing images of black athletes might scare white customers away, advertisers adopt "domesticating strategies" that depict, for example, the black athlete as a harmless, cuddly fat kid, craving nothing more forbidden than "a dozen bags of potato chips and a watermelon." Hoberman refers to an "anxious oscillation between idealized and demonized images of blacks" that perpetuates the invisibility of the black middle class and restricts the availability of salutary role models for young African Americans.

A book that comes perilously close to exemplifying the stereotyping tendencies analyzed by Hoberman is *Public Heroes, Private Felons* by Jeff Benedict (1997). Benedict described approximately a dozen cases of sexual assault on women perpetrated by athletes, as well as the legal aftermath of these assaults. With the exception of a group of white high-school football players who are briefly mentioned in his opening paragraph, virtually every athlete described by Benedict is a black professional or college athlete. His paradigmatic black athletes display a "diminishing sense of shame over their socially degenerate behavior," along with a "link" between their "unbridled sexual appetites and their crimes." In a disclaimer that appears to reinforce prejudicial thinking, Benedict stated that "the fact that so many athlete-offenders are black is not a function of race, but rather a result of the rising recruitment of poorly prepared young men, the majority of whom are black, whose social backgrounds are rife with problems." Like the pseudoscientific claims for African inferiority popular in the nineteenth century, Benedict's stereotypes are supported by an almost silly imitation of scientific method (Benedict & Klein, 1997).

The possibility of a statistical association between athletic participation and violence is worthy of study, if not of scapegoating. Currently, negative findings like the *Los Angeles Times* survey that uncovered only 72 athletes and 7 coaches among 3 million cases of assaults on women in 1995 (Lapchick, 1998) are based on an epidemiology only slightly more advanced than those of authors such as Benedict. The whole area needs more study using a variety of methods, including longitudinal case studies as well as statistical methodologies that employ prospective sampling procedures and that control for such factors as substance abuse, anabolic steroid use, and previous criminal history, among others.

Without this, studies that inadvertently stereotype merely repeat the common tendency for attacks on members of a particular race or ethnic group to disguise themselves as attacks on something else, such as violence toward women, pollution of academic standards, or rampant drug abuse. An example of poorly disguised racism was the accusation of drug abuse leveled against an outstanding black pitcher who had not missed a turn on the mound for five years and suddenly complained of a feeling of "deadness" in his arm. Shortly after the accusations were made this athlete suffered a cerebral vascular accident resulting from an occlusion of a carotid artery (Lapchick, 1991).

A confluence of racial stereotyping with athletic scapegoating was illustrated in a soccer game for 13- and 14-year-old girls. In this game, the only black athlete on one of the teams, named Jenny, repeatedly worked her way into position to score, but on every occasion kicked the ball over the goal rather than into it. Each time she would do this her coach, who was the father of one of Jenny's teammates, would shout in ever more insistent tones, "Jenny, keep your head down." Now in kicking, the position of the head is just one manifestation of a complex configuration of timing and balance, and attempting to correct a habitual error of technique in the middle of a game is a futile coaching exercise. Nevertheless, as Jenny's failures mounted, her teammates took up the coach's chant, vehemently commanding the young girl to keep her head down. When the team was beaten, one of the athletes said, "Jenny lost the game. She wouldn't keep her head down." In this case, the unfairness of making one athlete the scapegoat for a team's loss was compounded by a racial implication, since in the history of American race relations, keeping one's head down has been an unambiguous symbol of submission.

It is especially sad to see unfair practices based on race inflicted by adults on young athletes. Similarly unfair practices based on gender have been described. Joan Ryan (1995), for example, has suggested that young girls who participate in gymnastics are victimized by harmful attitudes and training methods that are systematically embedded in the sport. Ryan described preadolescent female gymnasts who are habitually subjected to dangerously intense physical training that includes severe nutritional restriction.

The basis for this abusive training is the collective athletic ambition of parents, coaches, and athletes. Together, they share an obsession with the athletes' maintaining a prepubertal physique, since this physique appears to maximize athletic potential by satisfying the esthetic predilections of tournament judges. "In staving off puberty to maintain the 'ideal' body shape," Ryan (1995) wrote, "girls risk their health in ways their male counterparts never do" (p. 9). The risks are physical, such as the overuse injuries described by Micheli (1984), and psychiatric, especially the eating disorders, which may become fatal (see chapter 4 of this volume). It is Ryan's opinion that while gymnastics and figure skating provide special opportunities for girls in sports, they also attempt to arrest the development of a girl's body, binding it in a prepubescent state like "the Victorian waist or the Chinese woman's foot" (p. 6).

The systematic abuse of young girls in gymnastics is concealed, according to Ryan (1995), by a "code of silence" among the participants, including the athletes themselves. She quotes one victim as saying that she felt "let down" by her own "inability to say no" to her coaches, who preferred "small, mute creatures who look at the coach as an idol and perform everything without ever talking back" (p. 24, quoting Elena Moukina in an interview in *International Gymnast*, 1987). The relative inability of female athletes to verbally protest their handling and express whatever they may think and feel about themselves and their situation may be part of a more general phenomenon of women's loss of voice that Carol Gilligan (1982) spoke of in her book, *In a Different Voice*.

Gilligan's book is both a critique of male-centered theories of psychological development and an alternative account of female development, emphasizing a "struggle for connection" and a developing "ethic of care." Particularly relevant to athletics is Gilligan's discussion of the adolescent girl's passage into an adult world oriented to the concerns of powerful males. This psychological passage is characterized by the beginning of self-doubt, the establishment of a "dissociative split" between experience and reality, and mind and body, and a difficulty in "listening to one's own voice."

Although Gilligan documents examples of successful defiance of gender expectations, the psychological impact of expected gender roles on athletic girls seems to become especially burdensome in adolescence, much as Gilligan describes. Athletic girls, even today, are often expected in adolescence to either relinquish participation or reduce the value they attach to sports. They may be taught that an athletic physique is unfeminine, a confusing prejudice capable of infecting the most routine activities of basic athletic training with doubt and embarrassment. In addition, the differential effects of developing secondary sex characteristics creates a gap between the girls and their former peers among athletic boys, even though they continue to display physical superiority over nonathletic boys. Many girls simply quit competing in adolescence, and the athletes studied by Ryan (1995) suffered frequent episodes of confusion, loss of a sense of self, and an inability to articulate their inner states.

Interest in women's sports and participation in sports by women have increased significantly in recent years. It is said that between 1970 and 1996, participation in sports by high-school girls has grown from 1 in 27 students to 1 in 3. There are successful professional leagues for women in the United States in basketball and softball. Corporations are estimated to have spent $100 million a year in 1997 to sponsor women's sporting events, and various kinds of sports equipment designed for women, such as a softball helmet with an opening for a pony tail, are being marketed (Fahri, 1997).

It remains to be seen whether the growing popularity of women's sports will result in athletics acquiring a female voice, one that emphasizes, to use Gilligan's (1982) concepts, connectedness and a caring ethic. A recent television advertisement that depends for its effect on a little girl's edgy remarks to a well-known female athlete indicate that advertisers, at least, may not quickly welcome the voice Gilligan describes. No doubt there are factors other than gender at issue here, as indicated by manifestations of "connectedness" displayed by men. It is customary, for example, for the male rugby players of opposing teams to gather in a postgame singing of traditional songs.

But studies that compare caring behaviors or manifestations of connectedness within and across gender need to be carried out in order to shed light on this issue. It would be interesting, for example, to measure the frequencies with which male and female athletes interrupt their play to care for an injured teammate or opponent, or the mean number of passes that occur among men and women before a basketball is shot at the hoop. It is not yet clear whether sports will permanently acquire a distinctive women's voice, or whether that voice will turn out to be little more than a weak echo of the sound of masculine heroics.

THE INSECURITY OF THE HERO

The loss or impairment of voice among young women participating in sports exemplifies a paradox with broad implications for the mental health of athletes. It is clear that athletic participation may have a beneficial effect on psychological development, enhancing self-confidence (Brook & Heim, 1991), contributing to moral reasoning (Shields &

Bredemeier, 1995), and perhaps counteracting pressures to behave in a deviant manner (Hastad, Segrave, Pangrazi, & Peterson, 1984). Sports have been used as a therapeutic modality for the treatment of depression and anxiety (Kostrubala, 1984), and for the treatment of hospitalized patients (Moore, 1966) as far back as the early decades of the 1800s (Windholz, 1995). It appears, however, that athletic participation has the potential for contradictory effects, directly promoting healthy development, on the one hand, while casting a person in a pathogenic role, on the other.

Various observers have suggested that the role of the professional athlete, in particular, has deleterious psychological consequences. In the fifth century B.C., Euripides described athletes as "slaves to their belly and their jaw" and blamed "the custom of the Hellenes who, honoring useless pleasures, gather to see such men" (Olivova, 1984, p. 102). Bradley (1976) has described how social adulation may mask an athlete's personal deficiencies until the end of one's career, when the athlete realizes, too late, that his "sense of identity is insufficient" (p. 123). It has been proposed that a triad of "aggressivity, promiscuity, and narcissistic grandiosity and vulnerability," which has been labeled "the Achilles complex," may represent an occupational hazard for professional athletes, resulting from developmental distortions of their role (Begel, 1992). One athlete has coined the phrase "terminal adolescent syndrome" to describe the professional athlete's deficits (House, 1989).

It is possible that a generic diminution of voice analogous to that of women athletes afflicts male professionals as well. Various observers have commented on the apparent rarity with which African American professional athletes publicly discuss the subject of racism in sports (Lapchick, 1991; Rhoden, 1998). Almost certainly, this conspicuous public silence is not a direct reflection of discourse among the athletes themselves, since the personal opinions of athletes on most matters, not only social and political ones, tend to be concealed from the public. In part, this may be due to the risks of speaking out, as Lapchick has observed, and Williams (1996), in her legal analysis of the racially hostile work environment of professional sports, has elaborated. Williams described how the deference required of pioneering black athletes in years gone by has been resurrected as a requirement for "professionalism," a new standard that has itself become a tool to effectively suppress legitimate protest. Although public silence may not directly reflect private discourse among athletes themselves, it might be instructive to compare the public responses of athletes to a prominent episode of racism, with the public responses of, say, musicians, actors, or other entertainers to the same episode. In this way, the impact of subordinating tools on athletes as a group might be assessed.

Whatever the results of such a study turn out to be, the average contemporary observer considers the attribution of personal shortcomings to prior mistreatment to be little more than a lame excuse. This is especially true when a person is accused of doing something wrong. The claim that graft among politicians caused a particular politician to take a bribe is not acceptable reasoning. Nor does a boxer who bites the ear of an opponent during a match receive any special sympathy for playing a sport that permits unusually direct expressions of aggression. But as Durkheim (1895) pointed out long ago, and as social scientists have repeatedly shown (Erikson, 1966), the factors that lead a particular individual to behave in a certain way are both psychologic and sociologic.

In his *Rules of Sociological Method*, first published in 1895, Durkeim pointed out the coercive influence of society on the thought and conduct of individuals. Such influence is obvious when considering the type of currency people use, the language they speak, and the clothes they wear. But even in behaviors that are intensely personal, such as suicide, Durkheim (1897) discerned the influence of society. The relative stability of suicide rates from year to year indicated, he said, a collective cause of some sort, almost a need, if you will, for societies to have a certain number of people kill themselves.

Durkheim also believed that social phenomena that are usually regarded disapprovingly are in fact required for the health of society. Crime, he suggested, helps the members of a community to maintain a collective awareness of the law. Strictly applying this principle to athletes would perhaps result in some absurd oversimplifications, such as that the female gymnast's loss of voice is a reminder to people to speak to one another, or the black athlete's subdued protest is an indirect catalyst for liberating activities. But it is reasonable to believe that how an athlete behaves depends in part on how that athlete is expected to behave. An individual cast as a hero in a complex social drama of race, gender, and sports will inevitably be transformed by the role.

One of the primary adaptations seems to be that taken by anyone of celebrity status. Athletes are continually beseeched by people who want material or emotional sustenance from them, and who will go to great lengths to get it. As a result, privacy becomes extremely important, and some athletes will confine their social interactions almost entirely to other members of their guild and to the narrow circle of their entourage. By becoming overly isolated, however, the athlete will inevitably become even more of an abstraction to his or her fans. The public will be all the more likely to misunderstand the athlete, who becomes entirely as an object of entertainment or, as one athlete put it, "like an animal in a zoo." Thus deprived of the normal range of social interactions, a versatile repertoire of ego skills becomes elusive, conspicuously so at retirement.

A peculiar twist to the isolation of the prominent athlete occurs during adolescence. At an age when a person normally detaches from public obligations and immerses oneself in the idiosyncrasies of one's group of peers, the athlete is prematurely thrust upon the social stage. People recognize him, seek out his opinion, and invite him to their social functions. Even within the athlete's family, the loosening of familial dependence loads the shared interest in the athlete's performance with extra significance. As the athlete's career progresses, this loss of privacy will become burdensome. But in adolescence, the status of hero provides ballast for the normal fluctuations of self-esteem.

The malignant factor in the athlete's role may very well be that for the public he or she is little more than a "self-object," to borrow Kohut's term (Kohut, 1971). The only thing the public knows for sure about an athlete is whether that athlete wins or loses. The rest is rumor, conjecture, and fabrication. In the public's eye, the athlete does not exist as a complex human being, but exists only to serve society's needs. The public's attachment to the athlete is intense, but superficial, fickle, and narcissistic. According to Singer (1994), "levels of emotional experience normally forbidden in daily life find easy expression in the fan's unbridled hatred, sadism, gloating, ridiculing, and murderous rages" (p. 54). As one of Bradley's (1976) informants aptly put it, "when the fan is kissing your ass and telling you that you're the greatest, he hates you" (p. 193).

This fickle, exploitative treatment can only lead, if anywhere, to a replication of narcissistic problems in the athlete. Little else could be fostered by such a peculiar blend of worship and contempt than a complementary one of grandiosity and insecurity. Kohut attributes a wide variety of psychological states to narcissistic regressions, among them "trance-like" states, unrealistically grandiose moods, and "cold, imperious" behavior. Further regression, he says, brings extreme tension, low self-esteem, shame, hypochondria, autoeroticism, loss of a sense of self, depersonalization, and estrangement. It is possible that psychological states like these contribute to the eating disorders, depressions, and other mental illnesses of athletes. They may also contribute to such common performance problems as choking and slump, and to drop-out rates, outbursts of group violence, and contagious injury. If this is so, then the specific psychological problems of athletes may originate, in part, in their role as hero and villain, a role played willingly.

One sport psychiatrist wisely asked his colleagues if "anyone is feeling sorry yet" for a young golfer who had just turned in a magnificent record-breaking performance (Burton, 1997). There is something tragic about the impact of a hero's role on the mind of the actor who enthusuastically plays it. Especially in sports, where the joys are so obvious, it is sad to see how the potential for lasting satisfaction becomes tainted by factors that have nothing to do with the game. A famous metaphor penned by Frederick Douglass (1881) might apply to the contemporary athlete, before the consequences of his role have dawned on him. Describing a solitary seven-mile journey from one slaveholder's farm to that of another to whom he had been sold, Douglass wrote: "Like a fish in a net, allowed to play for a time, I was now drawn rapidly to the shore, secured at all points" (p. 94).

REFERENCES

Begel, D. (1992). An overview of sport psychiatry. *American Journal of Psychiatry, 149*(5), 606–614.

Beisser, A. (1967). *The madness in sports*. New York: Appleton-Century-Crofts.

Benedict, J. (1997). *Public heroes, private felons, athletes and crimes against women*. Boston: Northeastern University.

Benedict, J., & Klein, A. (1997). Arrest and conviction rates for athletes accused of sexual assault. *Sociology of Sport Journal, 14*, 86–94.

Birrell, S. J. (1988). Discourse on the gender/sport relationship: From women in sport to gender relations. *Exercise and Sport Sciences Review, 16*, 459–502.

Bradley, B. (1976). *Life on the run*. New York: Quadrangle/The New York Times Book Co.

Brook, U., & Heim, M. (1991). A pilot study to investigate whether sports influences psychological parameters in the personality of asthmatic children. *Family Practice, 8*, 213–215.

Burton, B. (1997). Editor's choice. *The International Society for Sport Psychiatry Newsletter, 7*(3), 1.

Douglass, F. (1881). *Life and times of Frederick Douglass: His early life as a slave, his escape from bondage, and his complete history: An autobiography*. New York: Gramercy.

Durkheim, E. (1895). *The rules of sociological method*. (S. Lukes, Ed.; W. D. Halls, Trans.). New York: Free.

Durkheim, E. (1897). *Suicide: A study in sociology* (G. Simpson, Ed.; J. A. Spaulding & G. Simpson, Trans.). New York: Free.

Erikson, K. T. (1966). *Wayward puritans: A study in the sociology of deviance*. New York: Wiley.

Fahri, P. (1997, November 17). Courting the women. *The Washington Post National Weekly Edition*, p. 17.

Gilligan, C. (1982). *In a different voice: Psychological theory and women's development*. Cambridge, MA: Harvard University.

Greene, L. S. (1984). The new NCAA rules of the game: Academic integrity or racism. *St. Louis University Law Journal, 28*, 101–151.

Grove City College et al. v. Bell, Secretary of Education et al. (1984). *Supreme Court Reporter* (104), 1211.

Hastad, D. N., Segrave, J. O., Pangrazi, R., & Peterson, G. (1984). Youth sport participation and deviant behavior. *Sociology of Sport Journal, 1*, 366–373.

Hoberman, J. (1997). *Darwin's athletes*. Boston: Houghton Mifflin.

Hoch, P. (1972). *Rip off the big game*. New York: Doubleday.

House, T. (1989). *The jock's itch*. Chicago: Contemporary.

Kohut, H. (1971). The analysis of the self. *The Psychoanalytic Study of the Child, Monograph 4*. New York: International Universities.

Kostrubala, T. (1984). Running and therapy. In M. L. Sachs & G. W. Fuggone (Eds.), *Running as therapy: An integrated approach*. Lincoln, NE: University of Nebraska.

Lapchick, R. (1984). *Broken promises, racism in American sports*. New York: St. Martin's.

Lapchick, R. E. (1986). *Fractured focus: Sport as a reflection of society*. Lexington, MA: D. C. Heath.

Lapchick, R. (1991). *Five minutes to midnight: Race and sport in the 1990s*. Lanham, MD: Madison.

Lapchick, R. (1998, May). *My life in sports*. Address to the International Society for Sport Psychiatry, Toronto.

Leonard, W. M. II (1988). *A sociological perspective of sport* (3rd ed.). New York: Macmillan.

McCrone, K. (1988). *Sport and the physical emancipation of English women, 1870–1914*. London: Routledge.

Micheli, L. (1984). *Pediatric and adolescent sports medicine*. Boston: Little, Brown.

Moore, R. A. (1966). *Sports and mental health*. Springfield, IL: Charles C. Thomas.

Olivova, V. (1984). *Sports and games in the ancient world*. London: Orbis.

Plessy v. Ferguson (1896). *Supreme Court Reporter* (16), 1138.

Rhoden, W. C. (1998, January 31). In the NFL, justice is still denied. *The New York Times*, p. B17.

Rust, E., & Rust, Jr., A. (1985). *Art Rust's illustrated history of the black athlete*. New York: Doubleday.

Ryan, J. (1995). *Little girls in pretty boxes*. New York: Doubleday.

Shields, D. L., & Bredemeier, B. L. (1995). *Character development and physical activity*. Champaign, IL: Human Kinetics.

Singer, T. (1994). Baseball as the center of the world. In M. Stein & J. Hollwitz (Eds.), *Psyche and sports*. Wilmette, IL: Chiron.

Weiss, P. (1969). *Sport: A philosophic inquiry*. Carbondale, IL: Southern Illinois University.

Williams, P. W. (1996). Performing in a racially hostile environment. *Marquette Sports Law Journal, 6*(2), 287–314.

Wilson, W. (1996). The IOC and the status of women in the Olympic movement: 1972–1996, *Research Quarterly for Exercise and Sport, 67*(12), 183–192.

Windholz, G. (1995). Psychiatric treatment and the condition of the mentally disturbed at Berlin's Charite in the early decade of the nineteenth century. *History of Psychiatry, 6*(2), 157–176.

Yoemans, E. (1979). *The shady hill school: The first fifty years*. Cambridge, MA: Windflower.

II

CLINICAL ISSUES

4

Mental Illness in Athletes

Robert W. Burton

THE COUNTENANCE OF MENTAL ILLNESS is often indistinguishable from that of normalcy. The most profound aspect of mental illness is that it occurs in people who are otherwise functioning well, even in those possessing outstanding abilities in specialized and creative endeavors. Nowhere is this truer than in sports. Whether it is the multisport, collegiate woman athlete, a relentless competitor who one day stunningly commits suicide, or the brazen star quarterback who grudgingly reveals his chemical dependence only after having a seizure, the athlete suffering from a psychiatric disorder is the ultimate human paradox. Sport participation is supposed to promote health and well-being. In addition, the natural selection process in sport would seem to be designed to sort out the psychologically flawed as well as the physically inferior. And yet, athletes at the highest level of competition continue to come forward to speak of their symptoms and suffering.

Mental illness does occur in athletes and while definitive demographic data are not available, there is evidence suggesting that athletes suffer from the same types of psychiatric disorders as the general population in roughly the same distribution. It has been documented that highly accomplished athletes suffer from all of the major diagnostic groups, including mood disorders, psychotic illnesses, psychoactive substance abuse, and others (Deykin, Levy, & Wells, 1987; Johnson, Powers, & Dick, in press; Pope & Katz, 1988). In addition, athletes are at increased risk for certain illnesses, such as eating disorders, and are more likely to receive treatment for still others, like chemical dependence and anxiety disorders. The reasons for these tendencies are directly related to the human experience of being an athlete. Lifting the mask of mental illness in athletes will help clinicians not overlook it in even the most unsuspected places, and it will further our understanding of the forces at play in the process of individuals, athletic or nonathletic, developing a psychiatric disorder.

For many reasons, good demographic data do not yet exist for athletes with psychiatric illnesses. Some of these will be discussed later. First, however, we must consider our definitions. How does one define being "an athlete"? How athletic does one have to be to be included in that group? This chapter considers an athlete to be anyone who regularly devotes significant amounts of time to the pursuit of specific athletic performance goals or to the health-enhancing effects of training. This definition allows us to use a sufficiently broad range of the available literature, until such time that more highly refined studies are available. It also sets a minimum threshold for the effects of being athletic and the potential for that lifestyle to influence the athlete's mental health.

Just as important are the questions of defining "mental illness." Do we limit ourselves to syndromes sanctioned by the *DSM-IV* (American Psychiatric Association, 1994)? Since most behavioral and psychic disturbances can be described and conceptualized within that framework, and since that manual has been developed explicitly for the purpose of allowing us to compare and contrast data in the people that we treat, it provides an important organizing framework. But do we restrict our focus to Axis I? Axes I and II? What about V-codes? To debate the boundaries of mental illness along these lines would exceed the limitations of this chapter. However, the issue is relevant to any discussion of athletes because research has revealed a concerning incidence of behavioral and psychological features of mental illnesses beyond the *DSM*-sanctioned syndromes, as well as various "subclinical" syndromes. The significance of these findings is not yet entirely clear. A similar diagnostic situation exists within the realm of affective disorders. Specifically, the spectrum of bipolar affective disorders, along with the utility of the *DSM-IV* designations for these, has been and will continue to be debated (Akiskal, 1996).

We will focus our discussion on the *DSM-IV* Axis I disorders because they are the syndromes most people associate with mental illness. The exclusion of Axis II is in spite of the evidence suggesting that biological factors influence temperament and personality but, again, such a discussion is beyond the scope of this work. Undoubtedly, personality plays an important role in the genesis of many of the Axis I disorders and this is as relevant in athletes as it is in the general population.

THE DEVELOPMENTAL PROCESS AND NATURAL SELECTION OF ATHLETES

Before embarking on a review of the evidence of mental illness in athletes, it is imperative to establish a developmental perspective. Any discussion of an athlete or a group of athletes must be considered within the context of the overarching psychosocial developmental process of that individual or individuals. Just as the *DSM-IV* differentiates between disorders that occur in children and adolescents from those that occur primarily in adults, the important psychological issues in youth sports are different from those at the college or professional level. While this may seem obvious to most clinicians and educators, it bears being made explicit. No matter how prodigious or talented a young athlete may be and how, as a result, he or she may appear older and further along in his or her development, one must always remember that children are still children and not miniature adults.

In our earliest stages of human development, we are all athletes. Struggling to execute the degrees of difficulty associated with sitting up, rolling over, and first attempts at walking, infants universally warm to the cheers of the audience and supportive judges. The pure joy of movement and the acquisition of early motor skills form the foundation for all future athletic movement and for fans' appreciation of the performance of others. Our ability to identify with the performer and to observe with knowing awe is the basis for the tremendous popularity of sports.

Almost as soon as the process of developing as an athlete begins, however, a countervailing process stirs as well. Potential athletes of all shapes and sizes are discouraged and directed away from certain activities in a manner that complements yet opposes the support and nurturing attention that helps other athletes grow and develop and discover what they do well and enjoy. Each athlete's story of how he or she came to be is therefore unique, and for every successful survivor of the rigors of the various levels of competition, there are multitudes left behind.

The process of selection—and deselection—of athletes, then, is ongoing and of a dual nature. Athletes are selected for and excluded from further participation based on psychological as well as physical strengths and limitations. As a result, the more severe an athlete's psychiatric symptoms and the more highly competitive the level, the less likely he or she will be able to continue to participate and compete. This process, in effect, operates to exclude most athletes with more serious disorders. A certain degree of reality-testing and problem-solving, an ability to relate to others, and some self-directed impulse control are required. In contrast, few delusional or otherwise psychotic or severely anxious or depressed individuals will be able to continue to participate.

In more subtle ways, less seriously symptomatic individuals will be removed from any group of athletes as well. For example, an outstanding adolescent athlete who develops a mysterious psychosomatic illness associated with a moderate degree of anxiety and, as a result, is unable to maintain sufficient weight, muscle mass, strength, or endurance, will be discouraged from competing by his family and coaches.

THE EVIDENCE AND THE RESISTANCE

Although our epidemiological data is incomplete, the studies do provide glimpses of the reality behind the closed locker-room doors, and when compared with our clinical experience, they give us something substantial upon which to base our conclusions.

In general, psychiatric disturbances in athletes are underreported, and individuals, couples, and families are undertreated (Pierce, 1969). The athletic community's mental health needs are vastly underserved. There are simply too many forces opposing an athlete's getting adequate treatment. The individual athlete is afraid to disclose any psychiatric symptom for fear that it will be revealed and exploited as a sign of weakness and used as a reason for his or her deselection. The culture of sports and athletes is still decidedly "macho," especially when it comes to emotional vulnerabilities. Athletes have to be physically strong and mentally tough to win. To admit to a psychological or emotional problem not only threatens the individual's own confidence, so players' conventional wisdom goes, it also threatens one's status with teammates and coaches. This negative halo effect, with the athlete's suffering and a zone of silence spreading over the teammates and others around him or her, is a major concern in itself and presents a major health hazard to athletes. To the extent that it impedes the athlete from getting the professional help he or she needs, it puts that person at risk for greater suffering, potential morbidity, and even mortality.

Given this level of resistance to athletes receiving the treatment they deserve, and the collusion that takes place on the part of the nonparticipant significant others in sport, let us consider the various types of psychiatric syndromes and how often they present in athletes.

MOOD DISORDERS

Athletes appear to be more susceptible to depression than to bipolar affective disorder. Perhaps the physical rigors and mental discipline of athletic training ultimately selects out almost anyone with manic episodes or a severe degree of mood instability. Whatever the cause, manic-depressive athletes are not often reported in the literature. Exceptions are the substance-induced mood disorders that present with manic symptoms. Specifically, anabolic androgenic steroids have been reported to induce mania, along with a host of other psychiatric signs and symptoms (Pope & Katz, 1994). Fortunately, once substance use is interrupted, the mood disorder typically resolves, or at least becomes amenable to treatment.

On the other hand, many athletes have been reported to have suffered from depressive disorders, including major depression (Olney, 1997), and these are some of the most common emotional problems encountered by athletes (Deykin et al., 1987; Nicholi, 1987). While this may not be surprising given the high-stress environment that envelops most elite sports, there are several sports-specific factors that are worth noting.

1. Severe forms of depression very often preclude sport participation. One simply cannot train adequately or compete effectively when extremely depressed. Those prone to depressive illness will often be eliminated in the selection process. Although athletes have recovered from an episode of illness and returned to their sport, it is not at all clear how often this occurs.
2. Exercise and sport are therapeutic agents against depression and possibly other mood disorders. They have antidepressant effects of their own (Morgan, 1985) and often become a preferred defensive strategy for an individual athlete's psyche. Athletes commonly train

or exercise when sad, angry, or frustrated in order to feel better—at least temporarily. Exercise or sport participation can be health promoting if it is not the only defense mechanism used and it is not used to completely avoid dealing with a serious underlying issue.

3. Overtraining can lead to athletic burnout, referred to as overtraining syndrome, the symptoms of which are remarkably similar to depression (Kuipers, 1998). The physical demands of the athletic activity could conceivably deplete necessary biological factors, such as neurotransmitters, and cause symptoms. A certain group of athletes will respond to their less than satisfactory performance by pushing themselves even harder in their training, leading to a state of chronic fatigue and a depression that may be physiologically-based (Puffer & McShane, 1992).
4. Alternatively, an athlete with an inadequately developed repertoire of defenses might rely too heavily on exercise, overutilize it, find it inadequate or its effects too transient, and become depressed. Often an underlying depression will only become manifest years later. As an example, a youth threw himself into training for a sport in an attempt to deal with the tragic loss of a sibling and to escape the family's shared depression. After years of success as an athlete, his competitive career came to an end and a full-blown episode of major depression ensued.
5. Athletes often present for treatment of depression two or three years after retirement from their competitive sport. It is not always simply the loss of that meaningful activity that accounts for the sadness and despair. It is, instead, a combination of losses: the positively reinforcing activity itself, the preferred coping mechanism, and the physiological benefits of the exercise.

Additional evidence for this formulation is that when athletes begin to train or compete in some manner again, their depressive symptoms often remit, even if it is in a quite different type of sport or exercise activity. Examples are the career swimmer who becomes a triathlete, the baseball and basketball players who have taken up golf, and the former skiers and football players who have turned to automobile racing. Clearly, the type of training does not have to be the same as the previous sport. In most instances, however, athletes will be drawn to sports that share either an affective component or physical skill set reminiscent of their previously chosen sport. They can be counseled to consider these choices thoughtfully and taught to keep the new sport in perspective. The painful reality is that it is extremely rare for an athlete to become highly successful in more than one sport in his or her lifetime.

Beyond these factors, the inevitable losses that occur during competition and the injuries associated with athletic participation pose additional risks for depression. The more successful the athlete and the more serious the injury, the more likely the athlete will experience an episode of severe depression, even to the point of contemplating or attempting suicide (Smith & Milliner, 1994). Athletic participation is actually an added risk factor for suicide in young men and women. Other aspects of athletic injury that add to the risk are the lack of a return to the previous level of athletic functioning and the experience of being replaced by a teammate. For those familiar with the harsh realities of sport, these latter two consequences of injury would seem to be extremely common. While a certain percentage of adolescents and young adults would undoubtedly have become depressed anyway, post-injury depressive disorders are not merely reflections of a disturbed pre-injury mood or, in today's jargon, of a pre-existing condition (Smith et al., 1993).

Other factors thought to have a role in promoting the development of depression in athletes are the expectations of coaches and teammates, value incongruencies, heightened public visibility, time demands, social isolation, fatigue, academic pressures, and racial and gender stereotyping and discrimination (Lopiano & Zotos, 1992.)

SCHIZOPHRENIA AND OTHER PSYCHOTIC DISORDERS

While schizophrenic illnesses occasionally have been reported in elite athletes, the process of selection probably operates most mercilessly on the individual suffering acutely from these disorders. The developmental time course for the onset of these illnesses has individuals becoming most symptomatic at the very time that the pressures to perform as an athlete are the greatest. This also happens to be the time when many athletes are at or near the peak of their physical skills. It is nonetheless conceivable that a highly talented athlete with either mild positive symptoms or a late onset of a schizophrenic illness could reach an elite level of competition before being diagnosed and, hopefully, treated.

According to the scientific literature, the most likely cause for a psychotic disorder among athletes is substance-induced psychosis. Again, the psychiatric complications of anabolic androgenic steroid use have been well-researched (Pope & Katz, 1988), and clinicians must rule out this etiology before entertaining other diagnoses. My clinical experience, however, suggests that steroid use may be overrepresented in the literature. Nevertheless, when an athlete experiences a psychotic episode, suspicion must be high for all types of substance abuse. As toxic and withdrawal syndromes are ruled out, more obscure substances must be searched for, and the possibility of a primary psychotic illness seriously considered. While still a diagnosis of exclusion, a psychotic decompensation, characterologically based and precipitated by overwhelming situational stress, occurs in athletes without the confounding influence of substances. Given the propensity toward depressive illnesses, the possibility that some of those episodes might be associated with prominent psychotic features would also seem quite plausible.

Overall, then, psychotic illnesses are rare in athletes. When they do occur, particularly in the initial episode, they should be evaluated thoroughly, ruling out the more common causes such as schizophrenia and substance-related psychoses. A prior episode of psychosis is probably the most powerful predictor of subsequent episodes, regardless of the final diagnosis. Elite athletes who suffer from recurrent brief psychotic episodes, for which no additional cause can be determined, should be able to return to training at the professional level between episodes.

ANXIETY DISORDERS

The anxiety-performance relationship has been discussed extensively in the sport psychology literature (Jones, 1995). Perhaps as a result, anxiety is one emotional experience that athletes are willing to discuss with some level of comfort. While most will still deny any problem with anxiety when asked, athletes do suffer from anxiety disorders. A more effective approach is to consider the anxiety as a symptom, one that can be an indication of a variety of problems as well as an opening for the clinician to talk about other issues. Within the culture of athletes, it is a relatively acceptable reason for an athlete to talk to a psychiatrist, even if it is casually or informally.

Since athletes are judged on a moment-to-moment basis for their performance, it should not be surprising that they are very likely to present with performance anxiety as their chief complaint. Which psychiatric diagnostic entity might account for it, if any, can be quite variable. The first level of assessment, therefore, is whether the anxiety is of clinical concern or whether it is a natural response to the pressures to perform at a high level. Beyond the anxiety that is generally appropriate to the situation, athletes' anxiety can run the gamut from being an indication of a success neurosis to a symptom of marital discord to being a harbinger of an impending panic disorder.

Anxiety can also be a complication of injury, as injured athletes are more anxious (Kolt & Kirkby, 1994). Just as depression has come to be an understandable consequence of injury due to the real or implicit losses involved, anxiety can also be expected to accompany injury. Any injury can be expected to increase the amount of anxiety that an athlete might feel about whether or not he or she is going to be able to perform adequately. This dynamic is really an extension of performance anxiety itself. In certain instances, normalizing the athlete's experience of heightened anxiety following an injury may be therapeutic enough. For those who experience persistent or intense anxiety, other standard treatment modalities should be entertained.

Clinically, the important thing is to evaluate carefully an athlete presenting with performance anxiety. One must rule out other common and treatable disorders and not leave the presenting problem as the diagnosis and reflexively embark on a course of treatment or nontreatment.

While antianxiety medications may not be an option due to restrictions at various levels of competition, it is still important to understand exactly what it is that you are treating. Treatment may be quite frustrating, as in the case of managing an athlete with precompetitive anxiety of panic proportions without the benefit of medication. And yet, an acceptable alternative can often be found, providing symptom relief and performance benefits, which naturally follow. Relaxation techniques and a coherent psychotherapeutic approach to the anxiety are effective and illustrate how therapeutic interventions must often be modified due to limitations imposed either by the governing bodies of sport or the individual athlete.

EATING DISORDERS

The eating disorders are the psychiatric illnesses most studied in the sports medicine literature. While much has been written, not enough insight into the relationship between sports and eating disturbances has been developed.

Athletes are clearly at a greater risk for developing eating disorders than the general population (Stoutjesdyk, 1993; Sundgot-Borgen, 1994;

Wilmore, 1996), and this is true for men more than for women (DePalma et al., 1993; Johnson et al., in press). While the prevalence of both anorexia nervosa and bulimia nervosa is to some extent heightened in athletes, sports participation exerts its influence in some unique ways.

The syndrome of anorexia athletica (Sundgot-Borgen, 1994) illustrates this influence and is perhaps the prototypical sports-related psychiatric illness. This syndrome would be classified as an "Eating Disorder, Not Otherwise Specified," according to the *DSM-IV*. Athletes who would otherwise qualify for a diagnosis of anorexia nervosa are able to avoid that designation by virtue of their increased muscle mass that is a result of their intensive athletic training. They are thus able to keep their weight above the 85 percent of the accepted minimum body weight required for the diagnosis.

A more accurate name and one more consistent with the classic eating disorders, anorexia nervosa and bulimia nervosa, would be athletica nervosa which would identify the exercise as the pathogenic behavior. Athletes who are afflicted with this form of mental illness seriously overtrain and become so psychologically dependent on exercise as their preferred coping mechanism that they lose objectivity about their bodies and their behavior. As a result they practice extreme methods of weight control and develop medical complications. In terms of the latter, consider the athletic woman who has already had 10 knee surgeries but can't stay out of the gym, searching for that escape or release that only comes with vigorous exercise. She also suffers significant hip instability as a result of attempts to compensate for her knee problems, which causes her to fall unexpectedly during her normal daily activity. Not surprisingly, she refuses to use a cane.

In essence, such a person becomes the antithesis of the healthy athlete, one who exercises or is athletic to the point of compromising one's health. This feature is potentially a very useful clinical test in the assessment of a variety of behaviors that become distorted as a result of an individual's involvement in sports. Clearly, a broader spectrum of behavioral disorders exists in the sports world than was once thought, including abusive behaviors (physical, verbal, sexual, and substance-related), as well as impulse-control disorders and conduct problems.

In terms of the eating disorders, the literature indicates that there is a wide range of disordered eating behavior common among athletes of both sexes. Sundgot-Borgen (1994) found that more than 20 percent of all elite female athletes in Norway qualified for an eating disorder, either anorexia nervosa, bulimia nervosa, or anorexia athletica. The prevalence was highest in the so-called "aesthetic sports," such as gymnastics, figure skating, sports dance, and diving, where leanness or a specific body weight is most important. The athletes who began their careers at very young ages were at greatest risk. Sundgot-Borgen identified the triggers to the development of these disorders as prolonged dieting, frequent weight fluctuations, sudden increases in training volume, and traumatic losses, such as injuries, other physical illnesses, or the loss of a coach.

A large study of 11 NCAA Division I schools across 11 sports found that more than 13 percent of all athletes had clinically significant problems with anorexia and bulimia, based on self-report measures and strict criteria for these disorders (Johnson et al., in press). The mean percentage of body fat in the female athletes studied was below that required for normal menses. Johnson and colleagues concluded that their estimate of pathogenic eating behaviors was conservative. Further, they considered 25 percent of female athletes and 9.5 percent of male athletes to be at risk for anorexia and 58 percent of the females and 38 percent of the males to be at risk for bulimia.

In another study, 60 percent of normal-weight gymnasts met criteria for one of the disordered-eating syndromes, while only 22 percent could be considered normal or nondisordered (Petrie, 1993). Not surprisingly, eating disorders were more highly associated with athletes who had a desire to weigh less, who suffered from low self-esteem, and who endorsed the sociocultural views of female attractiveness.

Endurance athletes, due to their time-intensive training methods, have also been shown to be at risk (Wilmore, 1996). With the new "high-tech" training methods, virtually any sport that is being taken seriously by the participant should be considered a risk factor. This type of training encourages exceptionally close scrutiny of athletes' physiology, beyond their exact caloric intake and expenditure, and calculation of their body fat percentage, maximum heart rate, VO_2 max, and other parameters. It is easy to imagine how athletes can develop an unhealthy preoccupation with their bodies and bodily functions. As they try to satisfy their ideal training parameters, which are less and less directly linked to their subjective experience of physically performing in their sport, boundaries become less clear. As their experience of themselves becomes more detached and distant, it becomes more and more likely that their body image will become distorted and their behavior more aberrant.

While typically the province of women, in sports men are actually at significantly greater risk when compared to their nonathlete counterparts. While 1 percent of the men in the general population may have an eating disorder, among athletes the prevalence may approach that of women, at nearly 11 percent (Thiel, Gottfried, & Hesse, 1993), making their relative risk more than 10 times that of their nonathletic peers. Lightweight male rowers undergo serious weight fluctuations during the season and have significantly greater weight gain in the off-season than heavier teammates and their nonathletic classmates, respectively (Sykora, Grilo, Wilfleyl, & Brownell, 1993). Football players and wrestlers binge-eat to keep their weight up as it is believed to confer a competitive advantage over their opponents (Wroble & Moxley, 1998). The hazardous practice of wrestlers starving and dehydrating themselves shortly before weighing in has proven to be potentially lethal. Even jockeys engage in the risky behavior of purging. Clearly, when considering eating disorders and athletes, it is a major mistake to only think of the women as being at risk.

While the psychiatric morbidity and mortality of eating disorders is recognized, there are also links between eating disorders, mood disorders, and osteoporosis (Gadpaille, Sanborn, & Wagner, 1987) and between eating disorders, amenorrhea, and osteoporosis (Yeager, 1993). Since such serious consequences occur, there must be a search for a causal explanation. What are the pathogenic mechanisms that result in athletes becoming ill with an eating disorder? While a simple explanation is not possible, it can be surmised that the various intense pressures on athletes' performance (Brownell, 1995) and appearance, coupled as they are to high-risk behaviors, create a stressful yet fertile environment in which susceptible individuals will develop an eating disorder. Additional factors that make a particular athlete vulnerable are the same ones that apply to the general population: low self-esteem, prior mood disturbance, control issues with parents, a limited repertoire of defense mechanisms, and high socioeconomic status with its attendant pressures.

The amount of time athletes spend contemplating the appearance and functioning of their bodies, often in exquisite detail, puts them at risk for developing an unhealthy preoccupation with their physical selves, another hallmark feature of eating disorders. As training techniques become more sophisticated and the levels of competition more and more intense, to where winning and losing hinge on minute performance increments—or worse, on the more subjective judgements of others—the challenge to remain objective about one's weight or body shape becomes increasingly difficult. Accordingly, the temptations to use extreme means to control these variables rise.

ADJUSTMENT DISORDERS

In addition to the real and potential losses that contribute to athletes' susceptibility to depression and anxiety disorders, their often sheltered lifestyle leaves them with limited coping mechanisms. The defenses and personality structure that they do have are often rigid and concrete, while their personalities tend to be strongly goal-oriented and perfectionistic. A narcissistic personality disorder can be considered an occupational hazard (Begel, 1992). Beyond that, athletes would seem to be at risk for a variety of other forms of personality difficulties, all of which would predispose them to adjustment disorders. Athletes deprived of the usual type of hardening experiences of childhood, adolescence, and early adulthood would be likely to have limited or inadequately developed abilities to cope with life's more difficult moments and may become symptomatic. In addition, their athletic success may burden them with excessive expectations, sometimes at an early age when they are more unlikely to handle them effectively.

This kind of a situation, where an individual becomes symptomatic and suffers from an identifiable psychiatric syndrome, should be differentiated from the athlete who is forced to go through normal development in the public eye. Life is inherently stressful, and normal development includes periods of stress and discomfort where people become mildly or transiently symptomatic without qualifying for an actual episode of illness. In these instances, it is the responsibility of the clinician to rigorously apply the rules of diagnosis and to base a diagnosis only on a thorough evaluation that has been done in person. As an aside, nothing is more unethical or potentially damaging than the public pronouncement of an athlete's illness based on secondhand knowledge, an event that appears in the various media all too often.

ATTENTION DEFICIT DISORDERS

Athletes with attention-deficit/hyperactivity disorder (ADHD) may be overrepresented when compared to the general population. Young people with ADHD are more inclined toward physical activity, probably as a way of managing affect and/or anxiety. They may rightly or wrongly perceive their physical skills as more substantial than their mental or verbal ones, and in this way are drawn to athletic activities. The case of the professional athlete who grew up playing a wide array of sports, sometimes during overlapping seasons, as a way of dealing with his boundless energy is probably fairly typical. Stumbling upon one in which he excelled and in which he could make a nice living was extremely fortunate.

Unfortunately, for many, their behavior outside of the sport setting will get them into serious trouble that will threaten, if not preclude, their continued participation. Coaches and others are often required to have more patience and make extra efforts to encourage the verbal and social interaction that is a necessary and inherent part of sport.

The principles of rigorous diagnosis as well as creative, yet reasonable and coherent treatment approaches apply to the challenge of working with athletes with attention deficit disorders as they do to those afflicted in the general population. However, a clinician's treatment options are often limited further by national governing bodies of sport, as many of the pharmacological methods of managing these illnesses are not allowable for athletes wishing to compete at the higher levels.

POSTTRAUMATIC STRESS DISORDER

The same vulnerabilities that predispose athletes to eating disorders, depression, and adjustment disorders apply to the syndrome of posttraumatic stress disorder (PTSD). PTSD has been reported in athletes, using the usual criteria of encountering a major threat to one's life or self (Nicholi, 1987).

In addition, injuries to athletes are very often career-threatening and any serious injury, defined as one requiring surgery or a significant withdrawal from participation or training, should be considered traumatic until proven otherwise. The injury-causing incident can become an intrusive memory, analogous to the precipitating event in other cases of PTSD, and avoidant behavior may result. The condition may be conceptualized along a continuum of psychological responses to injury. The more severe, painful, or threatening the injury to the athlete, the greater the potential for it to be traumatizing. Fortunately, listening closely to an athlete talk about his or her experience of an injury will give the clinician plenty of clues that he or she has been traumatized. Working through the trauma successfully in a therapeutic relationship is feasible, but it can also be extremely difficult. A strong therapeutic alliance is absolutely necessary.

SUBSTANCE-RELATED DISORDERS

Because athletes become such high-profile celebrities, professional and collegiate athletes are scrutinized for their use of alcohol and other drugs. Since these are also major public health concerns and thus potential public relations nightmares for some of the academic and business interests surrounding sports, most leagues and conferences have fairly well-developed systems of care for chemical dependence treatment. Compared to other psychiatric illnesses, athletes in general have greater access to this component of the mental health care system and as a result will be more likely to receive treatment for these conditions. Whether the treatment provided is optimal or even efficacious is unclear, since no data have been published. With so many interested others involved in the process, including family, friends, teammates, coaches, athletic directors, and even agents, treatment is often extremely difficult. Not everyone will keep the athlete's best interest in mind.

There are data suggesting that certain groups of athletes are less likely than their nonathlete counterparts to abuse substances. Collegiate athletes clearly engage in high-risk behaviors, including the use and abuse of substances. Female college athletes appear to use more alcohol, while the men use more drugs (Johnson et al., in press).

Overall, alcohol is still the most frequently abused substance in sports as it is in society. In the sports medicine literature, however, the greatest attention has been paid to anabolic androgenic steroids (AAS). Athletes are 10–20 times more likely to abuse these substances than nonathletes, who tend to use them for their masculinizing effects on appearance. Nearly 7 percent of all high-school seniors, athletes and nonathletes, have used or are using them (Buckley et al., 1988).

The athlete using AAS often fits the pathogenetic pattern that has been described for the eating disorders. Some order of success along with the attendant external or internal pressure leads an athlete to explore various questionable practices for becoming faster, stronger, or more aggressive in order to gain a competitive advantage. Perhaps, initially out of frustration, after conventional or acceptable methods fail to produce clear benefit, the athlete decides to try these other means. Once established as a behavior with predictable effects, either physically or emotionally, they become potentially addictive substances with patterns of use consistent with that of dependence according to *DSM-IV* standards (American Psychiatric Association, 1994).

An important element in the situation with AAS is the belief, or at least the suspicion, that other athletes against whom one may be competing are already using them. It is often difficult for athletes to simply accept that another athlete is better than they are. In fact, this denial is often promoted as a cognitive strategy by coaches and others, including sport psychologists, camouflaged in the name of the power of positive thinking or self-talk. Unfortunately, it is an inherent part of sport that not everyone can be the best. On a given day in a given contest, only one person can be the victor. As a result of an athlete's denial of this reality and of being painfully and unavoidably confronted, an athlete may resort to doing something that is unacceptable by most standards. Athletes' ability to rationalize these choices is often remarkable, particularly in this area of substance abuse and dependence. It can make such behavior seem justifiable. It is also an interesting type of peer pressure, subtle and clandestine, but still based on the notion that "everyone else is doing it."

Another interpersonal aspect to AAS abuse is that invariably there is a "significant other" involved in either introducing the practice of using or actually helping to administer the substance. The presence of this significant other not only makes it a social activity of sorts but it also offers an opportunity for intervention. Knowledgeable and experienced coaches or others involved with an athlete's training should be alert and sensitive to an athlete's frustration or lack of progress and suggest ways of improving performance and actively discourage the use of things like AAS. Only by other significant people talking to these athletes about the risks, dangers, and unacceptability of a variety of training methods can there be any hope of changing this behavioral manifestation of the "win at any cost" mentality.

The subjects of substances of abuse and performance-enhancing drugs are addressed in greater detail in chapters 7 and 8. They are mentioned here as an acknowledgement of their proper designation among the mental illnesses affecting athletes. It is important to remember that AAS abuse can mimic many other psychiatric illnesses, especially mood disorders and psychoses. When considering psychiatric illness in athletes, one must maintain a high level of suspicion for these and other substances, such as stimulants. It is also prudent to anticipate extreme denial and intense resistance, especially rationalization.

Evidence continues to mount to support the notion of addictions as being strongly biologically determined illnesses. While this formulation may still be debatable, that they are among the better-studied and -defined psychiatric syndromes athletes may encounter is not. They clearly occur in significant numbers of athletes.

It is tempting to speculate further as to why this is. Like most of the conditions that have been discussed and described in this chapter, the occurrence of substance abuse in athletes has much to do with the very experience of being an athlete. In addition to the pressures of competition, training rituals, and influence of others, the risk-taking aspect of sport would also seem to have an important role in making it likely that athletes would abuse drugs or alcohol, and, in the process, their bodies. There is a process of letting go and of testing and trusting one's body that takes place with substance misuse and abuse that is akin to pushing oneself to the limit athletically. This inner experience of athletes and the abuse of substances have received some attention in the literature (Nattiv & Puffer, 1991). Discussed as sensation-seeking or risk-taking, it is probably to some degree a necessary ingredient for athletic success. With it comes the improvisation that is often a competitive advantage, as in basketball, for example. This creativity and spontaneity are inherently pleasurable, and this too reinforces and promotes the continued participation and involvement in sport, prolonging athletes' careers. Unfortunately, with drugs and alcohol, too often the outcome is, instead, injury or self-destructiveness.

CONCLUSION

Sport participation incurs a certain amount of stress on athletes. This stress, along with certain behaviors promoted in the name of training or competition, puts individuals at risk for developing a mental illness. That risk is greater than if the athlete had chosen not to participate. The capable individual responds to the stress and works to achieve his or her potential and is rewarded with degrees of success that would not have been attained without accepting the challenge and daring to try. Others will become ill with one of the various psychiatric syndromes that have been discussed and may or may not attain a level of success in sport and, unfortunately, may or may not ever receive adequate treatment for their illness.

Fortunately there are ways to limit some of the stresses and pathogenic behaviors and therefore protect many sport participants. The challenge is to identify the vulnerable individuals as soon as possible and to recognize when the stresses are becoming overwhelming, the behaviors are presenting risk, and actual symptoms are developing. Early detection and intervention can allow athletes to recover from their illness and resume training and competition if they wish to do so. Athletes should always be encouraged to play with emotion, feeling, and passion. In order to do so they need to realize that it requires taking care of themselves so that their emotions are managed and expressed constructively and productively through their sport.

The nagging question is, Why isn't our data better? Why haven't better studies been done? Why haven't the definitive, large-sample, broadly-based, multicenter surveys been done so we know more precisely what the incidence and prevalence of the various disorders are for this highly visible, yet highly representative subpopulation? The reasons must be multifactorial. Most likely the larger reasons are political and economic in nature. Sports are big business, especially at the higher levels of competition. Selfish interests of nonparticipants often prevail. The professional sports leagues, players associations and unions, collegiate athletic conferences, even high-school athletic departments could all easily obtain the data concerning participants' diagnoses and treatment for psychiatric illnesses. They are reluctant to gather such information, however, for some reason. Perhaps they fear that if they found that a certain sport or player was afflicted or in a high-risk category, public opinion might turn against them, their popularity would diminish, and their very reason for being would be threatened. On the other hand, if studies were allowed and supported, perhaps a number of young gymnasts or wrestlers, among others, would still be alive.

There is, in addition, some type of collective, perhaps unconscious, collusion in support of the popular myths that sport participation promotes mental health, and that, as a result, successful athletes are healthier psychologically than nonathletes. These beliefs are myths because they have been typically unassailable and have not been tested. The clinical reality is that sports cut both ways. They can be terrific training grounds for life's important lessons, where skills can be learned and developmental tasks can be accomplished. They can also be detrimental and destructive, depending largely on how the authorities presiding over them—from parents and coaches to governing bodies—carry out their responsibilities. The positive and negative potential are tremendous, and it is this range and polarity that draws us to them as both participants and spectators. They reflect our own dual human nature, of being capable of doing incredible good or of being harmful and destructive. Well-designed studies and an accurate disclosure of the statistics will benefit everyone involved by better defining the scope and nature of the problems, thereby allowing resources to be allocated and organized effectively for those in need of help. Such disclosure would actually enhance sport's popularity by making the athletes and their achievements ever more human.

We must also consider the role of sport in society to provide an outlet for our aggressive nature. Perhaps we recognize on some level the importance of this social benefit and so we overlook the aberrant acts of some athletes and allow them to continue to entertain us.

Consider also, the myth that professional athletes dislike or even hate their opponents. Many professional athletes form friendships with players on other teams because they too are subjected to the same scrutiny and stress that celebrities everywhere are and therefore have a natural bond. In addition, with free agency and athletes being likely to have several employers over the course of a career instead of being bound to a single team, they have greater opportunity to play with other athletes who may become opponents on the field in a subsequent season. Off-season activities also offer athletes a chance to get to know other athletes, even those who participate in other sports. Granted, a few athletes still harbor a dislike for their opponents, but this seems to be more a manufactured affect to justify their aggressive behavior during competition.

Another reason that good data are not available is the decidedly "antipathologizing" stance of sport psychologists. As a group they have been reticent to diagnose athletes, and the players, their athletic conferences, professional leagues, and the national governing bodies of sport have been happy to go along with this approach. As greater awareness and acceptance of mental illness in our society continue to grow, this stance becomes increasingly untenable. To their credit, some of their certification efforts have included experience in clinical assessment and diagnosis.

Clearly, good studies must be done. Accomplishing this task will require the cooperation and teamwork that characterize the positive aspects of sport. It will require individuals to put aside their selfish interests and to work together in pursuit of the common goal of understanding each other. It will also require some insightful individuals and enlightened institutions to initiate the studies and follow them through. The ultimate goal is to make appropriate treatment available to athletes. Psychiatrists with an interest in this area must be willing to take an active and visible role. An added benefit of studying this population is that the results will reveal much about the general population. Athletes can provide a mirror with which to examine ourselves and a lens with which to see a little more clearly how we operate internally.

REFERENCES

Akiskal, H. S. (1996). The prevalent clinical spectrum of bipolar disorders: Beyond DSM-IV. *Journal of Clinical Psychiatry, 16* (Suppl. 1), 4–14.

American Psychiatric Association. (1994). *Diagnostic and statistical manual of mental disorders* (4th ed.). Washington, DC: Author.

Begel, D. (1992). An overview of sport psychiatry. *American Journal of Psychiatry, 149*, 606–614.

Brownell, K. D. (1995). Eating disorders in athletes. In K. D. Brownell & G. F. Fairburn, (Eds.), *Eating disorders and obesity: A comprehensive handbook* (pp. 191–195). New York: Guilford.

Buckley, W. E., Yesalis, C. E., Friedl, K. E., Anderson, W. A., Streit, A. L., & Wright, J. E. (1988). Estimated prevalence of anabolic steroid use among male high school seniors. *Journal of the American Medical Association, 260*, 3441–3445.

DePalma, M. T., Koszewski, W. M., Case, J. G., Barile, R. J., DePalma, B. F., & Oliaro, S. M. (1993). Weight control practices of lightweight football players. *Medicine and Science in Sports and Exercise, 25*, 694–701.

Deykin, E. Y., Levy, J. C., & Wells, V. (1987). Adolescent depression, alcohol, and drug abuse. *American Journal of Public Health, 77*, 178.

Gadpaille, W. J., Sanborn, C. F., Wagner, W. W. (1987). Athletic amenorrhea, major affective disorders, and eating disorders. *American Journal of Psychiatry, 144*, 939–942.

Johnson, C., Powers, P. S., & Dick, R. (in press). Athletes and eating disorders: The NCAA study. *International Journal of Eating Disorders.*

Jones, G. (1995). Competitive anxiety in sport. In J. H. Biddle (Ed.), *European perspectives on exercise and sport psychology* (pp. 128–153). Champaign, IL: Human Kinetics.

Kolt, G. S., & Kirkby, R. J. (1994). Injury, anxiety, and mood in competitive gymnasts. *Perceptual and Motor Skills, 78*, 955–962.

Kuipers, H. (1998). Training and overtraining: An introduction. *Medicine and Science in Sports and Exercise, 30*, 1137–1139.

Lopiano, D. A., & Zotos, C. (1992). Modern athletics: The pressure to perform. In K. D. Brownell, J. Rodin, & J. H. Wilmore (Eds.), *Eating, body weight, and performance in athletes* (pp. 275–292). Philadelphia: Lea & Febiger.

Morgan, W. (1985). Affective beneficence of vigorous physical activity. *Medicine and Science in Sports and Exercise, 17*, 94–100.

Nattiv, A., & Puffer, J. C. (1991). Lifestyles and health risks of collegiate athletes. *Journal of Family Practice, 33*, 585–590.

Nicholi, A. M., (1987). Occasional notes: Psychiatric consultation in professional football. *The New England Journal of Medicine, 316*, 1095–1100.

Olney, B. (1997, August 6). At long last, Harnisch is back to being a pitcher. *The New York Times*, p. C23.

Petrie, T. (1993). Disordered eating in female collegiate gymnasts: Prevalence and personality/attitudinal correlates. *Journal of Sport and Exercise Psychology, 15*, 424–436.

Pierce, R. (1969). Athletes in psychiatry: How many, how come? *Journal of the American Collegiate Health Associations, 17*, 244–249.

Pope, H. G., & Katz, D. L. (1988). Affective and psychotic symptoms associated with anabolic steroid use. *American Journal of Psychiatry, 145*, 487–490.

Pope, H. G., & Katz, D. L. (1994). Psychiatric and medical effects of anabolic androgenic steroid use: A controlled study of 160 athletes. *Archives of General Psychiatry, 51*, 375–382.

Puffer, J. C., & McShane, J. M. (1992). Depression and chronic fatigue in the college student athlete. *Clinics in Sports Medicine, 11*, 327–338.

Smith, A. M., & Milliner, E. K. (1994). Injured athletes and the risk of suicide. *Journal of Athletic Training*, *29*, 337–341.

Smith, A. M., Stuart, M. J., Wiese-Bjornstal, D. M., Milliner, E. K., O'Fallon, W. M., & Crowson, C. S. (1993). Competitive athletes: Preinjury and postinjury mood state and self-esteem. *Mayo Clinic Proceedings*, *68*, 939–947.

Stoutjesdyk, D. (1993). Eating disorders among high-performance athletes. *Journal of Youth and Adolescence*, *22*, 271–282.

Sundgot-Borgen, J. (1994). Risk and trigger factors for the development of eating disorders in female elite athletes. *Medicine and Science in Sports and Exercise*, *26*, 414–419.

Sykora, C., Grilo, C. M., Wilfleyl, D. E., & Brownell, K. D. (1993). Eating, weight, and dieting disturbances in male and female lightweight and heavyweight rowers. *International Journal of Eating Disorders*, *14*, 203–211.

Thiel, A., Gottfried, H., & Hesse, F. W. (1993). Subclinical eating disorders in male athletes: A study of low weight category rowers and wrestlers. *Acta Psychiatrica Scandinavica*, *88*, 259–265.

Wilmore, J. (1996). Eating disorders in the young athlete. *Encyclopaedia of Sports Medicine*, *6*, 287–303.

Wroble, R. R., & Moxley, D. P. (1998). Acute weight gain and its relationship to success in high school wrestlers. *Medicine and Science in Sports and Exercise*, *30*, 949–951.

Yeager, K. (1993). The female triad: Disordered eating, amenorrhea, osteoporosis. *Medicine and Science in Sports and Exercise*, *25*, 775–777.

5

The Psychopathology of Everyday Athletic Life

Daniel Begel

In the course of any athlete's career, psychological problems will occasionally interfere with efforts to train productively and compete successfully. The types of psychological problems that interfere with performance range from the relatively mild to the dangerously severe. The most common problem, according to one experienced football coach (C. Cozza, personal communication, 1985) is that of inaccurate self-assessment or "kids who think they are better than they are and kids who think they are worse than they are." This is usually a mild difficulty, one that is easily solved by coaches and athletes themselves. The most severe problems are the mental disorders, especially the psychoses, mood disorders, and eating disorders. As Dr. Burton points out in chapter 4, symptoms of these disorders among athletes often appear first in the athletic setting, where they may become disabling.

Between these extremes of severity lie an array of problems in training or performance that are so common that they can be considered part of the psychopathology of everyday athletic life. For example, most athletes know the embarrassment of failing suddenly and unexpectedly in a simple task at a crucial moment of competition. Others have experienced prolonged periods of subpar performance or failure to improve beyond a certain plateau despite proper training. Athletes may be unable to resolve dilemmas regarding such questions as how soon and how hard to test a recovering injury, or when and how to extricate oneself from an unproductive training situation. There are a wide variety of uncertainties, pitfalls, paradoxes, and slip-ups well known to the athletic community as being frequently encountered concomitants of training and performance, and considerable energy is devoted to dealing with them. Although these problems of everyday athletic life may not qualify as mental illnesses according to strict nosological definitions, they are psychopathologic in their departure from optimal states of symbolic functioning (Edelson, 1971) and will tax the psychological resources of any athlete who suffers them.

FIVE TYPES OF PERFORMANCE PROBLEMS

The psychological problems that frequently interfere with training and competition may be divided into five types:

- sudden performance failure, or "choke"
- prolonged performance failure, or "slump"
- untimely injury or prolonged recovery from injury
- interpersonal problem with coaches and teammates
- training dilemma

This division is not based on a formal nosology, but is one that conveniently labels the usual manner of presentation.

Sudden Performance Failure

The sudden performance failure, or "choke," is perhaps the most humiliating experience an athlete can have in sports, since it often occurs at a time when spectators are most interested in the action. It consists of a sudden failure to perform at a customary standard at a crucial moment of competition. The athlete may or may not feel anxious, but will usually have the sense that his or her body is not moving freely and smoothly. The routine nature of the failed task may be an indication that an athlete has choked, rather than simply failed, as, for example, when a placekicker in football shanks an extra point that would win a hard-fought game.

An outstanding American athlete tore her Achilles tendon six weeks prior to the Olympic trials, the competition that would determine places on the Olympic team. As one of the world's best heptathletes, who compete in a seven-event track and field competition, she stood a good chance to win a medal in the Olympics if she was able to compete effectively in the trials. As a result of her injury, however, she was not able to prepare in the way she had planned, having been able to put on her spikes again just two weeks prior to the competition. Although physically able to compete, her confidence was compromised and she felt under "enormous pressure."

In the first event she hit several hurdles but managed to stay among the leaders. Her warm-ups for the second—and one of her best—events, the high jump, were "beautiful, awesome, huge, excellent." But by the time her turn to jump came, an hour later, "everything changed." Television cameras had been set up within inches of where she began her approach, in order to film certain running events at the nearby finish line. A piece of plywood to cover the cables used by these cameras lay in her path. She felt angry, but not entitled to "make a big scene." She "lost contact" with her warm-ups and began to feel "lost" and "completely disoriented." It was like a bad dream. She was shocked when on the first jump she hit the bar with her feet after her torso had cleared by a large margin. "Total panic, dizzying and out of control," set in. As if "trying to get there on a spare tire," she missed her two remaining jumps and received no points for the high jump. With her opportunity to qualify for the Games gone, she soon dropped out of the competition altogether.

Prolonged Performance Failure

The "slump," or prolonged performance failure, is characterized by an inability to perform at a reasonably respectable level over an extended period of time. The primary emotional effect, and perhaps an intervening cause of a slump, is the loss of confidence. It is apparent that a slumping athlete does not truly believe he or she will accomplish the particular task he or she is facing. Though an athlete will often try harder to perform well during a slump than under normal conditions, his or her attitude at the moment of competition is one of resignation. In attempting to emerge from a slump, an athlete may make modifications of technique that lead to further disintegration of performance. In a confusing vicious cycle, measures taken to counter a slump may aggravate it. Off the field, the slumping athlete may be depressed and irritable.

A professional baseball player was "off to a crummy start" for the second consecutive year. Although his spring training went well, his batting average hovered near .225 one month into the regular season. He was "sick of everybody telling me what to do," tired of analyzing his swing, and he complained of a "chicken-shit reporter" who was "taking shots" at him. At home he was becoming withdrawn and sullen. His wife reported to the team's employee assistance counselor that he spent many hours alone in the den watching television late into the night. He explained his withdrawal as an effort to "shield" his wife and family from his troubles. In addition to wondering how he "got into it" and how he would "get out of it," he wondered, "Why me? What did I do?"

Injury

Injury may represent a psychological problem in several ways. It sometimes happens that an injury occurs at the worst possible time, preventing an athlete from participating in an important event. When such an injury is due to the intensity of training or a simple accident, the athlete suffers a profound and sudden emotional loss akin to the death of a friend. But such untimely injuries also occur when an athlete is unable to manage the fear of a particular competition, and in that case the injury is said to be a "strategic" one that solves an emotional issue.

Another way in which injury becomes a psychological event is in the work of recovery, which has various aspects. Physical pain must be endured, and subtle distinctions between the expectable soreness of rehabilitation and the pain of further injury must be accurately assessed. The athlete must be "smart," succumbing neither to pressures to return prematurely nor to irrational apprehensions about reinjury. The forced reduction of physical activity may be experienced as a narcissistic wound or failure. Downregulation of endogenous opiate and catecholamine systems may induce dysphoria. Other factors are the loss of competitive excitement and the diminished interest and adulation of others.

A professional basketball player, the star of his team, tore an anterior cruciate ligament in his knee. One year after his injury he had not yet resumed playing, and the fans and press began to question his determination to return. In order to insulate himself from the pressure to return prematurely, the athlete stopped going to his team's games and sitting on the bench, where he was frequently a target of critical remarks. Although this evoked an even greater round of criticism, it enabled him to recover much more effectively and resume playing at the appropriate time.

Interpersonal Problem

Interpersonal problems with coaches and teammates come in many varieties and are often mutual problems. The physical intimacy of the relationship between athlete and coach, in which the coach has unusual interest in and authority over the athlete's body, may lead to sexual violations of the relationship, especially if either party has other sexual disturbances. Coaches sometimes make decisions based on their own needs and personal preferences rather than on what is best for their athletes or teams. Such decisions will be obvious to the athletes, who may then fail as a conscious or unconscious form of protest.

In "prima donna syndrome," an athlete of special ability will make life difficult for those around him or her as well as, inadvertently, for him- or herself, by excessive demands for preferential treatment. Teammates and coaches may act as if they are being blackmailed, acquiescing to the athlete's demands more than they would like for the sake of winning. Reasonable requests may evolve into a standoff. It is not often easy to determine whether a conflict between a coach and athlete represents an unreasonable demand on the part of a prima donna athlete or the interference of a narcissistic coach.

An outstanding high-school sprinter was prevented by the rules of competition in her state from competing in more than three events. Her coach routinely entered her in one individual event and two relays, since relays earned more points for his team. The sprinter, who already held one state record, inwardly steamed at her coach for not letting her develop her talents in both the 100- and 200-meter sprints, and she ceased talking to him except in the most perfunctory manner. When the coach, who had a mediocre track career of his own, followed the same plan in the conference meet, the athlete threatened to boycott that meet, as well as the state meet several weeks later. The issue was partially resolved when the coach, in consultation with an administrator from the school, yielded to the sprinter's demand to enter the events of her choice.

Training Dilemma

Training dilemmas grow out of the fact that athletes must occasionally make major decisions about their careers, and it is not always obvious which decisions are the right ones. An adolescent athlete may have to choose between a familiar coach who is like a member of the family and a new coach who will be better for his career. A graduating high-school athlete may have to choose between a college program that effectively guarantees participation and a more competitive program where he risks sitting on the bench. Retiring athletes must balance their desire to continue playing with the potential unpleasantness of being cut. In addition to these decisions regarding the path of one's career, there are many other decisions to make, including what specific training regimens to follow and when and how to make major modifications in technique. Decisions about the course of one's personal life can also influence training. An athlete may wonder whether to interrupt training when her physical abilities are at their highest in order to have children. Inability to solve a major training dilemma can significantly impair an athlete's functioning and sometimes end a career. The decisions one makes may have unforeseen consequences.

A 1500-meter runner was faced with the choice of taking a full year off from school in order to train for the Olympics, or of taking only half a year to do so. By taking a full year she would be better able to build a foundation of strength and endurance in the fall for the competitive season the following spring. But doing so would also prevent her from graduating with her class at the prestigious Ivy League school she attended, one of her goals. She chose to remain in school for the fall semester, and although she graduated with her class, this decision may have cost her a place on the Olympic team. Running well coming into the final straight, her heel was nicked, intentionally she felt, by a desperate competitor. She stumbled and came in fifth, which was not good enough to qualify for the Games. Had she taken off from school and built a stronger foundation in the fall, she might have been less vulnerable to such a challenge.

The division of performance problems into these five categories—choke, slump, injury, interpersonal problem, and training dilemma—is somewhat arbitrary, and in natural settings they often merge into one another. An athlete recovering from an injury, for example, may appear to choke in his first few competitions, though this may merely be an expression of excessive caution. An ongoing conflict with a coach may discourage an athlete and lead to a prolonged period of mediocre performance. A retirement dilemma may be solved by a career-ending injury.

In addition, performance problems seem to come in many varieties. A choke, for example, can be prolonged without ever becoming a true slump, as when a star professional baseball player went hitless in his first 17 World Series at-bats, or when an athlete persistently performs worse in competition than in practice. There is even a kind of pseudo-choke, as when an adolescent athlete blames a defeat by a better opponent on his own exaggerated failure. Clinically, it is probably less important to categorize performance failures than to understand their origins.

THE SOURCES OF PERFORMANCE PROBLEMS

There are probably as many explanations for performance problems as there are beliefs about human nature, and in the athletic community there is no shortage of such beliefs. There, a "failure to execute" is often cited as an explanation for poor athletic performance. In spite of its redundancy, this explanation provides comfort for athletes and coaches who may be disconcerted by the prospect of a psychological malfunction. More psychological, but still not very explanatory, are those descriptive labels that point to a mental cause of failure, such as "loss of concentration" or "brain-lock." Character deficiencies, such as lack of effort, discipline, or "heart," are popular explanations for performance failure, as is the related problem of "poor preparation." Where an interpersonal situation interferes with performance, the cause is frequently thought of as being the refusal of one person to think or act in a way that another person knows is best. The rain, a bum call by a referee, subclinical illness, and just plain bad luck are all believed to contribute to performance failure. In addition, God Himself is said by many athletes to take a keen interest in the outcome of their games.

To these theories, all of which may contain an element of truth, sport psychiatry adds its psychologic, psychobiologic, and psychosocial perspectives. Our psychologic explanations identify emotional conflicts or self-defeating thinking, our psychobiologic explanations point toward disorders of neurologic and neurohormonal functioning, and our psychosocial explanations elucidate the stresses of playing a particular role or roles.

The idea, especially, that athletic performance is expressive often guides our thinking. In psychiatry, we tend to believe that physical actions can be a form of expression, and not merely a means to an end. Mahl (1987) discussed the communicative functions of nonverbal behavior in an interesting account of a patient's versatile use of "the finger." This idea that nonverbal behavior may be a form of communication may be traced to the work of Freud, who said, "no mortal can keep a secret. If his lips are silent, he chatters with his fingertips" (Freud, 1905, pp. 77–

78). The same idea is familiar to athletes, of whom it is sometimes said that their play "makes a statement."

In a professional baseball game, a second baseman made two identical throwing errors in plays at home plate. In each case, with an opposing runner charging down the third-base line and his own catcher protecting the plate, he had thrown the ball a few feet down the line, rather than to the spot where his catcher braced himself. As a result, the catcher was forced to step toward the runner along the basepath, placing himself in precarious circumstances. Twice, he was clobbered mercilessly by the advancing runner, who scored each time, costing the team a win. After the game the player's manager chewed him out. The manager was so angry, in fact, that he invited one of the larger coaches into his office to ensure everyone's safety. One error, he could understand, but an identical error three innings later was absolutely—and here the manager resorted to a string of profanities.

Two weeks later the episode still bothered this athlete enough to consult the team's psychiatrist. He wondered if he should bring the matter up with his manager to clear the air. During their conversation, the psychiatrist was struck by the tone of contempt and disgust in the athlete's attitude toward his teammate, the clobbered catcher. The player accused his catcher, who was having a bad year, of not trying hard enough to play well and of not being aggressive or tough. With a slightly sadistic smile on his face he called the man a "coward." It must have been a delight, the psychiatrist concluded, for this athlete to see his teammate crumble under the impact of the first collision. And the opportunity to arrange a second one was no doubt too good for his unconscious to pass up.

The psychiatrist asked the athlete if he might have been trying to "toughen the guy up," referring to the catcher. The athlete laughed at the suggestion, commenting that it was the type of thing you could expect a psychiatrist to say. But he was also intrigued by the possibility and reasoned that if his manager saw things the same way the psychiatrist did, that might explain the man's anger. In the interest of "diplomacy," he said, he thought he would "just let the whole thing drop."

Although performance problems in which impaired behavior is discovered to be meaningful appear to be quite common in sports, there are many other factors beside stray ideas and unresolved feelings that may contribute to the psychopathology of everyday athletic life. As Ron Kamm discusses in chapter 9 of this volume, consideration of these factors is part of the evaluation of the athlete. Various biological factors, psychiatric and otherwise, may play a role. An athlete with a family history of panic disorder, for example, may be predisposed to choking as a result of subclinical abnormalities in brain stem norepinephrine and GABA systems (Kaplan, Sadock, & Grebb, 1994). Any disease that causes fatigue, especially but not only infectious and metabolic diseases, can mimic slump. A football punter's outbursts of rage disappeared when his frontal lobe glioma was diagnosed and removed. A case of apparent choke in a dyslexic athlete who misunderstood his coach's frantic, end-of-the-game commands has been previously reported (Begel, 1992).

A complex interplay of biological and psychological factors is often present in what is called "overtraining" or "athlete fatigue syndrome." In this syndrome, the intensity of training exceeds the athlete's ability to recover between training sessions, with a variety of consequences. Mood may become depressed and sleep disturbed (Morgan, Brown, Raglin, O'Connor, & Ellickson, 1987), metabolic and hormonal functions may become abnormal (Urhausen, Gangriel, & Kindermann 1995), and performance will suffer.

Attempts have been made to identify diagnostic biologic markers specific to this syndrome. Measurements of HPA axis dysregulation (Lehmann, Baur, Netzer, & Gastmann, 1997), plasma glutamine concentrations (Rowbottom, Keast, Garcia-Webb, & Morton, 1997), and the testosterone/cortisol ratio have been proposed (Urhausen et al., 1995), the latter as an indication of anabolic/catabolic imbalance. None of these markers has been shown to be definitive, however, and like the dexamethasone suppresion test for depression, their value in supplementing a clinical evaluation is not well established (Kaplan et al., 1994). The diagnosis of overtraining is made by a history of excessive training intensity and a beneficial response to reduced intensity. Overtrained athletes often feel "burned out" and desire to quit, which may be nature's way of lowering the training demand. The role of the sport psychiatrist in overtraining is primarily a supportive—rather than interpretive—one of helping the athlete to listen to the body's message to "slow down."

But the importance of biological sources of performance problems should not conceal their psychologic aspects. A case in which a college sprinter's longing to return home unwittingly delayed her recovery from a hamstring injury has been previously reported (Begel, 1992). An endurance athlete blamed a sequence of fashionable illnesses—ferritin-deficiency anemia and diffuse intravascular candidiasis—and coaching mistakes that resulted in "overtraining" for three successive years of slump (Begel, 1992).

Misplaced blame, discomfort with ambiguity, and fear of what one may discover about oneself are among the reasons that the psychological origins of performance problems may go unrecognized. Often it is believed that dwelling on problems will simply magnify, rather than solve, them. As a result, prescriptions may be formulated that fail to take into account the unwieldy strength of emotional factors. An athlete who chokes, for example, may be told to relax, something he cannot do. In a slump, an athlete may be advised not to think about it but just go out and play. Facing retirement, an athlete may be told to prepare for a life he cannot conceive of. Even when such prescriptions appear to effectively alleviate the difficulty for a time, they tend to mask important personal issues.

Because of the connection between personal and performance life, a crisis in training or competition may become the occasion for tending to a neglected personal area. A respected and well-liked professional basketball player, for example, surprised his many fans one day by attacking, apparently without provocation, an opponent in the middle of a game. His private explanation was that the guy was a "cry-baby," constantly complaining to the referees about the calls. Two years prior to this incident, the athlete's father had been killed in a suspicious hit-and-run accident, and on the very day of the game the athlete was in court for the sentencing of the "redneck" who drove the car. Accustomed to keeping his emotions to himself, the athlete did not allow himself to express his grief or rage until his furious outburst at his opponent, the "cry-baby." His attack may have been, in part, a repudiation of his own impulse to cry, even as it gave him the opportunity to do so. Alone in the locker room after being ejected, he sobbed into his towel "like a baby," initiating, at last, his mourning of his father's death.

Athletes facing a disturbance in training or performance may benefit from exploring neglected personal and interpersonal issues and making restorative changes. A famous miler, who was considered "washed up" as a result of an injury, took the opportunity to reestablish a bond with his father, whom he previously held at a neutral distance. A college basketball player, who choked at the free-throw line in a crucial postseason tournament game, subsequently extricated herself from a romantic involvement with her coach. The baseball player with a repeating slump mentioned earlier faced his irrational guilt for the death of a family member who drowned in a backyard pool he had financed.

Even if there is no known problem or dilemma underlying a psychological failure of performance, a psychological benefit may ensue. The heptathlete who panicked during the Olympic trials feels "enriched by some of these remarkably twisted events" that have occurred in her athletic career. They have inoculated her, she feels, against "going out of my head" in the face of life's other unwelcome surprises. The kinds of accomplishments an athlete may make as a result of exploring, rather than rationalizing away, the psychopathology of everyday athletic life are often more important than athletic victories. The sport psychiatrist, and others associated with athletes, may play an important role in the exploratory process.

REFERENCES

Begel, D. (1992). An overview of sport psychiatry. *American Journal of Psychiatry, 149*(5), 606–614.

Edelson, M. (1971). *The idea of a mental illness*. New Haven, CT: Yale University.

Freud, S. (1905). Fragment of an analysis of a case of hysteria. In J. Strachey (Ed. & Trans.), *The standard edition of the complete psychological works of Sigmund Freud* (Vol. 7, pp. 3–124). New York: Norton.

Kaplan, H. I., Sadock, B. J., & Grebb, J. A. (1994). *Kaplan and Sadock's synopsis of psychiatry: Behavioral sciences, clinical psychiatry* (7th ed.). Baltimore: Williams & Wilkins.

Lehman, M., Baur, S., Netzer, N., & Gastmann, U. (1997). Training and overtraining: An overview of experimental results in endurance sports. *Journal of Sports Medicine and Physical Fitness, 37*(1), 7–17.

Mahl, G. F. (1987). Gestures and body movements in interviews. In G. F. Mahl (Ed.), *Explorations in nonverbal and vocal behavior* (pp. 7–74). London: Erlbaum.

Morgan W. P., Brown, D. R., Raglin, J. S., O'Connor, P. J., & Ellickson, K. A. (1987). Psychological monitoring of overtraining and staleness. *British Journal of Sports Medicine, 21*(3), 107–114

Rowbottom, D. G., Keast, D., Garcia-Webb, P., & Morton, A. R. (1997). Training adaptation and biological changes among well-trained male triathletes. *Medicine and Science in Sports and Exercise, 29*(9), 1233–1239.

Urhausen, A., Gangriel, H., & Kindermann, W. (1995). Blood hormones as markers of training stress and overtraining. *Sports Medicine, 20*(4), 251–276.

6

The Dilemma of Youth Sports

Daniel Begel

In a metaphorical sense, all sports are youth sports, regardless of the age of the participants. For kids and grown-ups alike, it is more important to have fun in sports than to achieve social or economic goals. Even in the realm of professional sports, where cynicism and commercial interests are dominant, a fresh and exuberant spirit like that of young children at play is often displayed by athletes in their competition. Adults may recapture the feeling of youth not only by playing a sport, but also by assisting in some capacity in athletic programs for youth. Perhaps this is why more adults volunteer to coach kids in sports than to serve in other areas where they are desperately needed, such as childcare or classroom teaching.

It is ironic, however, that adults who enjoy the youthful spirit of sports often unwittingly stifle that spirit by imposing on young people the methods and assumptions of adulthood. Kids in sports are often subjected to prematurely intense and systematic training in order to satisfy the competitive appetites of parents, coaches, and administrators. As a result, they are exposed to public shame, familial disappointment, and hazardous health conditions. It has been pointed out many times that youth sport programs that are organized by adults are caught in a dilemma: The involvement of grown-ups, to which organized youth sports owe their existence, inevitably carries the risk that the needs of the adults will take priority over those of the kids.

BENEFICIAL ASPECTS OF YOUTH SPORTS

The greatest endorsement for organized youth sports is the number of kids who play them. Estimates vary, but it is generally agreed that between 20 and 35 million people between the ages of 6 and 18 participate in organized sports in the United States (Ewing, Seefeldt, & Brown, 1996). These sports are sponsored by schools, sports clubs, and various agencies. This estimate of participation does not include children who play sports exclusively on their own, outside of the auspices of various sponsors.

Among adults, it is the nearly universal judgment that participation in sports as a child endows one with virtues that are necessary for success in "the game of life." Wellington's famous assertion that the battle of Waterloo was won on the playing fields of Eton expresses this view, and it is repeated ad infinitum in sports banquets annually. The notion that virtue is inherent in sports was a contributing factor to the birth of organized youth sports in nineteenth-century America. The concept of Christian manliness was one basis for the organizing of sports in such institutions as the YMCA (Wiggins, 1996), and as the field of social work blossomed at the turn of the century, an athletic offshoot sprung up in the form of the "boys work" movement (Berryman, 1996). A long list of character attributes are believed to be fostered in sports, including "leadership skills, cooperativeness, teamwork, self-discipline, . . . coping skills, . . . respect for authority, competitiveness, sportsmanship, and self-confidence" (Stryer, Tofler, & Lapchick, 1998, p. 702). The subjective nature of this belief has been pointed out by the sport psychologist, Rainer Martens (1978), who wrote, "Sports have brought me much happiness and taught me many useful lessons. I cannot prove it to others, but I believe it to be so" (p. iv).

Systematic studies of youth sports offer some support for the subjective impression of benefit. Sports participation has been associated with a reduction of criminal behavior among delinquents (Hastad, Segrave, Pangrazi, & Peterson, 1984), improved self-esteem among asthmatic children (Brook & Heim, 1991), and healthy emotional adjustment among adolescents with craniofacial anomalies (Kapp-Simon, Simon, & Kristovich, 1992). The injection of regular aerobic exercise into the physical education of children has been associated with enhanced creativity (Herman-Tofler & Tuckman, 1998). Traditional martial arts training, which combines introspection, moral teaching, and fighting techniques, has been shown to be of potential benefit in the treatment of juvenile delinquents (Trulson, 1986). In a clinical paper, Bell and Suggs (1998) proposed martial arts training as a vehicle for fostering psychologic resiliency among children exposed to sociologic disasters. Petitpas (1997) has used sports to teach assertiveness, teamwork, concentration, and other "transferable skills."

Although studies that endorse the values of youth sport are suggestive, they are not entirely conclusive. Shortcomings in the design or interpretation of these studies sometimes weakens them. A survey, for example, that shows a particular personality feature to be associated with athletic participation cannot be said to prove that athletic participation caused that feature to appear. Some of the studies that demonstrate a psychological benefit of a particular strategy or approach in sports fail to provide the nontreatment, comparison group with a sham treatment or placebo. Therapeutic advocacy is an unidentified contaminant in other studies, as is the statistical error of regression to the mean, by which a group selected on the basis of deviancy will appear more normal at the next measurement. Morgan, the author and coauthor of many original papers in sport psychology, showed in the midst of the jogging craze of the 1970s that sitting in a comfortable reclining chair on a regular basis is just as good for the soul as jogging (Bahrke & Morgan, 1978), and his work established a standard for assessing clinical methods in sport psychology that is not often met in youth sport research. Taken as a whole, however, experimental work, subjective impression, and the enthusiastic participation of kids strongly support the idea that sports have a beneficial effect on the mental health of young people.

In addition to beneficial effects on self-esteem and character, youth sports may be used to promote intellectual development. By requiring that students meet arbitrary academic standards in order to participate in sports, many schools use sports as an indirect educational tool. A more direct and less coercive use of sports involves the teaching of academic disciplines through the study of athletics. Concepts of physics, for example, can be taught by studying what happens when a ball carrier and tackler collide in football, or by studying the mechanisms of the ten-speed bicycle (Crotty, 1987). The historical method can be taught in any number of ways in sports, such as by studying the origins of particular athletic techniques or comparing athletic records from different eras. Andersen, Brewer, and Davis (1996) have discussed the use of sport and sport science to teach the subject matter of developmental psychology, social psychology, and statistics to college undergraduates. With students of elementary and high-school age, however, the use of sports as a source of educational subject matter appears to be less popular than the use of sports as a reward for academic achievement. Innovative teaching of academics within the athletic context may in the long run prove to be a useful method of reaching those students who find athletic subject matter more interesting than what is taught in conventional classrooms.

RISKS OF YOUTH SPORTS

The general enthusiasm for youth sports has been tempered over the years by warnings about the potential for harm in youth sports programs. The danger appears to be in the "premature imposition on young athletes of training that is excessively intense, systematic, result-oriented, and exclusive to a single sport" (Begel, 1998, p. 874). The American Association for Health, Physical Education, and Recreation approved a resolution against highly organized sports for children at their convention in 1938 (Berryman, 1996) and in the following decade the American Medical Association and the American Academy of Pediatrics cautioned against "highly organized competition of a varsity pattern for children of elementary and junior high school age" (Martens, 1978). More recently, the International Federation of Sports Medicine and World Health Organization issued a statement of caution, specifically citing "stress related reactions . . . following abnormal psychological settings in organized sports" (National Youth Sports Safety Foundation, 1998).

Physical trauma and illness in the form of overuse injuries and the poorly understood pain syndrome known as "reflex sympathetic dystrophy" have been attributed to participation in highly competitive youth sports (Stryer, Katz, & Cantwell, 1997). In addition, it appears that competitive athletic pressures have become a motive for the use of anabolic steroids by children as young as 9 years of age (Faigenbaum, Zaichowsky, Gardner, & Micheli, 1998).

The kids themselves are thought to provide a cautionary voice by dropping out of sports. Attrition rates are thought to be quite high. In a fine review of youth sports, Stryer and colleagues (1997) report that 75 percent of youngsters who begin organized sport participation by the age of 7 quit before they are 15. Ewing and others (1996) report similarly high attrition, which seems to peak at ages 14–15. Stryer and colleagues rightly point out that the changing interests of adolescents are partly responsible for attrition, but not entirely so. Children who dropped out of sports reported to Pooley (1980) that too much competitive pressure and criticism from coaches were among their reasons.

Anecdotal observation of the behavior of parents and coaches makes a stronger case, perhaps, for the dangers of adult-organized youth sport than can be made by statistics, surveys, or official statements. Adults have been known to verbally abuse and physically assault referees, coaches, other parents, and their own children as a result of competitive failures. One father wired his son with a remote listening device in order to trap a coach who had criticized his son's play in a career-ending gaff. One mother hired a thug to murder the mother of her daughter's strongest cheerleading rival, in order to impair that rival's performance in the tryouts. Subtle decisions based on competitive criteria may embarrass children, as Kamm (1998) noted in reporting how one T-ball coach positioned his players in a tight circle near the plate for a poor hitter's turn at bat. The embedding of adult obsession with competitive success in the culture of youth sports is indicated in Kamm's account of little league's "major league draft":

> As it is now practiced in many towns . . . the draft has virtually eliminated the possibility that adults could set a moral tone for children. Instead . . . it is modeled on professional lines and encourages secret scouting networks and inside information. First-year coaches, who volunteer with naive visions of a Norman Rockwell season, enter a Draft Room seemingly lifted from a Mario Puzo novel. Established coaches routinely dominate and bully new volunteers (especially if they happen to be women), fighting tooth and nail for the best players. What should be the beginning of a cooperative and fun experience for adult and child alike turns into a highly competitive, cynical exercise in which each coach, giving lip serve to creating fair teams, secretly hopes to fashion a powerhouse. Unfortunately, when powerhouses are created, so too are doormats." (p. 901)

THE ACHIEVEMENT BY PROXY PARADIGM

A compelling formulation of the problem is given by Tofler, Knapp, and Drell (1998), who see the difficulty as one of a failure of adults to differentiate their own needs from those of their children. Tofler and colleagues define a "spectrum" of "achievement by proxy" behavior, characterized by healthy supportive behavior on one end and abuse on the other. In an intermediate stage termed "risky sacrifice," parents display a mild loss of ability to differentiate their own "needs for success and achievement" from their child's "developmental needs and goals." In "objectification," a greater loss of this capacity is displayed, and the child becomes increasingly defined by one activity in which he or she is able to perform well. The objectifying parent may encourage the child to train at a potentially dangerous level of intensity, while rationalizing away that danger according to the principle that the end justifies the means. A family systems perspective on this problem is elucidated by Hellstedt in chapter 11 of this volume. Hellstedt notes that young athletes may become triangulated in order to provide stability to a problematic parental dyad, and that the difficulty may be multigenerational.

If, indeed, the pressure placed upon young people by grown-ups constitutes a syndrome endemic to youth sports, it is a syndrome that is peculiarly devoid of symptoms, at least in its early stages. Although a high rate of insomnia prior to competition has been noted, this may be no more clinically significant than, say, insomnia among children on Christmas Eve. Lewthwaite and Scanlan (1989) reported a statistical association between children's anxiety about sports and their perceptions of parental pressure without a determination of clinical significance. Presumably, highly competitive sports programs are potentially most harmful at relatively young ages. Observers believe that it is dangerous for 7-year-old gymnasts to train with the intensity of adult professional athletes (Ryan, 1995). And yet, in all the literature on the dangers of youth sport, it is nearly impossible to find a case of a prepubertal child who displays psychiatric symptoms as a result of psychological damage sustained in sports.

The case cited by Tofler and colleagues in their paper mentioned above is that of a 14-year-old girl. Four cases of exploitation cited by Ogilvie, Tofler, Conroy, and Drell (1998) are those of two 16-year-olds, a 19-year-old, and a 24-year-old. The cases reported by Begel (1998) that fit into the achievement by proxy category are all adolescents. Passer (1988) stresses that the health-related effects of excessive competition on young people are largely unstudied, and Kamm (1998) points out that in discussions of the potential harm of youth sports it is the behavior of the adults, not of the children, that seems critical. Apparently, the major consequences of excessive pressure on latency-aged children are subclinical anxiety and overuse injuries. Psychiatric symptoms of clinical significance are either not prominent or have been neglected for some reason by trained observers.

What appears to happen clinically is that symptomatic behavior resulting from achievement by proxy dynamics makes a delayed appearance. Between the ages of 6 or 7 and the onset of puberty, children are unwitting accomplices in creating the achievement by proxy syndrome. At this age they are more eager to learn whatever adults have to teach them about the right way of doing things than they are at any other stage of life. They do not protest twice daily swim practices if that's the way things are done, nor do they perceive that excessive and overly systematic training will deprive them of the opportunity to experiment athletically and socially on their own. Although the conditions of excessive training and competition may originate as an unconscious parental need to solve certain problems, the latency-aged child becomes an enthusiastic participant.

It is not until adolescence that child athletes with clinically significant problems come to the attention of psychiatrists. Some of the problems that adolescent athletes present are directly related to athletics, such as mixed feelings about wanting to continue in a sport, explosive relationships with coaches and teammates, or emotional turmoil related to injury. Other problems are defined by symptoms that lie outside of the athletic arena, such as drug use, sexual promiscuity, and school failure. As Burton points out in chapter 4, symptoms that satisfy diagnostic criteria for mental disorders may appear first in the athletic arena. If, in any given case, achievement by proxy dynamics are a relevant factor, the adolescent athlete's troubles will become a problem for the athlete's parents as well, regardless of whether the prominent symptoms appear within the context of athletics or outside of it. Even a problem as apparently mild as a failure to improve to an expected degree may precipitate a clinical evaluation by a psychiatrist in a family that has become highly invested in the athletic success of a child.

Although there is no a priori basis for assuming that the problems of adolescent athletes have their origins in the prior establishment of achievement by proxy dynamics, the relative absence of clinically significant psychiatric symptoms among younger athletes does not give us reason to assume that everything is okay. Like the symptoms of other kinds of trauma, the environmental and familial distortions imposed on young athletes may have effects that are delayed in their appearance or recognition. In families where parental needs are inadequately differentiated from those of an athletic child, symptoms may appear during adolescence. At that time, the normal processes of adolescent emancipation will carry the extra burden, for the athletic child, of disentangling self-esteem from athletic performance. A full assessment of the impact of participation in organized youth sports requires longitudinal, clinical study.

An example of delayed symptomatology occurred in a 16-year-old speedskater and only child who was brought to a sport psychiatrist by her mother. Since suffering a back injury in competition a year and a half previously, the girl was reluctant to resume competing. She had trained since the age of 7 and showed promise in both sprints and distance, and her mother devoted a great deal of time, money, and energy to her career. Although the athlete had carried out her rehabilitation following the fall and felt comfortable on the ice once again, she was undecided about resuming her career. In addition, she was displaying impulsive behaviors in other areas of her life, experimenting with drugs and sex, and skipping school. This conduct distressed her mother as much as the interruption of her athletic career, though perhaps not more so.

The girl's complaints were not about skating, but about her parents. She dismissed her father, a remote, chainsmoking man given to long visits to the bathroom, as a "nonentity." She described her mother, a school social worker, as "suffocating." Her mother had escaped from a dead marriage by pouring her soul into her daughter's skating, and for many years the daughter enjoyed the powerful bond between them. Now, however, the daughter was attempting to achieve some measure of independence from her mother who remained, in the daughter's words, "stuck to the ice like glue."

SOME SOLUTIONS

A number of suggestions have been put forth to ameliorate the unhealthy factors and promote the healthy ones in youth sports. One approach is to reduce the stress that derives from competition by changing the rules, equipment, or circumstances of play. In basketball leagues for very young children, for example, the baskets are lowered, smaller balls are used, and walking with the ball is permitted, all of which puts less of a premium on athletic precocity. Youth athletic leagues in various sports have eliminated playoffs and standings, placed restrictions on practices, and enforced the requirement that all children play for a significant period of time, regardless of ability. Some coaches have used a kind of buddy system in which a more competent player will teach a less competent one during the game itself, and the liberal use of time-outs for teaching by adults is also employed. Orlick (1982) has promoted games and sports of various kinds that are more cooperative than competitive. Playing a tennis match to tie, for example, rather than to win, can lead to a surprisingly spirited match, especially between unequal partners.

In addition to modifying the circumstances of play, the suggestion is often made to modify, by education, the behavior of coaches. It has been proposed that coaches be taught concepts of child development and athletic learning and to emphasize participation, effort, and social growth rather than winning. They should be trained to give positive reinforcement rather than criticism, and to listen to the concerns of the kids. The National Association for Sport and Physical Education (1995) has devised a set of national standards for athletic coaches. This rather labyrinthine scheme, consisting of 37 standards, 8 domains, 5 levels, and approximately 320 "competencies," essentially recommends that coaches possess a working knowledge of social, emotional, and athletic development.

A number of programs designed to educate coaches of young people have been developed. The lead author of the *National Standards* has developed a program used in the state of Michigan, the cornerstones of which are positive reinforcement and awareness of developmental abilities. The philosophy of this program is that "whether a child has a positive or negative sport experience is dependent on the coach's ability to use positive reinforcement, to match the challenges of the sport tasks to the abilities of the children and youth, and to teach children to respect and abide by the rules" (Ewing et al., 1996, p. 37). Smith, Smoll, and Curtis (1979) have developed a similar program called "coaching effectiveness training" (CET), which teaches coaches how to be supportive and positive, offer technical advice, deal with parents, and imbue an athletic program with a healthy philosophy.

These programs are probably beneficial, although the studies designed to prove it have not as yet matched experimental groups with meaningful controls. It may be that the value of these programs lies in a general heightening of coaches' awareness of the independent needs of their athletes, rather than retention of the content of a particular curriculum. In this regard, one study (Horn, 1985): suggests that criticism, in fact, may be as much of a boost to an athlete's feeling of competence as positive reinforcement: "Players who received relatively higher frequencies of criticism for skill error . . . may have perceived such evaluation to be an indication that their coach attributed their failure to lack of effort and that the coach expected them to perform at a higher level, thus facilitating higher perceptions of competence in these players" (p. 183).

In general, it is thought best for coaches to identify an optimal time for teaching their athletes particular skills, and that children be introduced to activities when they are ready for them (Magill & Anderson, 1996). Thus, basic skills are taught before complex ones, variety introduced before specialization, and participation encouraged before competition. Although it may appear obvious that teaching be aligned with development, it is not always clear at what age a given child is ready for a given athletic activity. It seems that both the acquisition of motor skills (Seefeldt, 1996) and psychological capacities (see chapter 1 of this volume) follow an orderly sequence, but the timing of this acquisition is subject to a degree of individual variation (Seefeldt, 1996).

There appears to be some ambiguity, for example, regarding the age at which competitive strivings become important. Passer (1996) refers to work that describes the emergence of activities in 3-year-olds that appear competitive, but discounts these as "autonomous achievement goals." In a paper published in 1988, Passer says that "children's understanding of competition will not be well developed until they are about 12," although this assertion disappears from a later version of the same paper (1996). Chapter 1 of this book takes an epigenetic view of competitive actions, suggesting that the toddler's willfulness is a foundation for the Oedipal child's competitive strivings. These strivings, in turn, become channeled into athletic competition during latency, as the rules of true sports are learned. In adolescence, competitive activities are imbued with passion. In any case, the recommendations of Passer (1996) and Coakley (1986) that participation in competitive sports not begin until approximately age 7 or 8 makes sense when we consider the fact that this is the age at which children devise and participate in competitive sports and games on their own, without the expert intervention of adults.

If a degree of ambiguity surrounds an assessment of a child's readiness to learn a particular athletic lesson, the coach's readiness to understand that fact is shrouded in mystery. As Tofler and colleagues (1998) and Hellstedt (see chapter 11) have pointed out, the ambitions of adults for the children under their care have unconscious origins. The more unreasonable the ambitions, the less accessible they are to modification. The expectation that parents and coaches will shed unreasonable ambitions in response to even a well-designed program of education may therefore have a wishful component. Coaching education may heighten an awareness of the needs and capacities of the kids, and help modify those aspects of behavior that are under conscious control, but it will be unlikely to alter achievement by proxy dynamics. It seems rather fanciful to suggest, for example, that a coach who seeks a sexual relationship with an athlete will refrain from it if equipped with a "sophisticated understanding of the nature of the transference-countertransference relationship distortions" (Ogilvie et al., 1998, p. 883).

Kamm (1998), expressing skepticism about the ability of relatively brief didactic presentations to alter ingrained and motivated behavior, borrows an idea from family therapy and suggests that the sport psychiatrist "join" the system and work to modify it from the inside. This can be done by volunteering to coach, participating actively in gatherings of parents, or simply helping out with whatever needs to be done. A number of interesting suggestions are made by Kamm about how a psychiatrist in this position might effect change. For example, he customarily invites parents and athletes to fill out a preseason checklist of what they want from the sport, and then compare their answers with each other. Like other observers, he finds that while the parents hope their child will improve athletically and develop character traits such as self-confidence and discipline, the kids primarily want to have fun and be with their friends. Comparing their checklists often leads to some interesting discussions between children and parents. An example of how a psychiatrist might "join" the athletic system and use it to foster healthy development is indicated in the following example.

A psychiatrist and former pole-vaulter volunteered to coach vaulting at a track club for boys and girls located in an impoverished section of the city. The school where this club trained provided the landing pit and runway, and a local brewery donated two fiberglass poles small enough for the kids to handle. On the first day, coach and kids hauled the huge blue landing pit to the runway outdoors, and no sooner was it in place than five or six kids from the neighborhood, who were not officially part of the club, tested its quality with spins and flips. To demonstrate the event, the psychiatrist ran a short distance down the runway, planted the pole in the box and took off. Then, with one end of the pole anchored in the box and a child gripping the other end, he pulled each boy and girl through, so that they could get the feel of swinging on the pole.

When one of the kids became disruptive by refusing to wait his turn, the psychiatrist stopped play and asked the group how to "help" the disruptive kid. One kid volunteered to take him to the water fountain for a "time-out." Several men, who were leisurely sipping something from containers in paper bags and who had been cheering the group on, admonished the youngster to "act right."

When the vaulting was over, the psychiatrist and athletes lay in the pit as vaulters do and talked about many things. Noticing the way the psychiatrist wore his hat with the brim backward, one of the kids warned him that he could "get shot," since his manner of wearing the hat signaled affiliation with a particular gang. A 7-year-old vaulter named Jamaris, who, along with his sister, Kamitra, displayed unusual talent at vaulting, began to discuss at length the evils of gangs, suggesting that the kids, especially the disruptive one, join "God's gang." Coach and vaulters listened raptly to the precocious sermon.

Psychiatrists who join the system are often impressed that parents complain about the fanatical behavior of "those coaches," even while coaches complain about the fanatical behavior of "those parents." For this reason, some psychiatrists have brought these camps together, along with the kids on whose behalf they presumably act, in discussion groups. In these groups parents, coaches, and athletes talk about matters of mutual concern in a flexible format. The psychiatrist may offer a vignette or propose a role-play to initiate conversation, but the idea is for the participants to work through their ambivalence about competition and other issues. Often parents or coaches who are concerned about excessive pressures and the behavior of persons in charge of athletic programs feel isolated and powerless. In groups, they may find a collective voice through which to express their concerns. By scheduling these groups over a period of months, and sometimes years, a restructuring of deeply embedded attitudes may be initiated. A variation of this method involves adding the presence of a well-known senior athlete to the group, both as role model and draw, and teaching the methods of running the group to "athlete coordinators."

THE PLAYGROUND ENVIRONMENT

One has to wonder whether therapeutic groups, programs to educate and set standards for coaches, and special rules to reduce competitive pressures would all be necessary if youth sports were not so highly organized by adults. When kids organize their own games, they don't enforce grueling practices on themselves, they don't play positions for which they are not yet prepared, and they are sheltered from the displaced ambitions of adults. On the playground, kids don't specialize. Sport-like games, such as double dutch, hackey sack, pom-pom, and horse comfortably coexist with true sports. The raison d'etre of their games is the opportunity to have fun, rather than win a medal or trophy.

In pom-pom, for example, children of different levels of ability play happily in the same game. This game starts with one person in the middle of a field of play and the rest of the players on one sideline. At the call of "pom-pom pole away, let your horses run away," or simply "pom-pom," the group on the sideline runs across the field, trying to avoid being "caught" by the person in the middle. When caught, a player joins the person or group of people in the middle, and the game continues until the last person is caught. Many ages can play this game, and there are many variations, including tackle, touch, on ice, and blindfolded.

The essential characteristic of autonomously organized playground games is that they are self-regulating. For this reason, they are excellent activities for learning. In his essay comparing sandlot baseball with Little League, Devereux (1978) discusses some of the characteristics of games and sports that kids play spontaneously that make them excellent learning environments. The participants feel "free" and "safe," he says, and the activity is "spontaneous, autotelic, and agent responsive." The activity is also "self-pacing" and feedback is "continuous and relevant." Solutions to social problems, such as how to "handle poor sports, incompetents, cry-babies, little kids . . . when the easy out of excluding them from the game (is) . . . impractical" must be invented by the participants themselves (Devereux, 1978, p. 123).

Echoing Devereux, Begel (1992, and chapter 1) has emphasized the importance of self-regulated athletics for moral development, and referred to the child's overall learning process in unregulated sports as "playground conditioning." In organized sports, arguments among participants that stop play are thought to be detrimental and pointless. It was during one such apocryphal argument that Carl Stolz, bored in center field, is said to have conceived the idea of Little League. But from a developmental perspective, the extended arguments that ignite on the playground are not wisely extinguished by adults, for in debating the rules kids are constructing them and, therefore, making them their own. In asking what we want to teach through sports, a distinction might be made between respect for rules and respect for authority. Playground games foster the former, while organized sports, where the rules are defined and enforced by powerful adults, foster, if anything, the latter.

Since so much of the athletic activity available to kids today seems to be the kind that is organized by adults, a degree of nostalgia surrounds discussions of playground sports. Idyllic accounts of childhood play can be found in the poetry of masters, such as Dylan Thomas (1939) and of hacks:

I swam the warm lake and skated the frozen pond
I ran basepaths etched in the corner lot by a Hand I took for granted
(Anonymous)

Indeed, it has been said that "spontaneous pick-up games in neighborhoods and on school playgrounds are rapidly becoming a thing of the past" (Libman, 1998, p. 740). In one sense, spontaneous games are indeed a thing of the past, for the impulse of young people to play them in defiance of their elders is ancient. Writing of his boyhood in fourth-century North Africa, Saint Augustine (4th century) wrote:

> But we loved to play, and punishments were imposed on us by those who were engaged in adult games. For the amusement of adults is called business, but when boys play such games they are punished by adults, and no one feels sorry either for the children or for thc adults or indeed for both of them. Perhaps some refined arbiter of things might approve of my being beaten. As a boy I played ball games, and that play slowed down the speed at which I learnt letters with which as an adult I might play a less creditable game. The school master who caned me was behaving no better than I when, after being refuted by a fellow-teacher in some pedantic question, he was more tormented by jealousy and envy than I when my opponent overcame me in a ball game. (p. 12)

A human impulse that persists over centuries is not easily extinguished and, opinion to the contrary notwithstanding, kids still like to play ball on their own. In their survey of over 8,000 young athletes, Ewing and Seefeldt (1996) found that significant numbers participated in sports outside of structured programs during their free time. Thirty percent of those surveyed played basketball on their own, for example, while 20 percent bowled, and 29 percent swam. The Sporting Goods Manufacturers Association (1998) reported that among sports played frequently by kids between the ages of 6 and 17, basketball, a sport that is played predominantly in unstructured settings, was the most popular in 1997. Other sports in the top ten included touch football, in-line skating, volleyball, freshwater fishing, and billiards, none of which have sufficient leagues to accommodate more than a small fraction of the number of kids estimated to play them. Indeed, if there is an expanding presence of adult-organized games in youth sports, data from the SGMA (1997) indicates that kids may be resisting the trend: The three fastest growing sports for kids between 1992 and 1996 were in-line skating, mountain biking, and weight lifting.

While it may be tempting to solve the dilemma of youth sports by making them off limits to adults, such a solution is probably neither possible nor wise. The joy of watching kids play sports is irresistible, and so is the instinct to get involved. Adults have an important role to play in ensuring safety, providing instruction, and offering encouragement. The delight taken by parents in the athletic performances of their children is a reassuring sign of their love.

An alternative to banning adults is for them to create, as much as possible, conditions that mimic the playground. One way to do this is by having the kids referee their own games, and have adults step in only when the kids have exhausted their efforts to resolve disputes on their own. Another method is to allow kids to manage their teams and leagues, selecting opponents and setting rosters, and letting them establish, in their own way, their practice agenda for the day. Activities on the playground are not confined to one sport, and so soccer leagues, for example, might mimic this circumstance by encouraging the kids, at practice and even at competitions, to play other sports of their own choosing. There are many possibilities for blending the environment of the playground with that of the adult-organized youth sport programs, and while such blending does not eliminate the impulse to project our needs onto our children, it may reduce the opportunity to do so.

REFERENCES

Andersen, M. B., Brewer, B. W., & Davis, S. F. (1996). Sport and exercise psychology in the undergraduate curriculum. *Teaching of Psychology, 23*(1), 40–42.

Bahrke, M. D., & Morgan, W. P. (1978). Anxiety reduction following exercise and meditation. *Cognitive Therapy and Research, 2*, 323–334.

Begel, D. (1992). An overview of sport psychiatry. *American Journal of Psychiatry, 149*(5), 606–614.

Begel, D. (1998). The psychotherapist and the adolescent athlete. In I. R. Tofler (Guest Ed.), *Child and adolescent psychiatric clinics of North America: Sport psychiatry* (Vol. 7, No. 4, pp. 867–878). Philadelphia: Saunders.

Bell, C. C., & Suggs, H. (1998). Using sports to strengthen resiliency in children: Training heart. In I. R. Tofler (Guest Ed.), *Child and adolescent psychiatric clinics of North America: Sport psychiatry* (Vol. 7, No. 4, pp. 859–866). Philadelphia: Saunders.

Berryman, J. W. (1996).The rise of boys' sports in the United States, 1900–1970. In F. L. Smoll & R. E. Smith (Eds.), *Children and youth in sport: A biopsychosocial perspective* (pp. 4–14). Madison, WI: Brown & Benchmark.

Brook, U., & Heim, M. (1991). A pilot study to investigate whether sport influences psychological parameters in personality of asthmatic children. *Family Practice*, *8*(3), 213–215.

Coakley, J. (1986). When should children begin competing? A sociological perspective. In M. R. Weiss & D. Gould (Eds.), *Sport for children and youth* (pp. 59–63). Champaign, IL: Human Kinetics.

Crotty, J. P. (1987). Bicycles. In *Science, technology and human physical needs: Curriculum units by fellows of the Yale-New Haven Teachers Institute* (Vol. VI, pp. 1–27). New Haven, CT: Yale-New Haven Teachers Institute.

Devereux, E. C. (1978). Backyard versus little league baseball: The impoverishment of children's games. In R. Martens (Ed.), *Joy and sadness in children's sports* (pp. 115–131). Champaign, IL: Human Kinetics.

Ewing, M. E., & Seefeldt, V. (1996). Patterns of participation and attrition in American agency-sponsored youth sports. In F. L. Smoll & R. E. Smith (Eds.), *Children and youth in sport: A biopsychosocial perspective* (pp. 31–46). Madison, WI: Brown & Benchmark.

Ewing, M. E., Seefeldt, V. D., & Brown, T. P. (1996). Role of organized sport in the education and health of American children and youth. In A. Poinsett (Ed.), *The role of sports in youth development: Report of a meeting convened by Carnegie Corporation of New York, March 18, 1996* (pp. 1–157). New York: Carnegie Corporation.

Faigenbaum, A. D., Zaichowsky, L. D., Gardner, D. E., & Micheli, L. J. (1998). Anabolic steroid use by male and female middle school students. *Pediatrics*, *101*(5), e6.

Hastad, N. N., Segrave, J. O., Pangrazi, R., & Peterson, G. (1984). Youth sport participation and deviant behavior. *Sociology of Sport Journal*, *1*, 366–373.

Herman-Tofler, L. R., & Tuckman, B. W. (1998). The effects of aerobic training on children's creativity, self-perception, and aerobic power. In I. R. Tofler (Guest Ed.), *Child and adolescent psychiatric clinics of North America: Sport psychiatry* (Vol. 7, No. 4, pp. 773–790). Philadelphia: Saunders.

Horn, T. S. (1985). Coaches' feedback and changes in children's perceptions of their physical competence. *Journal of Educational Psychology*, *77*, 174–186.

Kamm, R. L. (1998). A developmental and psychoeducational approach to reducing conflict and abuse in little league and youth sports: The sport psychiatrist's role. In I. R. Tofler (Guest Ed.), *Child and adolescent psychiatric clinics of North America: Sport psychiatry* (Vol. 7, No. 4, pp. 891–918). Philadelphia: Saunders.

Kapp-Simon, K. A., Simon, D. J., & Kristovich, S. (1992). Self-perception, social skills, adjustment and inhibition in young adolescents with craniofacial anomalies. *Cleft Palate—Craniofacial Journal*, *29*(4), 352–356.

Lewthwaite, R., & Scanlan, T. K. (1989). Predictors of competitive trait anxiety in male youth sport participants. *Medicine and Science in Sports and Exercise, 21*, 221–229.

Libman, S. (1998). Adult participation in youth sports: A developmental perspective. In I. R. Tofler (Guest Ed.), *Child and adolescent psychiatric clinics of North America: Sport psychiatry* (Vol. 7, No. 4, pp. 725–744). Philadelphia: Saunders.

Magill, R. A., & Anderson, D. I. (1996). Critical periods as optimal readiness for learning sport skills. In F. L. Smoll & R. E. Smith (Eds.), *Children and youth in sport: A biopsychosocial perspective* (pp. 57–72). Madison, WI: Brown & Benchmark.

Martens, R. (Ed.). (1978). *Joy and sadness in children's sports.* Champaign, IL: Human Kinetics.

National Association for Sport and Physical Education. (1995). *National standards for athletic coaches*. Reston, VA: Author.

National Youth Sports Safety Foundation. (1998). Sports and children. *Side Lines*, *8*(1), 1–2, 4.

Ogilvie, B. C., Tofler, I. R., Conroy, D. E., & Drell, M. J. (1998). Comprehending role conflicts in the coaching of children, adolescents, and young adults: Transference, countertransference, and achievement by proxy distortion paradigms. In I. R. Tofler (Guest

Ed.), *Child and adolescent psychiatric clinics of North America: Sport psychiatry* (Vol. 7 No.4, pp. 879–890). Philadelphia: Saunders.

Orlick, T. D. (1982). *The second cooperative sports and games book.* New York: Pantheon.

Passer, M. W. (1988). Determinants and consequences of children's competitive stress. In F. L. Smoll, R. A. Magill, & M. J. Ash (Eds.), *Children in sport,* (3rd ed., pp. 203–228). Champaign, IL: Human Kinetics.

Passer, M. W. (1996). At what age are children ready to compete? Some psychological considerations. In F. L. Smoll & R. E. Smith (Eds.), *Children and youth in sport: A biopsychosocial perspective* (pp. 73–86). Madison, WI: Brown & Benchmark.

Petitpas, A. (1997). *Athlete's guide to career planning.* Champaign, IL: Human Kinetics.

Pooley, J. C. (1980). Dropouts. *Coaching Review, 3,* 36–38.

Ryan, J. (1995). *Little girls in pretty boxes: The making and breaking of elite gymnasts and figure skaters.* New York: Doubleday.

Saint Augustine (4th century). *Confessions* (H. Chadwick, Trans.). Oxford: Oxford University.

Seefeldt, V. (1996). The concept of readiness applied to the acquisition of motor skills. In F. L. Smoll & R. E. Smith (Eds.), *Children and youth in sport: A biopsychosocial perspective* (pp. 49–56). Madison, WI: Brown & Benchmark.

Smith, R. E., Smoll, F. L., & Curtis, B. (1979). Coach effectiveness training: A cognitive-behavioral approach to enhancing relationship skills in youth sport coaches. *Journal of Sport Psychology, 1,* 59–75.

Sporting Goods Manufacturers Association. (1997, September 3). *Youth movement in sports* [Press release]. North Palm Beach, FL: Author.

Sporting Goods Manufacturers Association. (1998, September 17). *Youth at play in the USA* [Press release]. North Palm Beach, FL: Author.

Stryer, B. K., Katz, S. E., & Cantwell, D. P. (1997). Youth sports and adolescent development. In L. T. Flaherty & R. M. Sarles (Eds.), *Handbook of child and adolescent psychiatry: Vol. 3. Adolescence: Development and syndromes* (pp. 209–224). New York: Wiley.

Stryer, B. K., Tofler, I. R., & Lapchick, R. (1998). A developmental overview of child and youth sports in society. In I. R. Tofler (Guest Ed.), *Child and adolescent psychiatric clinics of North America: Sport psychiatry* (Vol. 7, No. 4, pp. 697–724). Philadelphia: Saunders.

Thomas, D. (1939). Fern hill. *The collected poems of Dylan Thomas.* New York: New Directions.

Tofler, I. R., Knapp, P. K., & Drell, M. J. (1998). The achievement by proxy spectrum in youth sports: Historical perspective and clinical approach to pressured and high-achieving children and adolescents. In I. R. Tofler (Guest Ed.), *Child and adolescent psychiatric clinics of North America: Sport psychiatry* (Vol. 7, No. 4, pp. 803–820). Philadelphia: Saunders.

Trulson, M. E. (1986). Martial arts training: A novel "cure" for juvenile delinquency. *Human Relations, 39,* 1131–1140.

Wiggins, D. K. (1996). A history of highly competitive sport for american children. In F. L. Smoll & R. E. Smith (Eds.), *Children and youth in sport: A biopsychosocial perspective* (pp. 15–30). Madison, WI: Brown & Benchmark.

The author wishes to thank Barri Katz Stryer, M.D., and Ian R. Tofler, M.D., for their indispensable contributions to this chapter

7

Substance Abuse and Athletes

Gregory B. Collins

ONE OF THE MORE DIFFICULT PROBLEMS confronted by physicians in the practice of sports medicine is that of the athlete who is abusing drugs. The athlete is playing a foolhardy game with his or her future by jeopardizing academic standing and subjecting him- or herself to arrest and conviction. In addition, the athlete's individual performance may be impaired by the drug abuse, which may have a detrimental effect on a team or an entire athletic organization. Often a problem with substance abuse may be well hidden because no one wishes to talk about it. Parents are concerned about their athlete's future, the athlete does not wish to risk detection or discipline, the school does not wish to endure embarrassment or public scrutiny, and the league may shy away from the expense and difficulty involved in enforcement. Often, rules prohibiting substance abuse are laid down by coaches, schools, or teams, but the talented athlete may feel unconstrained by such regulations and may directly or surreptitiously violate these rules with abusive substances, anticipating that discipline will be soft since the team can ill afford to have a star athlete benched for long.

Indeed these same issues make treatment problematical since it is the rare team that will be willing to sideline a valuable player in the midst of a hotly contested season so that treatment can be obtained for a substance-abuse problem. The team physician is also frequently put in a difficult dilemma by the presence of such problems. Is the physician the agent of the athlete, the team, the school, or the sports organization? Problems with confidentiality and the dilemma of treatment versus discipline can put the physician in a delicate position. Additionally, the team physician must know the league rules for testing and for the prescribing or use of prohibited substances since the presence of these substances in the urine can disqualify an athlete from competition. The physician's prescription of a substance is not generally a valid excuse. In a worst-case scenario, the physician may be compromised into prescribing controlled substances such as anabolic steroids, stimulants, or narcotic analgesics in a misguided attempt to keep the athlete playing even if in pain or to enhance performance through the boosting effects of chemicals.

Such practices are highly questionable from a legal and ethical standpoint and should be shunned by responsible sports physicians. Although no reliable data on the frequency or type of substance abuse among athletes have been published, the stream of publicity attached to athletes who get in trouble with substances demonstrates the reality of the problem. The tragic deaths of athletes at collegiate and professional levels have kept the problem of athletic substance abuse in the public eye. Substance-abuse programs for early identification, referral, and treatment, are now in place for virtually all professional sports organizations, and these programs generally operate from league-wide rules for consistency in regulations, detection, and enforcement. Most of these policies allow voluntary self-referral for treatment, but also for-cause testing, mandatory treatment, and probationary return or expulsion. At the amateur level, the National Collegiate Athletic Association has adopted a drug-testing protocol for postseason bowl games and tournament events (Duda, 1984). The International Olympic Commission (IOC) has been testing for drugs since 1968 (Becket & Cowan, 1979). At the secondary school level, many school systems are developing programs to prevent drug abuse by focusing on the needs of student athletes. These programs generally provide education and antidrug motivational presentations, often with the assistance of professional athletes, religious leaders, treatment professionals, or recovered young people. Some school systems even provide in-school counseling, referral services for professional treatment, and in-school support groups for non-use of substances. Many schools have had to reexamine their policies about drug detection, urine testing, athletic participation while on drugs or in treatment, and the integration of treatment and disciplinary approaches. In spite of all of this activity, there is very little prevalence or outcome data available, primarily because of concerns about confidentiality, adverse publicity, and lawsuits.

What emerges from this picture is a recognition that drug involvement in the world of sports has changed in the past few decades. While performance enhancers such as amphetamines were the popular drugs of abuse in the late 1960s and early 1970s, they have been largely replaced by the so-called recreational drugs, notably marijuana and cocaine. Alcohol has always been a problematic recreational drug and continues to be so at the present time. Work with professional athletes over the past 15 years in the departments of sports medicine and psychiatry at the Cleveland Clinic Foundation has revealed that the drugs most frequently seen in athletes are alcohol, marijuana, and cocaine. Anabolic steroids are another commonly abused drug, especially in the weight and strength sports, but their misuse will not be discussed in this chapter.

SUBSTANCE ABUSE—A SOCIETAL PROBLEM

Recent data gathered from surveys of the general population, young people, and athletes reflect some disturbing trends. According to the 1994 National Household Survey on Drug Abuse, the percentage of 12–17-year-olds who believe that there is great risk of harm in using marijuana occasionally has decreased. At the same time, findings indicate that monthly marijuana use among 12–17-year-olds rose to 7.3% in 1994, up from 4% in 1992. Despite the increase in marijuana use among youth, the total number of illicit drug users has remained constant since 1992. This leveling off follows more than a decade of decline since 1979, the peak year for illicit drug use.

The rate of "past-month alcohol use" declined between 1979 and 1992. Since then, the rate has increased slightly. The rate of heavy alcohol use has not changed since 1990. The survey defines "heavy alcohol use" as drinking five or more drinks per occasion on five or more days per month. The Household Survey also found that the number of underage drinkers, which included two million heavy drinkers, remained unacceptably high.

In an average month in 1994, the survey estimated that 13 million Americans (6.0% of those 12 years and older) used illicit drugs; 10 million Americans (77% of current illicit drug users) used marijuana, making it the most commonly used illicit drug; 1.4 million Americans (0.7% of the population) used cocaine; 13 million Americans (6.2% of the population) had five or more drinks per occasion on five or more days of the month; 60 million people (including 4 million adolescents, ages 12–17) smoked cigarettes.

Young people remain a source of concern since, in 1994, the rate of current illicit drug use was highest among persons 18–21 and 12–17 years old. Heavy drinking also was most prevalent among persons age 18–21 and 22–25 (National Household Survey on Drug Abuse, 1994). Other investigators have noted that adolescents who are most likely to use illicit drugs are more alienated from parents, more critical of society, more adventuresome and thrill-seeking, more extroverted, less traditional, and less oriented to religion than their peers (Smith, 1986). In view of these research findings on the frequency of substance abuse in general society, there is no reason to believe that young athletes are immune from the societal epidemic of alcohol abuse and dependency (Ryan, 1984).

In fact, there are factors involved in sport participation that may heighten the risk and misuse of drugs and alcohol. In a study (Nattiv & Puffer, 1991) of 219 undergraduate college students who were asked to participate in a confidential survey about personal lifestyle and health risk behaviors in 1989, including a subgroup of 109 undergraduate collegiate athletes (109 athletes vs. 110 nonathlete controls), it was noted that the athlete group had more "high-risk" lifestyle behaviors compared with the nonathletes. The lifestyle behaviors that placed the athletes at significantly higher risk included a greater quantity of alcohol consumed per sitting (athletes, 51%; nonathletes, 36%); more frequent driving while intoxicated from alcohol or drugs (athletes, 39%; nonathletes, 12%); more frequent riding with a driver who was intoxicated or under the influence of drugs (athletes, 49%; nonathletes, 26%); less frequent use of seatbelts (athletes, 47%; nonathletes, 29%); less frequent use of helmets when riding a motor scooter or a motorcycle (athletes, 49%; nonathletes, 33%); less frequent use of contraception (athletes, 40%; nonathletes, 26%); increased frequency of sexually transmitted diseases (athletes, 11.6%; nonathletes, 2.8%); increased number of sexual partners (athletes, 28%; nonathletes, 12.7%); and infrequent rest days from aerobic exercise (athletes, 25%, nonathletes, 9%). Family history of alcohol and/or drug abuse was also greater in the athlete group (athletes, 22%; nonathletes, 9.5%). There was no significant difference between the two groups with respect to frequency (not quantity) of alcohol consumption or use of marijuana, amphetamines, cocaine, anabolic steroids, cigarettes, or smokeless tobacco.

Why athletes expose themselves to more high-risk circumstances is a fascinating question. Sports psychologists have studied this matter and postulated that perhaps there is a predisposing personality type for high-risk sports (Bouter, Knipschild, Paul, Feij, Jan, 1988). A Type "T" personality has been described, which may perhaps characterize high-risk athletes such as sky divers and mountain climbers. Such individuals may actively pursue thrill-seeking behavior, excitement, and stimulation (Farley, 1986). Ogilvie (1973), another psychologist, also studied high-risk athletes and noted the strong stimulus-seeking component of their behaviors and personalities.

The 1989 report of the replication of the national study of the substance use and abuse of drugs by college student athletes (Anderson & McKeag, 1985, 1989) provides some survey data regarding the use of major pain relievers and weight loss substances by college athletes. Major pain relievers, including Tylenol #3 (McNeil), Percodan (DuPont), morphine, codeine, and Demerol (Winthrop Pharmaceuticals), are the most commonly used "perceived ergogenic" drugs studied in this report. Thirty-four percent of the athletes studied reported using at least one of these compounds within 12 months, an increase of 6% from the original study in 1985. The most common source of these medications is the team physician, accounting for 43% of the student-athletes' sources of these drugs. Other physicians provided these drugs to another 35% of the athletes studied. Although more than 20% of these athletes received their major pain medications from sources other than physicians, the reasons named for their use in the survey, 76.7% for a sport-related injury and 20% for a nonsport injury, do appear to be appropriate. Only 1.3% of athletes reported use of these drugs to improve performance. Weight-loss medications, especially appetite suppressants, are also commonly used by athletes, especially women. Overall, about 5% of college athletes surveyed in the 1989 NCAA study reported using a weight-loss product during the preceding 12 months (Anderson & McKeag, 1989).

The 1984 Michigan State Study of Athletes in Division I, II, and III colleges (Anderson & McKeag, 1985) revealed that 88% of the 2,039 respondents used alcohol within the prior 12 months, compared with 36% who used marijuana or hashish. Twenty-seven percent of those using alcohol consumed 3–5 drinks 2–5 times per week, while 23% had 6–9 drinks at least 2–5 times per week. Of those athletes using alcohol, 24% indicated they did so in junior high school or before.

The economic impact of alcohol in both amateur and professional sports cannot be overstated. Beer is perhaps the most important economic contributor to the sports economy. Consider this: Anheuser-Busch spends two-thirds of its advertising budget on sports ("Top T.V. Sports Advertisers," 1988). According to Anheuser-Busch's executive vice-president and director of marketing, each year the brewery sponsors on broadcast television, radio, and/or cable: 23 of the 24 domestic major league baseball teams; 18 of the 28 clubs in the National Football League; 22 of the 23 National Basketball Association franchises; 13 of the 14 domestic National Hockey League teams; and 9 of the 11 major indoor soccer league clubs. That's in addition to various direct, media, or fundraising scholarships of more than 300 college teams. Anheuser-Busch will also manage or promote about 1,000 secondary and tertiary sporting events (at the rate of three per day), ranging from hydroplane races to the Bud Light ironman triathlon (Gloede, 1988). It has been estimated that the average child is exposed to as many as 100,000 beer ads before reaching the legal drinking age (Gloede, 1988).

Another major consideration about alcohol and drug misuse relates to athletes and athletic figures as role models (Wadler & Hainline, 1989). For that reason, the National Football League (1989) adopted the following drug policy for all of its players, coaches, and other personnel:

> NFL players, coaches, and other employees should not endorse or appear in advertisements for alcohol beverages (including beer) and tobacco products. While fully recognizing that the use of alcohol and tobacco is legal, the NFL nevertheless has long been of the view that participation in ads for such substances by its employees, particularly players, who are prohibited by Federal Law from appearing in such ads, may have a detrimental effect on the great number of young fans who follow our game. Endorsements or other close identification of NFL players with alcohol or tobacco could convey the erroneous impression that the use of such products is conducive to the development of athletic prowess, has contributed to their success, or at least has not hindered them in their performance. For the above reasons, players and other club and League employees (including game officials) should not use alcohol or tobacco products while in the playing field area or while being interviewed on television.

In response to these concerns, schools and sports organizations at the amateur and professional levels have, in recent years, taken a more vigorous stance opposing drug abuse. The reasons for doing so are summarized as the following:

1. Drug abuse is physically and psychologically harmful to the athlete and may even be fatal.
2. Drug abuse is harmful to athletic performance and significantly detracts from the athlete's goal of maximal athletic achievement.
3. Drug abuse causes apathy, inattention, impaired memory, or negative attitude and is therefore harmful to the athlete's academic performance.
4. Drug abuse undermines the view of athletes as "positive role models" for young people and may supplant these images with "negative role models," influencing young people to take drugs because of their "status" or "safety."
5. Drug abuse detracts from the sport as a whole and soils the view of the sport as a wholesome example of competitive athletic/character rivalry. This last effect could conceivably result in questioning the value of organized sport to society and substantial loss of viewer interest or support.

In summary, most sports organizations have concluded that there is very little that is "good" and very much that is "bad" about substance misuse. Unfortunately, knowing this bad or harmful aspect of substance misuse doesn't necessarily translate into a clear administrative action plan for dealing with this issue. In practice, nearly any administrative response or action is likely to be met with a confounding variety of intense resistance, especially when these initiatives are directed toward athletes (Collins, Janesz, Bergfeld, & Pippinger, 1988).

The major resistance centers around concerns about confidentiality. Athletes themselves, parents, schools, and sports organizations all share a legitimate concern about the stigmatizing affects of labeling or identifying young people as "drug abusers," "drug addicts," or "chemical dependents." Will a pro team take a chance on a player who has been treated for drug dependence? Will that player still be worth a sizable signing bonus? Will that player be a reliable and consistent performer, or will he or she have frequent relapses, requiring long absences from the team for rehabilitative therapy? What will be the impact on colleges, coaches, pro teams, the media, and the community? Concerns about confidentiality violations have led the athletes themselves and their support systems to resist and avoid meaningful responses to the drug abuse problem.

Other resistances include concerns about costs of prevention, detection, and treatment, uncertainty about the legality of intervention, and anxiety from lack of knowledge about how to respond. Another major point of resistance is the athlete's and parent's fear that the drug-involved player will be disciplined and not allowed to play. Concerns about fairness or prejudicial application of rules and sanctions compound the problems of consistent enforcement. Often, attempts by coaches or schools to enforce discipline have resulted in legal challenges, lawsuits, and rescinded administrative actions. It is easy to come to conclude that addressing the problem of substance abuse in an athletic population is like stepping into an administrative minefield.

WHY DO ATHLETES START USING CHEMICALS?

Peer pressure is frequently cited as a major factor in the initiation and maintenance of chemical problems in young athletes. The desire to be accepted by one's athletic peers, friends, and teammates is enormously compelling. Emulating what appear to be macho, mature, risky behaviors seen in older siblings, friends, or teammates, these young athletes learn at the age of 13 or 14 that heavy, conspicuous group drinking confers a kind of macho status and acceptance among peers. The inherent violations of law, training rules, and social convention seemingly add stature to the young athlete as invincible, powerful, and a nonconformist. Drinking often continues during high school and is soon augmented by the smoking of pot. Much of this chemical activity is done in groups and is especially pronounced after games or competitions. Parents, coaches, and others may fall into the belief that chemical excesses are "normal" and to be expected under such pressured circumstances, and the athletes are expected to "blow off steam." The exceptional athlete may have such an abundance of natural athletic ability, size, or speed, that this level of chemical use does not diminish his performance noticeably, and he might still remain an outstanding performer relative to his less-gifted peers. Unfortunately, this only serves to reinforce the delusion that substances are not harmful to him and that he can use them with impunity indefinitely into the future without detracting from his athletic performance. In this way, substance misuse reinforces a self-delusion of power and invincibility which only serves to blind the athlete to the need to adhere to rules and norms of responsible behavior with substances. This blindness turns into pathological entrenched denial, which may require intensive psychotherapy to undo at a later date.

At the college level, now using marijuana and alcohol heavily, the athlete is introduced to cocaine by older peers or friends, such as, in one case, a bar owner who provided cocaine free to all of the collegiate athletes who would hang around his establishment since their presence would attract customers. Still, cocaine use is generally quite limited during college years. Generally, lack of money to purchase the drug is the reason given for this restraint. Alcohol and marijuana remain the mainstays of recreational drug abuse during college days for most youngsters. At this point, a few collegiate athletes are identified as drug abusers by college coaches on the basis of erratic performance, drug-related misbehavior, or association with drug-involved peers. Rarely, however, is any serious attempt at counseling or rehabilitation therapy attempted during college years. At the present time, random urine testing is done on some athletic collegiate teams, where school policy directs it and where league policy allows it. One notable example is the drug program at Ohio State University, formerly under the guidance of Dr. Robert Murphy (personal communication, 1986). The Ohio State University program and others like it offer hope that drug-involved athletes will be identified at an early point and promptly given appropriate treatment and counseling before the problem becomes well-entrenched ("Ohio State," 1986).

At the professional level, the athlete often undergoes a personality change. While he might have been a pleasant, coachable, and easily directed youth, he may now come to feel that he has "made it." He has achieved his lifelong goal of acceptance into the ranks of the world's top professional athletes. The temptation to play the role of a macho superstar is overwhelming. In time, peer influence and peer competition begin to change the athlete's personality and behavior. Although in school athletics the appearance of conformity to societal expectations is maintained, at the professional level there is pressure to compete in nonconformist, macho behaviors. Drug abuse fits into this nonconformist behavior pattern. Cocaine, with its phenomenal expense, glamorous allure, and severe legal penalties, is an attractive vehicle for demonstrating wealth, status, and power. One player summed this up nicely when he described himself as "King High." The need to construct and maintain this super-macho persona is a powerful psychological inducement to use and abuse dangerous substances. Thus, for many players, cocaine becomes the drug of choice, which is either "snorted" or smoked "powder," "freebase," or "crack." In my experience, patterns of cocaine abuse range from sporadic to repeated daily, almost constant, administration of the drug.

Drug use appears to affect the player's athletic performance on several levels. Most pro-players involved with drugs experience some impaired concentration, more mental errors, sleepiness, lethargy, loss of desire to play, and greater proneness to injury. Many players experience physical deterioration as well, ranging from fat accumulation and loss of speed and strength to weight loss and declining fitness.

Many factors appear to be involved in the "blossoming" of the problem at the professional level. Personality changes, nonconformist peer pressure, and enlarged disposable incomes are just a few of these. We have observed that in most cases, it takes about two years for the effects of drug abuse to become apparent in athletic performance and team participation. Marijuana alone has also been shown to impair performance in a number of sports-related parameters (general performance, standing steadiness, reaction speed, and psychomotor performance). When combined with alcohol, performance on marijuana is even worse (Belgrave et al., 1979; Bird et al., 1980). Marijuana has also been shown to decrease peak exercise performance (Tashkin, Soares, Hepler, Shapiro, Rachelefsky, 1978). Dr. Forest Tenant, a physician who has treated many athletes, also believes that marijuana use is particularly harmful to athletes and can permanently impair their visual perception and their ability to do fine-muscle or mental tasks; the timing that is so critical in many sports may be affected just enough to make the small difference between success and failure in professional sports participation (Cowart, 1986).

Once the problem is established, the drug-involved athlete becomes a multiproblem individual whose personal affairs are in chaos. All of the drug-involved players we have treated had serious financial problems resulting from the neglect of financial responsibilities and the expenses associated with a drug-involved lifestyle. Passivity bordering on paralysis with regard to social responsibility was not unusual. For example, some players had been so immobilized by drugs that a simple payment on an auto loan was beyond their motivation or interest. Many had totally abdicated the management of their personal affairs to distant agents or friends of the family. In spite of high salaries, several players were more than $100,000 in debt, with nothing to show for it. Players' attitudes toward this financial chaos were generally passive and uninvolved. Since many were accustomed to having all expenses paid for them throughout their school years, debts and costs were rarely a deterrent to drug use. Players generally reported that they could obtain drugs even when they had no money. Pushers and dealers considered prominent athletes to be "high-status customers" who conferred status on the dealer and who tended to attract more business. Many dealers would simply write off the player's bad debts as business losses. Other dealers were not so forgiving; occasionally a dealer would threaten an athlete to obtain payment, but no significant violence was ever noted in our experience, probably because the dealers did not wish to attract unwanted police or media attention. Generally, players' debts were in the form of unpaid bills. Drug-using players were hopelessly far from achieving their dreams of financial security and material reward for themselves and their families. Few had anything at all to show for their lavish spending. The problem of sudden affluence in athletes has been described elsewhere (Cohen, 1982).

Idle time is a serious risk factor for the drug-involved athlete. When the Cleveland Clinic program for the Cleveland Browns began in earnest in the early 1980s, football players generally worked only six months a year. The unstructured time during the rest of the year could have been put to productive use such as education or off-season employment; but for the drug-involved athlete, idle time was another "enabling" circumstance, permitting even more drug use. Players had little accountability for time. A player could stay up all night and all day doing cocaine, and then he could "crash" for long periods. Even during the season, as long as he would show up for a few meetings, practices, and games, he thought nothing would be discovered or said. Indeed, the problem of drug abuse presents a serious dilemma for teams at all levels. How much supervision should the team provide? Is the team's supervision of the athlete limited to training, preparation, and sports-related activities, or should this supervision extend to "free" time, even in the off-season? Drug-involved players generally resist this accountability and try to keep it to a minimum. It was soon evident that involved players required far more stringent and consistent supervision on a daily basis year round, or at least until stable sobriety was achieved and emotional maturity was in evidence, generally 18–24 months after treatment began.

Negative reinforcers often have no impact on professional athletes. Arrests and convictions for alcohol and drug offenses are few relative to the magnitude of the problem. Only one of our athletes had ever been arrested for a drug-related offense. If few are arrested, fewer still are convicted and sentenced. Many drug-involved athletes know that prosecution is unlikely, so "scare tactics" about arrest and conviction have little preventative value. Similarly, the threat of job loss is a weak motivator for avoiding drugs. The players believe that their athletic ability is always in demand. If the player is cut, he can usually go to another team or even to a competing league. The best players also perceive that their positions are secure because a team is unlikely to cut a talented player. Thus, threats of benching or cutting players for drug abuse or for treatment noncompliance are seen by players as bluffs. At the high school or college level, these disciplinary tactics or dismissals would seemingly be more feared by players since switching schools is not so easily done and players must be actively playing in order to showcase their talents for professional scouts. Unfortunately, the pressure to play is so strong at the academic level that benching is likely to be met by extremely tough resistance from parents, alumni, and players. Few coaches are in a secure enough position to bench or suspend a top player for drug abuse. For this very reason, top players and outstanding athletes seem more at risk for the development of drug problems. Seemingly immune from the corrective and disciplinary pressures that provoke fear and conformity in their less gifted peers, these athletes comfortably defy training rules and school policy with the realization that negative consequences are unlikely to follow. Dr. Joseph Pursch, a noted authority, has commented that addicts often tell him that they have a "right to use illegal drugs recreationally. Most addicts, however, say this in the beginning. Whether they are athletes, board chairmen, military personnel, physicians, or housewives, they feel that they are able to handle them and that they have a right to use them" (Cowart, 1986).

Drug-involved players have few plans for their post-competition careers. All recognize the short career of a professional athlete and the constant risk that their careers could be abruptly ended by injury, yet only a small percentage take concrete steps to prepare for the future. In general, it seems that drugs blind players to reality in this regard. Although transition to nonathletic career status is often a difficult step for the lifetime athlete, drug involvement makes this even worse. Drug-involved athletes do nothing to prepare, do not acquire skills in the off-season, and do not cultivate business contacts or concern themselves about keeping a "clean" reputation. While athletic life provides insulation from the real world, drugs further drive the player into a cocoon of isolation and unreality. Drug-involved players do not attempt to develop educational credentials, business experience, business contacts, or an understanding of the competitive marketplace. Long-term occupational goals are dramatically stunted by heavy drug abuse.

THE PROBLEM PLAYER SYNDROME

The psychosocial backgrounds of the drug-involved players in my sports psychiatry practice are strikingly similar. Virtually all were reared in very impoverished circumstances. When working with them, I am struck by the multidimensional nature of poverty. Drug-involved football players are generally from poor, small towns in the South, and drug-involved basketball players are mostly from the large, urban ghettos of the North. Very few had any stable father figure in the home when they were growing up. Many did not know their fathers at all, and among those who did, fathers were often very unhealthy role models. One father was the town bootlegger; several were alcoholic "bums" who seldom came around except to look for money. Many of the athletes' brothers had drug problems; several were in trouble with the law and were in and out of jail. Brothers often looked to the athletes to supply drugs, bail money, or lawyers' fees when in trouble. The athletes' mothers, however, usually were hardworking, self-sacrificing women who took on most of the financial responsibility of the family, and who fostered the religious, academic, and social values within the home. As a result, virtually all of our players felt a strong sense of responsibility and loyalty to their mothers and all expressed a sincere desire to be better fathers than their own had been. Many of the athletes had had extensive religious training (fundamentalist Christian) when young. Many could quote chapter and verse of scripture fluently, yet had a difficult time incorporating spiritual, moral, and religious values into their daily lives. They were far more influenced by peer pressure and drug-cultured norms than by religious training. Most felt guilt and anxiety about deviating from parental expectations and went to great lengths to conceal their drug involvement, especially from their mothers.

All of the players had been lifelong athletic standouts. Many were from small towns in which their athletic talent dominated all local competition. Virtually all had been on outstanding scholastic teams; several had won state and national championships. At the professional level, drug-involved players ranged from marginal to outstanding, and from rookies to seasoned veterans. In general, the drug-involved players were highly social and outgoing. They were outwardly affable, relaxed, and self-confident. A few, however, were extremely introverted and shy, and some suffered from speech and reading impediments.

Academically, the drug-involved players were marginal at best. Forty percent had completed college, primarily with athletic majors. As a group, they had little serious academic interest and generally saw school only as a vehicle for demonstrating their athletic ability. In college, a few had been drug-free, but most had extensive experience with marijuana and alcohol, while some had used cocaine recreationally. In general, colleges provided no special counseling or academic help for these athletes, a situation that is receiving more media criticism (Klein, 1986).

At the professional level, a frequently seen scenario is described by Dr. Joseph Pursch, who has treated many famous athletes:

> When I have a sports star in my office for the first time, I can expect all of the buttons on my telephone to be lit up. . . . His agent is on one line to tell me he has a beer commercial lined up for his client that can't be shot if it is known he is an alcoholic, and the income loss will be multiple thousands of dollars. The coach wants to know how soon he can play; the hospital administrator wants to make a public announcement; and the star's lawyer wants it quiet. A TV network demands a full report. Agents for the Players Association and the team have their interests, and his wife and ex-wife (and maybe a girlfriend) want to be assured his income will continue, and all of this is before I have even taken his blood pressure. (Cowart, 1986, p. 2646)

Forest Tennant, M.D., the former drug czar for the National Football League, noted that the outlook for an athlete with drug addiction is poorer than average:

> They cannot be expected to do well. You have to have certain elements in your treatment program, self-help groups, counseling, urine testing, monitoring, and social supports. An athlete is on the road all of the time. Most of the time he can't obtain what he needs to stay clean. Not that many athletes don't do well in spite of this; it is just more difficult for them. (Cowart, 1986, p. 2645).

There may be special considerations in treatment as well. According to Dr. Pursch:

> We as therapists have to be aware that people will want to do something they do extremely well and avoid doing things they don't do well. Athletes perform well physically and like to, and often don't perform so well emotionally and intellectually in the sense of being open and honest in group therapy or with spouses or lovers. They don't do well talking, sharing, and taking emotional risks. (Cowart, 1986, p. 2649)

For that reason, Dr. Pursch will not allow an athlete unlimited exercise time, in the same way that he tells physician-addicts under treatment that the medical library is off limits to them.

> If you leave the schedule open, the jocks will be in the gym all day. If physical exercise helped these people, they wouldn't be here in the first place. They have to learn what it is that is defective about their lifestyle. A well-known jock has to be watched or the minute he gets on the running track, he takes over and everybody gravitates around him and treatment is just that much more difficult. (Cowart, 1986, p. 2649)

THE CLEVELAND BROWNS AND CLEVELAND CLINIC PROGRAM FOR DRUG-INVOLVED PROFESSIONAL ATHLETES

How then can an athletic organization deal with the destructive problem of drug use among resistant players who are at high risk and who have extensive problems, no psychological insight, and virtually no effective external motivating factors? In 1980 the Cleveland Browns football team approached the problem by mobilizing a *total organizational commitment* aimed at prevention, identification, and treatment, not only for the drug abuse itself, but also for the problem of the "whole person" (Collins, Pippenger, & Janesz, 1984). Since the problems of the drug-involved athlete are so complex, the "links in the chain" of effective response resources within the team include the owner, coach, team physician, team psychiatrist, players (the "Inner Circle"), employee assistance consultant, administrative assistant, security agent, players wives, and spiritual counselor (figure 7.1). "Links" outside the team's resources included rehabilitation centers, specialized self-help groups, and urine toxicology laboratory monitoring. The approach was specifically directed to *help the players*, not to appease management, and it was directed not only at football, but also at postfootball success. Only by attacking the entire matrix of internal psychological and external environmental problems could gains against drug abuse be made and maintained. The total organizational commitment demonstrated by this professional football team was a highly successful model that met the specific needs of the drug-involved athlete, and it has been adapted for use by schools and other industries.

The Owner

The team owner came to recognize that alcohol and drug abuse was a major problem that could adversely affect team performance. He readily

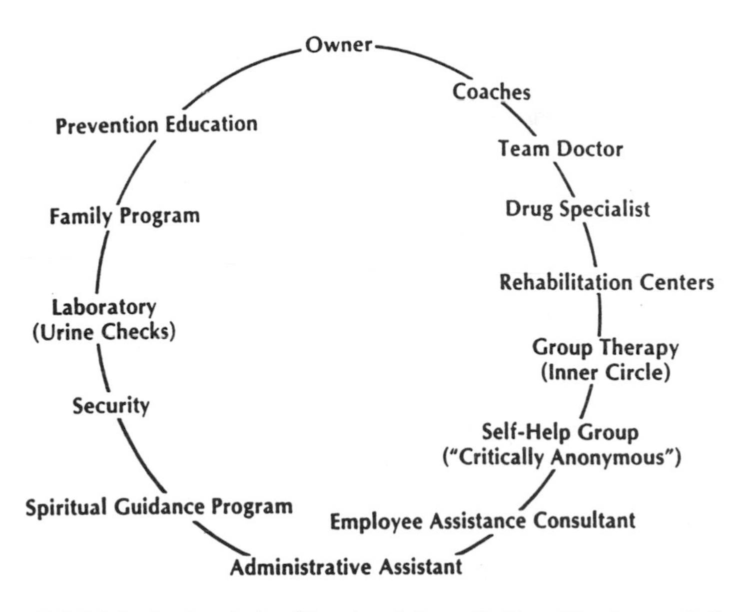

Figure 7.1 Links in the chain. (Reprinted from Collins, Pippinger, & Janesz, 1984, with permission.)

agreed to endorse all of the team's drug-treatment and prevention efforts, including paying for all costs incurred. Subsequently, the league's insurance program provided reimbursement for most of the treatment provided to the athletes.

Coach

The coach proved to be the central figure in the overall antidrug effort. The coach knew the players well and could best judge if performance was being affected by drugs. He consistently took a helping, and not a punishing, approach to the drug-involved players and, on the basis of a long-established relationship of trust, was responsible for several players voluntarily coming forth for help. In some cases, when voluntary participation was not forthcoming, involuntary referral was made for evaluation. The coach was in a relatively strong position of power and influence over the players, so that they generally dared not defy his recommendations for participation. The coach did not see himself as a medical director or a psychiatrist, and in every case he avoided diagnosing and treating problems himself. Rather, he would notice impaired performance and refer the player to the psychiatrist/specialist for evaluation and recommendations. The coach then required the player to follow the psychiatrist's treatment recommendations. Interestingly, the coach became a regular member of the group therapy sessions. The players reacted for a time with distrust and apprehension, but eventually the coach's perseverance and enthusiasm overcame their resistance. The coach served as an invaluable resource and inspiration for the players, and his presence also provided stability to the group. In his absence, maintaining an orderly discussion was difficult. The players would revert to "cutting up" in the sessions at first. Some drifted away. We eventually had to ask the coach to return to restore order and control. A year later, when the coach was called away for other duties, the players had progressed enough so that "cutting up" and other forms of misconduct did not occur.

The Team Physician

The regular team physician, an orthopedic surgeon, had been involved in preliminary discussions with the coach and team owner, which led to the recognition of drug abuse as a significant problem to the team. The team physician then assisted in recruiting the psychiatrist specializing in drug abuse, and he convinced management to provide an ongoing drug treatment program. Since all outsiders are initially greeted with suspicion by players and management, his endorsement and support of the specialist in the drug treatment program were vital to the establishment of trust and cooperation. He recognized that drug-abuse problems are complicated, requiring specialized help and a complex, long-term solution.

The Team Psychiatrist

The psychiatrist initiated the program with educational lectures about drug abuse and an offer of confidential treatment to any player with a problem. The treatment usually began with a comprehensive, psychiatric assessment, giving careful attention to the player's drug and alcohol history. Treatment recommendations were formulated promptly and were usually given to the player, his spouse (if he had one), the team doctor, and the coach. These recommendations eventually came to include any or all of the following: inpatient drug rehabilitation, outpatient group and individual therapy, family therapy, hospital-sponsored self-help groups, and urine monitoring. The psychiatrist had primary responsibility for the organization and maintenance of all aspects of the treatment program, with the approval of the coach and owner. The psychiatrist conducted all group and individual therapies, collected all urine for testing, and established a self-help meeting for players. At its height, the program came to occupy approximately one-third of the psychiatrist's total professional activities.

The Inner Circle

The Inner Circle was a group of identified drug-involved players. When the program was initiated, they participated in one group therapy session at the workout facility, one individual therapy session at the psychiatrist's office, and one self-help meeting, all to be done weekly. The group therapy session, or Inner Circle meeting, was similar in format to Narcotics Anonymous meetings, but emphasized open discussion of the individual players' problems rather than testimonials or topics. There was also an "Outer Circle" of non–drug-involved helpers, including the psychiatrist, coach, team administrative assistant, employee assistance consultant, and spiritual counselor. Initially, group therapy was often undermined by peer group loyalties so that open discussion was difficult. Generally, players were reluctant to confront each other or to reveal much about themselves. The progress of the players was highly variable. Some were able to abstain permanently from drugs from the first day of treatment. Others had periodic relapses, and others failed to alter their patterns of frequent use. Players who failed to modify their use were eventually either ejected from the group, or were a loss to the team. No factors were identified that could predict success or failure. Relapses were initially recorded by self-disclosure, but subsequently were reported by sharing results from therapeutic urine monitoring. Group discussions typically dealt with who was relapsing and why, and the need for changes in the individual's lifestyle to support staying "clean."

The players' attitudes about sobriety were highly variable due to the instability of mood and attitude that is part of their illness. At times, participation was enthusiastic and sobriety was stable. At other times, attitudes were negative, antagonistic, resistant, and deceptive. After approximately a year of intensive therapy, including the use of inpatient chemical dependency rehabilitation centers, the group was able to achieve a stable, therapeutic attitude in which sobriety was valued as a positive good for the players themselves rather than as a necessity to please the coach, owner, or physician. With this turning point in attitude came the replacement of a "conspiratorial peer code" by healthy teamwork. Rather than participating in cover-ups and deceptions, the players saw that relapses were "contagious" and that when one member was in trouble, others would soon follow. Eventually, open confrontation about old drug-related behaviors, friends, environments, and attitudes ensued. The group eventually became responsible for much of its own therapeutic work in keeping individual members away from drugs. Resentment, deception, and hostility were replaced by pride, gratitude, and loyalty. Relapses, once frequent, eventually became extremely rare. Eventually, senior players with longstanding sobriety became role models for younger players. Thus, positive peer pressure came to be a major force in one teammate helping another.

Therapeutic Urine Monitoring

Urine monitoring for drugs proved to be an *indispensable* treatment modality. Urine was initially tested weekly, but players soon learned to time their drug use immediately after urine collection so they would be drug-free by the following collection. The sampling frequency was therefore increased to two samples per week. In addition, a policy was established wherein the physician could ask for a urine sample at any time. Urine was always collected under direct "eyeball to penis" supervision. Prior to establishment of this rigorous collection supervision policy, some players attempted to frustrate the urine monitoring by bringing in urine from their girlfriends or by authorizing one clean member to urinate for everyone, or by sharing urine among themselves. Once these "games" were discovered, the policy of rigorous collection supervision was put in place without further incident.

These urinalyses came to be regarded as part of the therapy for the players in the drug program. They are not collected by the club, but by the treating psychiatrist. Urine samples were screened for the presence of opiates, marijuana, cocaine, benzodiazepines (minor tranquilizers), amphetamines, methadone, propoxyphene, and phencyclidine (PCP) by homogenous enzyme immunoassay (CIBA Company, Palo Alto, California) and by thin-layer chromatography (Toxi-Lab Analytical Systems, Laguna Hills, California). Confirmation of positive specimens was carried out by gas-liquid chromatography or gas-chromatography/mass spectroscopy. Alcohol was not checked. The results of the urine tests were openly discussed at the group meetings in which the coach was present. A discussion of legal issues in urine-testing protocols has been written by R. T. Chamberlain (1986).

Additionally, the players elected a system of self-imposed fines as a deterrent to prevent "dirty" urines and to penalize missed urine checks or missed appointments. These self-imposed fines were relatively severe: $200 for a "dirty" urine or a missed urine collection, and $100 for a missed appointment or meeting. Fines were saved for a contribution to charity at the end of the year.

The Employee Assistance Consultant

The consultant was hired by the team to assist players with personal problems, including housing, debts, taxes, hangouts, financial management, girlfriends, and other matters relating to the "outside world." The team hired a former outstanding player for this position, and he also became a nonaddict member of the therapy group (the Outer Circle). His assistance was invaluable because it was discovered that the drug-involved athlete is a multiproblem person whose affairs are in chaos and whose initiative has been undermined by the drug-involved lifestyle. Rebuilding a healthy, supportive social matrix for these players is a time-consuming, frustrating endeavor. Their own resistance, distrust, and passive noninvolvement made this rebuilding a formidable task. Getting the player to accept some personal responsibility for his financial obligations and for undoing the chaos created by years of neglect was no small matter. As these problems were resolved, attention could be directed toward future financial planning for postfootball years. The employee assistance consultant also mobilized competent attorneys, accountants, and banks to help players resolve their complex financial and legal problems. Eventually, players were able to cooperate actively in their social rehabilitation with reasonable resolution of their financial, legal, environmental, marital, and family problems. Being a former outstanding player, the consultant also served as a role model for a healthy, totally committed, achievement-oriented, well-rounded life for the drug-involved athletes. He embodied the reality that drug and alcohol avoidance was possible and would pay large dividends and nonathletic rewards.

The Administrative Assistant

The owner's administrative assistant, a Hall of Fame former NFL player, was also a member of the Outer Circle of nonaddict group therapy members. He frequently clarified administrative questions relating to the status of players on the team. Often these problems related to apprehension about salary negotiations, team policies, or being cut from the team. His constant presence in the group was a reminder of the owner's complete support for the program. The administrative assistant also coordinated continuing education, since several players had not completed their college undergraduate degree requirements. Helping the player to identify his educational needs, contacting his former school for records, and arranging enrollment in scheduling of additional coursework in the team's city were critical undertakings. The educational program was very successful and some players went on to enroll in Master's level programs in marketing or counseling. Once again, the presence of a truly outstanding, successful, and non–drug-involved player-peer was critically important in the identification of healthy role models for young, immature athletes.

Team Security

The team hired a full-time security agent, not to provide surveillance of the players, but to protect the players and the staff. Players were constantly exposed to security problems, including threats on their lives and property, harassment of their families, and exposure to drug pushers. By avoiding direct surveillance of the team members, we were able to minimize antagonism and foster trust, such that eventually players were identifying to the security agent their former drug sources at games and practice sessions. The security agent was able to discourage the presence of such undesirables, minimizing temptation for the drug-involved players and promoting a healthier environment for the team. Prior to his arrival in the organization, drug pushers were extremely brazen in their approach to players. They would hang around the practice field and attempt to see the players after practice sessions and games. Many would use women as inducements and some of the pushers themselves were women. Some pushers even used children to seek autographs and to befriend the players enticing them into dialogue that would end in a drug offer. Pushers and criminal elements frequently attempted to befriend the players and to obtain tickets and other favors.

Specialized Rehabilitation Centers

These centers were used to provide "total immersion therapy" in the initial phases of treatment for some players. Centers were especially selected if they had expertise in drug rehabilitation, rather than an approach geared solely to alcoholism. Because of confidentiality problems, centers were chosen that were not located in either the player's hometown, college town, or professional team town. On one occasion when this principle was violated, newspaper coverage of the player's treatment soon followed. It proved to be difficult to contain the excitement and notoriety of a player in treatment. We attempted to "match the personality" of the treatment center and its major emphasis on treatment with the specific personality needs of the individual player. As a result, players went to a number of different facilities around the country. Some facilities were highly confrontational and dealt with highly resistant, antagonistic drug dependence. Other centers were more psychologically inclined, and offered supportive, nonthreatening, insight-oriented, and Alcoholics Anonymous milieus. Generally, the results achieved through the rehabilitation centers were striking. The players returned from the centers with an improved attitude and a strong desire to remain abstinent. However, this motivation was not long sustained without rigorous outpatient follow-up treatment. In fact, even the slightest weakening of the support network, such as a schedule change or a vacation, often led to relapses. In all cases, the athletes regarded the treatment provided at the rehabilitation centers positively. At the time of discharge, the centers verbally communicated to the team psychiatrist a status report on the athlete's evaluation and treatment, as well as a recommendation for aftercare. In general, aftercare was provided by the team's Inner Circle program and additional support groups and counseling.

Self Help Group

An unsupervised self-help group, similar to but not affiliated with Narcotics Anonymous, was started at the Cleveland Clinic Foundation hospital specifically for the needs of the professional athlete. By identifying a need for additional support and access to a self-help program, and being limited by concerns for confidentiality, this "Critically Anonymous" self-help group was developed, consisting of recovering chemically dependent players at risk for recognition of name or face in the community. This group met at the hospital on a weekly basis in an unmarked room. The meeting was also attended by recovering physicians, dentists, lawyers, judges, and other prominent community figures. This mixture worked well. In general, the nonplayer professionals had more education and more intact social supports, and they were able to provide a stabilizing influence. No therapist or team management representatives were present, so the players could be more open about their problems in a group session without fear of administrative consequences. It was hoped that the absence of a professional therapist would foster more independence and personal responsibility for recovery. These hopes proved difficult to actualize. For months, the same resistances appeared in the self-help group, including the conspiratorial peer bond, covering up, defensiveness, and resentment. Eventually, however, the quality of the meetings also improved, and motivation for sobriety began to emerge with players taking a more active role, even to the point of helping others.

Concerned Others

The involvement of "concerned others," including wives and girlfriends, was believed from the outset to be critical to the success of the program. In general, professional football is not conducive to stable relationships. The players are constantly exposed to the adulation and availability of women, and many of the drug-involved players had never developed any longstanding relationships with emotionally healthy women. Often the women were also involved with drugs, ranging from drug sharing to selling. At the outset of the program, only one player was married. After a year of treatment, half were married. Invariably, marriage to a non–drug-involved woman was viewed as a healthy step for the player and signified a transition from a hedonistic, immature lifestyle to a more responsible, goal-directed one. This transition was generally not made smoothly, however. Often players had concealed their heavy substance use and chaotic personal financial affairs from their fiancées who typically were in distant parts of the country. Generally, the fiancée was a "girl from back home." Once married, when the full reality of the problems became apparent, the wives often reacted with anger and disillusionment. Invariably, these reactions were healthy, for they forced the athlete to reassess his conduct and make changes to preserve his fragile marriage. The team began to foster entertainment for couples such as visits to baseball games, church activities, and family barbecues. The hospital also promoted spouse/girlfriend involvement by starting a separate self-help group for significant others, which met at the same time as the meeting for the players. In this way, attendance at the self-help meetings could be a "family night out." In all cases the Inner Circle attempted to build a healthy alliance between the spouse and the program, to surround the athlete with healthy influences, and to promote communication about day-to-day progress or setbacks.

Spiritual Counseling

Spiritual counseling emerged as a powerful source of strength for the professional athlete. To capitalize on the athlete's prior childhood religious training, the team instituted a voluntary, weekly Bible study conducted by a lay minister. He was invited to be a participant as a group therapy member, and he assisted in rebuilding individual spiritual support systems for each player. Over half of the players became regular churchgoers and virtually all attended Bible study. The players generally related very well to spiritually-oriented counseling with scriptural and moral guidelines. This emphasis blended in nicely with the 12-step approach of Alcoholics Anonymous, and with the behavior-change-oriented psychiatric counseling that the players received.

Results

The Cleveland Browns' Links in the Chain–Inner Circle Program continued for 16 years until the team moved to Baltimore and disbanded the program. This comprehensive approach, involving active therapy of the involved players for many years, led to substantial improvement in 75 percent of the cases. This improvement had been characterized by drug-free status and marked improvement in a number of other psychosocial and biologic parameters. Ninety percent of the involved players became married while in treatment, and all developed a stable, nonhedonistic lifestyle. Most developed long-term career goals that included pursuit of additional education or training. All went on to a significantly improved financial footing, and several became engaged in financial planning for postfootball careers and investments. Improvement in physical conditioning was notable, as demonstrated by annual, rigorous workout testing. Overweight players lost weight and improved speed. Underweight players gained weight through vigorous participation in a weight-training program. Most players improved their playing ability as a result of participation in the program, and several assumed prominent leadership positions on the team. Unquestionably, the members of the Inner Circle contributed significantly to the team's strong win/loss record. In the seven years before the initiation of the Inner Circle Program, the team's overall record was 46 percent with only one play-off game in seven years. In the seven years following inception of the program, the team's winning record improved to 56 percent, with 9 play-off games. The team reached the semifinals for the Superbowl twice during the seven-year treatment follow-up period.

APPLYING THE LINKS IN THE CHAIN–INNER CIRCLE MODEL TO SCHOLASTIC DRUG PROGRAMS

At first glance, the extensive list of treatment resources available for professional athletes would appear to be beyond the reach of most schools. Experience has shown, however, that the Links in the Chain–Inner Circle model is a useful conceptual framework for organizing school-based drug programs. Interestingly, many schools seem to begin their drug and alcohol programs by focusing on athletes. Schools generally report that this is because of the strong peer influence that athletes have over the rest of the student body. Thus, a program aimed at changing student attitudes toward chemical misuse seemingly has a better chance of success if it begins with an athletic focus. Also, professional athletes are often willing to go to schools to talk about avoidance of drugs and alcohol, and can generally deliver a presentation emphasizing achievement and discipline, completion of school, and spiritual values. Professional athletes continue to exert strong influence on young people, and are often willing to "kick off " a school-based drug program.

The strength of the Links in the Chain-Inner Circle model is the total organizational commitment mobilized by such an approach. It should involve every component of the organization in order to have maximal effectiveness. The starting point for most programs, however, is the development of an administrative policy with respect to chemical misuse in the school. All too often, school-based programs flounder over the discipline vs. treatment dichotomy. Traditionally, schools have approached drug and alcohol misuse from a disciplinary perspective. Discipline may be mild or harsh, but the disciplinary framework has traditionally mandated some type of punitive response in reaction to substance misuse. Chemical misuse is frequently seen as a rule-breaking (or law-breaking) behavior, which seemingly must be followed by punitive consequences. School administrators often fear the "ripple effect" of unpunished drug or alcohol misuse on other students. Also, there may be fear that the school administration will be made to look weak if students "get away" with chemical misuse without disciplinary consequence. When the offender is a student athlete, the dilemma over discipline vs. no discipline is made even more acute. Should the student be allowed to participate in sports or in other recreational/competitive activities if he or she has been involved in substance misuse? This will often prove to be an emotionally charged issue. Those on the pro-discipline side will assert that something must be done to discipline the offender, discourage future offenders, and maintain school discipline. On the other side, the student athlete, his family, and many others will insist that he be allowed to play because of fear of overreaction to immature behavior, possible breach of confidentiality if the athlete is conspicuously missing from play, possible long-term damaging effects from labeling the athlete as a substance abuser, and even detrimental effects to the scholastic win/loss record if a valued performer is not allowed to play.

LINKS IN THE CHAIN IN SCHOOL

Unfortunately, the stage is set for the discipline-no discipline dichotomy when a school has few or no resources committed to responding to the drug-involved student. With the total organizational commitment, and with a clearly defined policy in place, the school has a wide variety of responses available. These resources allow more flexibility and suitability and enhance student and parent acceptance.

Since total organization commitment is the key to a successful school-based program, virtually all facets of the school-related community must be involved. The school board must adopt a policy, promulgated widely, and support reasonable expenditures for program costs. The school administration, especially the principal, should conspicuously endorse and support the program and be persuasive in rallying dissenters to a unified approach. Teachers and coaches should receive education about the policy, the drugs of abuse, alcohol misuse, and early identification of substance misuse. Coaches should be encouraged to allow athletic participation by students who are making a reasonable effort to follow the treatment program of substance avoidance and counseling. Students who are repeat offenders and who are noncompliant with treatment/prevention efforts should be subject to disciplinary measures including, if necessary, suspension or cessation of athletic participation. School counselors should obtain specialized training in early identification of substance problems, foster education/prevention programs within the schools, and develop an awareness of professional treatment facilities and community self-help programs for students.

The school should encourage or develop in-school non-use support groups that develop positive peer pressure for chemical avoidance and that provide a "safe harbor" and support for non-use. These groups should have faculty supervision, and can incorporate input from local doctors and mental health professionals. A chapter of S.A.D.D. (Students Against

Drunk Driving) should be started. Educational materials encouraging drug avoidance by clarifying risks and consequences should be incorporated into school educational curricula. School nurses should become sensitized to indications of substance misuse or intoxication. A system for referral of individuals for evaluations/assessments should be clearly defined. Local religious groups should be approached to add their endorsement and support to this school-based effort. Local law enforcement officials and school security officers should be part of the total organization of response. If their approach is to *protect* the student from drug pushers and drug influences, as well as to lend their support to early identification of drug-involved students, their input can be extremely valuable. If they are bent on prosecution at all costs, they will generate much system resistance and have limited effectiveness. Most important, perhaps, parents must be major participants and sustainers of the school-based program. They must have access to educational materials and presentations, and should have the school-based policy clearly explained to them. Parent organizations such as PTA and M.A.D.D. (Mothers Against Drunk Driving) should have an opportunity to participate vigorously in promoting the program among parents. The students themselves should be given an opportunity to exercise constructive involvement and leadership in the development and implementation of this program. If they have some ownership in its development and implementation, they will be more likely to regard it as their own, to refer their peers to it, and to use it themselves when substance misuse is a problem. Since most substance abuse is highly secretive in schools, promotion of self-referral and peer-referral is of vital significance for program efficacy. The program must be oriented toward helping the students and must be clearly for their interest, or they and their parents will not support it. Agreed-upon disciplinary aspects should be defined in advance of implementation, as much as possible.

Although the program with the Cleveland Browns involved total organizational commitment and marshalled tremendous human resources, little real expense was involved. Most of the "work" in setting up such a program was involved in attitude restructuring, policy development, and education. Because of the relatively low cost and because of the large numbers of young people that can be influenced, school-based programs may be the wave of the future as opposed to relying on professional resources outside of the school.

Although much of the foundation for this Links in the Chain approach lies within the school, there is an important component that must generally be accomplished in a professional setting. Consultation and advice for the planning and development phase of such a program should involve professional drug-abuse consultants. An alliance with one or more highly reputable treatment centers will prove valuable in a variety of ways. A high-quality treatment resource, in our view, is one that is versatile in its approach, has a highly individualized approach to young people, and does not rely excessively on a "canned" or "cookbook" approach to substance problems in young people.

Sadly, many programs offer a seemingly quick and easy solution to complex problems. While many young people might be helped in such programs, others can be hurt by an overzealous diagnosis of addiction or alcoholism and by a lack of appreciation of the complexities of adolescent maturational and psychological issues. Many of these programs market vigorously with sensational advertising campaigns to keep their treatment beds filled with "adolescent alcoholics." A high-quality treatment center offers the school an objective resource for student/parent evaluations. Such evaluations will generally provide a treatment plan, which can be integrated into the school response and insisted upon by school administrators. Such an approach will often overcome student or parent resistance to dealing realistically with a substance misuse problem.

Treatment options should be many; family therapy is often of prime importance with adolescents. Adolescent substance abusers often have parents with substance problems. Families in turmoil are not uncommon. Family tensions can often be extreme, and without resolution of these problems, chemical misbehaviors will continue. Outpatient counseling specifically targeted at substance involvement provides accountability and guidance against "backsliding." Special groups of young people to foster identification with the program, develop new nonusing friendships, and provide peer support are often helpful. Urine monitoring should be offered for diagnostic purposes and for monitoring of therapeutic compliance. Urine monitoring is best done in the professional setting, and information from the urine results should be made available to parents, the school counselor, and the principal. If outpatient treatment and urine monitoring do not prove successful, more intensive inpatient treatment in a rehabilitation center is advisable. Adolescent treatment centers with comprehensive, individualized approaches, including psychological/psychiatric input, often provide effective care if done at the hands of an experienced, well-trained staff. The treatment center should have frequent communication and information sharing with school-based support resources during and after the acute phase of treatment.

A NOTE TO SCHOOL TEAM PHYSICIANS

Jonas, Sickles, and Lombardo (1992, p. 384) described the role of the team physician as follows:

> Identification of the use and/or abuse of therapeutic agents in athletes often requires little more than a careful clinical history during the athletes' preparticipation evaluation and thorough medical recording methods. Athletes are often unaware of the abuse potential of many of these agents and need to be counseled regarding their appropriate use, not only as it relates to athletic competition, but also regarding the appropriate use of medication to treat medical illnesses and their symptoms. Athletes frequently utilize over-the-counter products without considering them to be medications. It is especially important for athletes who are competing in events where drug screening is performed and detection of banned substances is possible that they are carefully counseled regarding what medicines they may or may not be permitted to take. When it is not readily apparent from the history, it becomes much more difficult to detect inappropriate use of therapeutic agents in athletes other than through random drug screening programs. The use of these medications should be tightly controlled by the team physician. Athletes who need these potent medications should be counseled regarding their appropriate use. Most of these compounds are on a banned substance list of many athletic governing bodies. Athletes' access to most prescription medications is through either their team or primary care physician. Education programs encouraging athletes to communicate with members of the health care team regarding their use of any drug is important. Primary care physicians should be aware of the appropriate use of therapeutic drugs of athletes and participate as an active member of the health care team to ensure safe, ethical, and legal participation of athletes who require medical treatment.

AN OPEN LETTER FROM THE INNER CIRCLE

The members of the Cleveland Browns Inner Circle wrote the following letter to students in an Ohio high school:

It begins with a couple of beers after the "big game" or drinking some wine with the fellows on the corner. It ends with a dependency on cocaine and pot and destroys marriages, salaries, and athletic careers. This is how it started and almost ended for most of us in the Inner Circle. For many different reasons, and we will discuss a few of them, we, the members of the Inner Circle became involved in a lifestyle that was leading us to jail, bankruptcy, and possible death. The biggest reason a number of us got involved was acceptance. Peer pressure is tough in today's society. In order to become "one of the guys" we felt we had to do as they did. That is not true; your friends will respect you a lot more if you stand up and be your own man. The second reason is coping with stress and failure. We used chemicals to ease external and internal pressure, as well as the problems of everyday life. It doesn't work. When you finish taking your last drink, your last toke, or your last snort of coke, your problems are still there. Finally, the feeling of chemicals giving you status. The people that hang around you because you have the drugs or other source, or who are able to acquire alcoholic beverages are not your true friends and you will soon find that out. If you don't drink or use drugs, don't start. If you do, then today will be a great time to stop and seek help and, in our opinion, the best help you can get is from your family members. Remember: Chemical dependency doesn't discriminate. Soberly yours, The Inner Circle

SUMMARY

The student athlete and young athletic professional are at high risk for substance abuse. In the absence of an effective, well-planned, total organizational response, a downward spiral of evergrowing drug involvement and negative consequences is likely to ensue. The end result is often deterioration of athletic performance and even total personal devastation. The drug-involved athlete presents a complex problem, requiring a complex, long-term, and organizational commitment to help him or her. The Links in the Chain–Inner Circle Program developed jointly by the Cleveland Browns and the Cleveland Clinic Foundation offers a useful and adaptable model for responding to this complex challenge.

REFERENCES

Anderson, W. A., & McKeag, D. B. (1985, June). *Substance use and abuse happens in college student-athletes.* Presented to National Collegiate Athletic Association Counsel, College of Human Medicine, Michigan State University.

Anderson, W., & McKeag, D. (1989). *Replication of the national study on substance use and abuse habits of college student athletes: Technical report.* Mission, KS: National Collegiate Athletic Association.

Becket, A. H., & Cowan, D. A. (1979). Misuse of drugs in sports. *British Journal of Sports Medicine, 12,* 185–194.

Belgrave, B. E., Bird, K. D., Chesher, G. B., Jackson, D. M., Lubbe, K. E., Starmer, G. A., & Teo, R. K. (1979, March 29). The effect of transdelta tetrahydrocannabinol, alone and in combination with ethanol, on human performance. *Psychopharmacology, 62*(1), 53–60.

Bird, K. D., Boleyn, T., Chesher, G. B., Jackson, D. M., Starmer, G. A., & Teo, R. K. (1980). Intercannabinoid and cannabinoid-ethanol interactions on human performance. *Psychopharmacology, 71*(2), 181–188.

Bouter, L. M., Knipschild, P. G., Paul, G., Feij, J. A., & Jan, A. (1988). Sensation seeking and injury risk in downhill skiing. *Personality & Individual Differences, 9,* 667–673.

Chamberlain, R. T. (1986). Drug screening in the workplace: Medical legal implications. *Therapeutic Drug Monitoring Toxicology, 7*(12), 1–7.

Cohen, S. (1982, September). The problem of acute affluence: The high-priced athlete. *Drug Abuse and Alcoholism Newsletter, 11*(7), 1–4.

Collins, G. B., Janesz, J. W., Bergfeld, J. A., & Pippenger, C. E. (1988). Recreational drug use in sports. In J. Lombardo (Ed.), *Advances in Sports Medicine and Fitness* (pp. 97–120). Chicago: Yearbook.

Collins, G. B., Pippenger, C. E., & Janesz, J. W. (1984). Links in the chain: An approach to the treatment of drug abuse on a professional football team. *Cleveland Clinic Quarterly, 51*(3), 485–492.

Cowart, V. (1986, November 21) Road back from substance abuse especially long, hard for athletes. *JAMA, 256*(19), 2645–2649.

Duda, M. (1984). Drug testing challenges college and pro athletes. *Physician and Sports Medicine, 12*(11), 109–118.

Farley, F. (1986, May). The big T in personality. *Psychology Today, 20,* 44–52.

Gloede, B. (1988, September 5). What if beer were banned? *Sports, Inc.,* 14.

Jonas, A. P., Sickles, R. T., & Lombardo, J. A. (1992, April). Substance abuse. *Clinics in Sports Medicine, 11*(2), 379–401.

Klein, F. C. (1986, February 21). Student jocks deserve better teaching. *The Wall Street Journal,* p. 16.

National Football League. (1989). *Drug policy of the National Football League.* New York: Author.

National Household Survey on Drug Abuse. (1994). Rockville, MD: National Clearinghouse for Alcohol and Drug Information.

Nattiv, A., & Puffer, J. C. (1991). Lifestyles and health risks of collegiate athletes. *Journal of Family Practice, 33*(6), 585–590.

Ogilvie, B. C. (1973). The stimulus addicts. *Physician and Sports Medicine, 1,* 61–65.

"Ohio State to implement new drug testing program." (1986, July 19). *OSU Sports.* Columbus, OH: Ohio State University Sports Information Office.

Ryan, A. J. (1984). Causes and remedies for drug misuse and abuse by athletes. *JAMA, 252*(4), 517–519.

Smith, G. M. (1986). Adolescent personality traits that predict young adult drug use. *Comprehensive Therapy, 12*, 44–50.

Tashkin, D. P., Soares, J. R., Hepler, R. S., Shapiro, B. J., & Rachelefsky, G. S. (1978). Cannabis, 1977: UCLA conference. *Annals of Internal Medicine, 89*, 539–549.

"Top T.V. sports advertisers." (1988, February 29). *Sports, Inc.*, 35.

Wadler, G. I., & Hainline, B. (1989). *Drugs and the athlete.* Philadelphia: F. A. Davis.

8

Athletes' Use of Performance-Enhancing Drugs

Todd P. Hendrickson   Robert W. Burton

SPORT IS DEFINED AS "a source of diversion: recreation" and "physical activity engaged in for pleasure" (Webster, 1996). Competitive sport refers to sporting activities that are contested. In competitive sports, athletes, coaches and athletic administrations continually search for new ways of gaining a competitive advantage over their opponents.

Doping is the administration to, or the use by, a competing athlete of a substance foreign to the body or any physiological substance taken in abnormal quantity or by an abnormal route of entry into the body, with the intention of increasing in an artificial and unfair manner his or her performance in competition (Green & Puffer, 1997).

Historically, there have been a number of influential incidents reported in the sport context (Puffer & Green, 1990). In 1960, Danish cyclist Kurt Enemar Jensen died during the Summer Olympics in Rome from amphetamines and Ronicol. In 1964, Tokyo became the first Olympiad to perform drug testing. The International Olympic Committee (IOC) adopted the definition of "doping," and established a "banned substance list." In 1968, formal drug testing was adopted at the Olympic Games. In 1972, United States swimmer Rick Demont was stripped of his gold medal for using ephedrine to treat underlying asthma. The death of Maryland basketball player Len Bias in 1986 led to the expansion of drug testing to include intercollegiate athletics. In 1988, Canadian Olympian Ben Johnson was stripped of his gold medal following a positive drug test for the anabolic stanazolol. In 1990, US track and field athlete Randy Barnes was suspended for two years following a positive drug test for steroids. In 1998, St. Louis Cardinals slugger Mark McGwire publicly discussed his ergogenic use of androstenedione.

A number of studies illustrate substance abuse in athletes. An NCAA study in 1981 showed that alcohol and marijuana use are similar in athlete and nonathlete groups (Duda, 1983). Anabolic steroid use was noted to be 2% higher in athlete groups. In the 1984 Los Angeles Olympic Games there were 11 positive drug tests; 10 samples proved positive for anabolic steroids. In a study of Big 10 schools, over 1500 athletes were tested and questioned (Anderson & McKeag, 1985). Table 8.1 shows the study results.

TABLE 8.1
Prevalence of Drug Use

DRUG	*PERCENT OF ATHLETES*
Alcohol	88%
Amphetamines	.08%
Anabolic steroids	6.5%
Antiinflammatories	31%
Caffeine	68%
Cocaine	17%
Marijuana	36%

In a study that surveyed twelfth-grade students, 7 percent admitted they use or had used anabolic steroids (Buckley et al., 1988). This chapter will focus on the various performance-enhancing substances, their various effects and epidemiology, and an athlete's decision to use them.

ANDROGENIC ANABOLIC STEROIDS

Androgenic anabolic steroids are synthetic testosterone-like substances or testosterone preparations that have anabolic (increased protein synthesis) and androgenic (masculine sexual characteristics) effects. Oral and injectable forms are available. These drugs differ primarily in their solubility (water- vs. oil-based). Most oral preparations are taken on a daily basis, while intramuscular preparations are injected every 1–3 days during a period of use, known as a "cycle."

A common practice is to "stack" the drugs, taking more than one drug at time in a pyramid fashion, with a gradual buildup of drugs over a cycle of perhaps 6–8 weeks, followed by a taper-down. Table 8.2 lists common androgenic anabolic steroids.

Androgenic anabolic steroids activate DNA-dependent RNA polymerase to produce messenger-RNA for protein synthesis (Windsor & Dumitru, 1988). Anabolic steroids cause an increase in body weight and lean muscle mass when used in conjunction with adequate diet and resistance training. These substances have very restricted medical uses, which include the prescription-only treatment of aplastic anemia, hypogonadism, medical anorexia, and the management of severe burn patients. They are "banned substances" for athletic performance and are now primarily obtained through black market resources throughout the world. It is illegal to possess or distribute them nonmedically in the United States.

Side effects may vary from individual to individual, based on age, developmental level, and sex. In general they include the pathological involvement of the cardiovascular system with increased LDL cholesterol, decreased HDL cholesterol, hypertension, myocardial infarction, and cerebrovascular accident (stroke) (Marshall, 1988). Gastrointestinal and liver effects include hepatocellular damage, hepatocellular cancer, and hepatomas. Psychiatric morbidity includes mood swings, depression, mania, psychosis, aggression, and antisocial behavior (Pope & Katz, 1988). Miscellaneous effects include acne and spontaneous tendon ruptures (Kiraly, 1987).

Specific effects of the androgenic anabolic steroids include differential effects on men and women. The American College of Sports Medicine (ACSM; 1984) reported the following: in males, oligospermia, decreased testicular size, and gynecomastia; in females, decreases in LH, FSH, estrogens, and progesterone. Male pattern baldness, hirsutism, clitoromegaly, and deepening of the voice were also reported and may be permanent. Premature epiphyseal closure and stunted growth were medically reported in prepubertal youth athletes. The sharing of needles among users can be linked to a variety of infections and abscesses; however, athletes are likely to use injectable steroids in a meticulously clean fashion.

Androgenic anabolic steroids are used by athletes in a variety of power, speed, and endurance sports. There is also a growing number of individuals who are using them for masculinization at young ages (i.e., 11–13 years old). Drug testing is quite accurate in detecting steroid use and

TABLE 8.2
Androgenic Anabolic Steroids

ORAL AGENTS
17-a alkyl derivatives of testosterone

Generic Name	*Brand Name(s)*
ethylestrenol	Maxibolin
fluoxymesterone	Halotestin, Android-F, Ora-Testryl
methyltestosterone	Android, Metandren, Oreton, Testred, Virilon
oxandrolone	Anavar
oxymetholone	Anadrol, Anapolon 50c
stanazolol	Winstrol

INJECTABLE AGENTS
testosterone, testosterone esters, and 19-nortestosterone esters (nandrolone products)

Generic Name	*Brand Name(s)*
nandrolone decanoate	Anabolin LA-100, Androlone 50, Androlone D, Deca-Durabolin, Hybolin Decanoate, Kabolin, Nandrobolic L.A., Neo-Durabolic
nandrolone phenpropionate	Anabolin, Androlone, Durabolin, Hybolin-Improved, Nandrobolic
testosterone (aqueous)	Andro-100, Andronaq-50, Histerone-50, Histerone-100, Malogen, Testamone 100, Testaqua, Testoject-50
testosterone cypionate	Andro-Cyp, Andronq-LA, Andronate, depAndro, Depotest, Depo-Testosterone, Depo-Testosterone Cypionate, Duratest, T-Cypionate, Testa-C, Testojext-LA, Testred Cypionate, Virilon IM
testosterone enanthate	Andro L.A. 200, Andropository 100, Andryl 200, Delatest, Delatestryl, Durathate-200, Everone, Malogex, Testone L.A. 100, Testone L.A. 200, Testrin-P.A.
testosterone proionate	Malogen, Testex

Other anabolic steroids banned by the USOC include a number of oral and injectable agents: androstenedione, boldenone, clostebol, danazol, dehydrochormethyltestosterone, mesteronlone, methandienone, methenolone, norethandrolone, and oxymesterone.

Data from Narducci, Wagner, Hendrickson, & Jeffrey, 1990.

is now performed by a number of sport governing bodies and athletic associations (ACSM, 1984).

HUMAN GROWTH HORMONE

Human growth hormone (HGH) is a polypeptide hormone composed of 191 amino acids. Normally, 5–10 mg are stored in the anterior pituitary gland and adult males produce 0.5–1.0 mg/24 hours (McIntyre, 1987). Intramuscular injection is the route of administration. HGH is utilized medically in deficiency states such as growth hormone-deficient children. Deficiency state dosages are typically 0.06 mg/kg, three times a week, or 1 mg/day in a 50 kg individual. There are reports of athletes using 20 times this amount (Cowart, 1988).

Administration of HGH results in a positive nitrogen balance and stimulation of skeletal and soft-tissue growth. HGH reduces glucose and protein metabolism and produces a net anti-insulin effect by inhibiting the cellular uptake of glucose. HGH also stimulates the mobilization of lipids from adipose tissue, increasing protein synthesis. There are no controlled studies describing the effects of HGH in competitive athletes. HGH is recommended for medicinal use only in growth deficiency states (Underwood, 1984). Although there is currently no reliable method for detecting exogenous HGH administration in athletes, HGH concentrations can be measured in the plasma. Synthetic HGH preparations were first sold in the United States in 1985.

Side effects of HGH have been widely reported. The risk of acromegaly with its coarsening of the face, hands, and feet is significant, especially in large-dosage use. Complications of acromegaly may include diabetes, arthritis, and myopathies. These complications can be seen in dosages only two times the recommended dose for growth deficiency states. Hypothyroidism has also been described, as well as the formation of antibodies to HGH. Cadaver HGH (from pituitary glands) has been associated with Creutzfeldt-Jakob disease, a cause of dementia (McIntyre, 1987).

HUMAN CHORIONIC GONADOTROPIN

Human chorionic gonadotropin (HcG) is a glycoprotein with a molecular weight of 30,000. HcG is normally secreted by the syncytial trophoblast cells of the early fertilized ovum. The hormone can first be measured in the blood 6–8 days after ovulation; it peaks 7–9 weeks after ovulation.

HcG is naturally occurring in females and pregnant females. HcG is also present in the male fetus, causing the production of testosterone, which in turn causes the testes to descend in the scrotum during gestation. HcG has been synthetically reproduced and is typically given in an intramuscular form. Dosages are not well studied in athletes.

HcG stimulates production of estrogen and progesterone effects, which can be seen in both males and females. Male athletes utilize HcG to counter the effects of androgenic anabolic steroids, namely testicular atrophy and retraction, symptoms that are detested by athletes.

The side effects of HcG are largely unknown in athletes because it has been so poorly studied. Reports of water retention and mood swings have been anecdotally described.

ERGOGENIC AIDS

An ergogenic aid is an agent or procedure that enhances energy production, energy control, or energy efficiency during performance. Ergogenic aids are often non-FDA-approved substances, so these products are not held to the same standards as FDA-approved drugs. They fall under the same category as food, as long as the manufacturer does not make any specific health or performance claims. Ergogenic aids can have unpredictable effects within an individual's body. The athlete, coach, and athletic trainers should always investigate the contents of any ergogenic aid before utilizing any of them. Consultation with the sports medicine staff should be an important part of the decision when choosing to use an ergogenic aid. Organizations such as the NCAA and the USOC have created classifications of banned and regulated substances for athletic competition in various sports (Fuentes, Rosenberg & Davis, 1994). The NCAA policy regarding ergogenic is as follows: "There are no shortcuts to sound nutrition, and the use of suspected or advertised ergogenic aids may not provide a competitive advantage" (Fuentes et al., 1994). The USOC policy reads, "Use of any of these products is at the athlete's own risk, since exact ingredients cannot always be ascertained or guaranteed" (Fuentes et al., 1994). The following substances are currently classified as ergogenic aids.

ST. JOHN'S WORT

St. John's Wort (hypericum perforatum) is an herb typically packaged in 300–400 mg capsules or tablets; however, various dosages are available.

The standard 0.3% hypericum content usually also includes vitamin B6 and folic acid. Daily values have not been established for the hypericum extract. Industry recommendations are one capsule two or three times each day. "There is evidence that extracts of hypericum are more effective than placebo for the treatment of mild to moderate depression" (Linde et al., 1996). Athletes may use this preparation for mood evaluation, performance anxiety, and insomnia. The mood elevation reported by athletes using St. John's Wort correlates with increased energy that is believed to be beneficial for improving endurance training.

The side effects of St. John's Wort are relatively mild and may include photosensitivity, gastrointestinal symptoms, and restlessness (Linde et al., 1996). The specific mechanism of action remains unclear. Hypericum may inhibit serotonin, dopamine, and norepinephrine uptake in vitro. It also may inhibit the enzyme monoamine oxidase. St. John's Wort probably should not be taken with most antidepressant medications, including serotonin-specific reuptake inhibitors (SSRIs), and monoamine-oxidase inhibitors (MAOIs), as this may precipitate a serotonin syndrome. It is also recommended to avoid tyramine-containing foods until more is known about hypericum's mechanism of action.

Investigation of hypericum is currently underway at Duke University Medical Center under an NIMH grant. The European literature is difficult to interpret due to numerous study design flaws and nonhomogeneous study populations (Cott, 1997).

CREATINE

Creatine monohydrate is derived from lingonberries, found naturally in lean red meat and fish, or synthesized. Creatine is packaged in powder form and time-released capsules and it works best when kept refrigerated. One heaping teaspoon provides 5000 mg (5 g) of creatine monohydrate. Companies that market it often recommend a loading dose of 20 g/day for the first week, then 5 g/day for maintenance. A common practice would be a 6–8 week cycle with a 3–4-week break between cycles.

Creatine is an amino acid derived from the amino acids glycine, arginine, and methionine. It is naturally produced by the body in the liver and kidneys. Creatine is then phosphorylated to creatine phosphate, an important compound that converts food into energy, which is stored in muscle tissue. It serves as a reservoir that muscles can utilize in the process of converting ADP back to ATP. These processes occur during muscular contraction and physical exertion.

Creatine may benefit individual athletes in speed as well as endurance sports by making available more stores of creatine phosphate. This effect may help to improve endurance and delay muscle fatigue. Competitive athletes will often dose the creatine before and after workouts. Anecdotal reports in bodybuilders suggest that lifters are supplementing creatine in combination with androgenic anabolic steroids in order to decrease their overall steroid load. Controlled trials of this practice are not available. Continued noncycled use can be associated with decreased muscle mass and a weakened immune system. In addition, high doses of creatine can cause extreme dehydration and muscle cramping. One to three liters of water per day are recommended for those who use creatine-based products.

CAFFEINE

Caffeine is a naturally occurring plant alkaloid from extracts of coffee arabica and cola acuminata (Lombardo, 1986). Caffeine is a central nervous system stimulant found in coffee, tea, cola drinks, chocolate, and a number of prescription and nonprescription products. Structurally, caffeine is a methylxanthine similar to theophylline, a traditional bronchodilator. Caffeine is an ingredient of many natural products, and comes in tablet form. Peak levels are achieved in 30–60 minutes with a half-life of 3–4 hours. Athletes often use caffeine to increase work efficiency, alertness, energy, and power. These effects are likely due to increased mobilization of free fatty acids and an increased rate of lipid metabolism (Ivy, Costill, Fink, & Lower, 1979). Bronchodilator effects of caffeine are also prominent effects noted by athletes. Caffeine's enhancement of performance is controversial and has been questioned (Butts & Crowell, 1985). Some studies have shown it to be effective in endurance sports. Caffeine is a stimulant utilized in fatigue states, and in combination with analgesic compounds to reduce pain. Athletes will commonly use caffeine one hour prior to performance situations, and often prefer tablet forms over liquid forms. General side effects include increased gastric acid secretion, tachycardia, increased blood pressure, increased diuresis, insomnia, headache, tremors, shakiness, and tolerance. Anxiety and agitation are common at dosages above 600 mg ingested during a 2–3 hour period. The IOC allows caffeine at concentrations up to 12 mcg/ml. The NCAA allows a maximum of 15 mcg/ml. Caffeine can be detected by drug screening. The average daily consumption of caffeine is 200–300 mg/day, but some athletes will consume 2–3 times this amount prior to or during athletic competition. Some reports suggest it would take an ingestion of over 1,000 mg of caffeine within 3 hours of competition to exceed the tolerated threshold (IOC). Table 8.3 shows caffeine concentration in commonly used preparations (Puffer & Green, 1990).

KAVA KAVA

Kava Kava (piper methysticum) is a member of the Polynesian black pepper family, extracted from the roots of the kava plant. Phytochemical kavalactones are the active ingredient in this ergogenic aid. Kava comes in capsules, tablets, and powdered elixir forms. Manufacturer-recommended dosages vary between 300 and 500 mg/day. It is often taken at nighttime, but the dose can be split up during the daytime to reduce anxiety states. Kava Kava has been marketed by companies to decrease anxiety and help with insomnia, as well as to promote a sense of well-being. The number of athletes using Kava Kava are unknown. Anecdotal reports are confined to helping with sleep states, especially in athletes using androgenic anabolic steroids or during periods of high stress. The mechanism of action is largely unknown but it may work similarly to benzodiazepines such as alprazolam or diazepam with reduction of anxiety states,

TABLE 8.3
Caffeine Findings

SUBSTANCE	*CAFFEINE CONCENTRATION (MG/ML)*	*CAFFEINE LEVEL* (MG/ML)*
Coffee	55–85	1.5–3 (1 cup)
Tea	55–85	1.5–3 (1 cup)
Cola	10–15	0.75–1.5 (1 cup)
Medications		
Cafergot	100 mg/tablet	3–6
NoDoz	100 mg/tablet	3–6
Anacin	32 mg/tablet	2–3
Midol	32 mg/tablet	2–3

*Level in serum depends on size of athlete and rate of metabolism. These figures are general estimates based on average size and rate metabolism.

initiation of sleep, and mild disinhibition. Long-term use of Kava Kava can result in dry, scaly skin that takes on a yellow pigmentation, and excessive dosages can cause drowsiness and incoordination. Long-term use at high doses can impair liver function and may cause nerve damage. There are anecdotal reports of tolerance to Kava products similar to what is seen with benzodiazepines.

DEHYDROEPIANDROSTERONE

Dehydroepiandrosterone (DHEA) is a naturally occurring "pro-hormone" produced by the adrenal glands, testes, and brain. DHEA is converted into the steroid hormones estrogen, cortisone, and testosterone. Normally, an individual's DHEA levels peak around age 20 and decrease linearly with increasing age. DHEA is packaged in 50–400 mg tablets and administered once per day. DHEA may stabilize blood-glucose levels and enhance the immune system's ability to fight viral infections. DHEA does not appear to be very effective in individuals younger than 30 (ACSM, 1984).

Side effects have not been well studied, but they may include water retention and weight gain. Athletes often use DHEA in combination with creatine products. DHEA is currently being used in experimental medical treatments for multiple sclerosis and Parkinson's disease.

ERYTHROPOIETIN

Erythropoietin (EPO) is a synthetically produced substance that stimulates the production of red blood cells. It has been used medically to treat illnesses, such as the anemia from chronic renal failure, and other refractory causes of anemia (Ersler, 1991).

Physiologically, EPO results in an increase in red blood cell mass in a dose-response relationship. Athletes may benefit by increasing their ability to carry oxygen in the blood stream, subsequently experiencing less fatigue in endurance training. There is little empirical data suggesting that EPO is effective in power-related sport activities such as sprinting or jumping events.

It is unknown what dosages have been used when doping with EPO, but the abuse of this substance can result in marked polycythemia with the potential for subsequent thromboembolism, cerebrovascular accident, and myocardial infarction (Mellion, Grandjean, & Ruud, 1999).

Deaths have been reported among competitive cyclists who were known to use EPO, but they were never medically substantiated.

DRUG TESTING

Drug testing continues to be utilized in a number of different sports and by a number of different sports organizations throughout the world. Most ergogenic aids, however, are not banned substances and are commonly used by athletes to facilitate their athletic performance.

Table 8.4 lists the various restricted and banned substances, as detailed by the NCAA and the IOC respectively.

THE ATHLETE'S DECISION AND THE SPORT PSYCHIATRIST

The decision of an athlete to use or not to use a performance-enhancing drug is not an easy or an infrequent one. More and more substances are being tried, used, and abused, and information about them is rapidly, although often incompletely, disseminated. Psychiatrists working with athletes must be able to discuss the substances knowledgeably and address the dilemma that the athlete faces. The dilemma involves trying to use the available knowledge about training methods and techniques that will promote optimal performance without endangering the athlete's health or breaking the rules. The sport psychiatrist must be familiar with the substances in question and be willing to research them when they are unfamiliar. In addition, he or she must be able to get at and challenge the athlete's motives and his or her understanding of the drugs. It is not too dissimilar to the concept of informed consent. Does the athlete have the capacity as well as the information available to him or her to make an informed decision? If not, is more information needed or should someone else be making the decision?

The influence of significant others is important to assess, as well. The sport psychiatrist should attempt to discern when these powerful figures in an athlete's life are overstepping their boundaries. As an example, an athletic trainer who suggests or provides a drug or nutritional supplement without getting a physician's approval may be reaching beyond the limits of his or her expertise. It is under these circumstances that the sport psychiatrist must act as a patient advocate, making sure that potentially harm-

TABLE 8.4
Restricted and Banned Substances and Procedures

NATIONAL COLLEGIATE ATHLETIC ASSOCIATION

Banned Drug Classes

Psychomotor and central nervous system stimulants, including caffeine (urinary concentration > 15 mcg/ml)

Anabolic steroids, including testosterone (testosterone to epitestosterone ratio > 6)

Substances banned for specific sports

 Alcohol (e.g., rifle)

 Beta-blockers (e.g., rifle)

Diuretics

Street drugs: heroin, marijuana, and THC (urinary concentration > 25 ng/ml)

Drugs and Procedures Subject to Restriction

Blood doping

Growth hormone

Urine manipulation

Local anesthetics (procaine, carbocaine, and xylocaine, without vasoconstrictor may be used locally or topically when medically justified and submitted in writing to the NCAA crew chief in charge of testing; cocaine is not permitted)

INTERNATIONAL OLYMPIC COMMITTEE

Doping Classes

Stimulants

Psychomotor stimulants

Sympathomimetic amines

Miscellaneous CNS stimulants, including caffeine (urinary concentration ≥ 12 mg/ml)

Narcotics

Anabolic steroids

Beta blockers

Diuretics

Growth hormone

Human chorionic gonadotropin

Erythropoietin

Doping Methods

Blood doping

Pharmacologic, chemical, and physical manipulation of the urine

(*continued*)

TABLE 8.4
Continued

Classes of Drugs Subject to Certain Restrictions
Alcohol (levels may be requested by specific international federations)
Local anesthetics (permitted when medically indicated and documented in writing to the IOC Medical Commission)
Corticosteroid (banned except when used topically, locally, intra-articularly, or via inhalation and documented in writing to the IOC Medical Commission)
Beta-2 agonists (permitted in the aerosol or inhalant form for the treatment of asthma)

Data from Mellion et al., 1999.

ful substances are not taken by an athlete unknowingly. The media has reported numerous instances in which an athlete tests positively for a prohibited substance. The athletes routinely cry wolf and deny any knowledge of having ingested the illegal substance. And yet, retracing the steps carefully may reveal that a questionable substance was obtained from someone who was trusted, only to turn out to contain an illegal agent, and that the trusted individual may well have known—clearly should have known—before suggesting it to the athlete. This is the ultimate bottom line—that of culpability. Anyone that recommends an athlete take a substance should be held responsible for that recommendation. Unfortunately, that person usually will not have nearly as much to lose as the athlete. It is the sport psychiatrist's job, then, to help athletes make healthy decisions in these matters.

Further, as a trained observer and diagnostician, the sport psychiatrist should also be alert for behavioral changes that suggest that the athlete may be taking a performance-enhancing drug and suffering from adverse effects. Again, this will require familiarity with the substances in this chapter.

Unfortunately, the psychiatrist will often be called in to deal with the aftermath—after the athlete has tested positively and alerted various others to the problem. At that point, compassion for the dilemma that the athlete has faced and empathy for the suffering that inevitably has taken place will offer the best chance for rapport to develop.

In one case, an athlete's spouse served as coach and trainer. He suggested the athlete take a nutritional supplement that was alleged to be on the approved list with the national governing body. The athlete subsequently tested positive for a banned substance and lost eligibility for a year that was critical for her competitive career. As can be imagined, marital strife ensued, along with depression over the various losses. By consulting with a sport psychiatrist, a working-through process was initiated, with the hope of restoring peace and a resolution to the losses. Along with the risks associated with using a foreign substance, this case illustrates the hazards of blurring the boundaries in an athlete's important relationships.

CONCLUSION

Athletes' quest for the optimal training methods and performance techniques not surprisingly leads them to consider various chemical means. Applying the scientific method to athletic performance creates, however, the opportunity for misuse of the available information. It is the responsibility not only of sports' governing bodies, but also of everyone involved in sport and with any athlete to be vigilant for any means or method that might be unhealthy or unfair for the athlete or athletes to use.

Fairness in the sport is as inherent as the health-promoting quality of physical activity and exercise. When human behavior, and especially the knowing use of a physical substance, runs counter to these values it should be radically opposed. Sport psychiatrists, along with other sports medicine physicians and other knowledgeable and responsible people interested in sport, should not hesitate to get involved in the process of determining which practices are appropriate.

REFERENCES

American College of Sports Medicine. (1984). *Stand on the use of anabolic-androgenic steroids in sports*. Indianapolis, IN: American College of Sports Medicine.

Anderson, W. A., & McKeag, D. B. (1985). *The substance use and abuse habits of college student athletes*. Mission, KS: National Collegiate Athletic Association.

Buckley, W. E., Yesalis, C. E., Friedl, K. E., Anderson, W. A., Streit, A. L., & Wright, J. G. (1988). Estimated prevalence of anabolic steroid use among male high school seniors. *Journal of the American Medical Association, 260*(23), 3441–3445.

Butts, N. K., & Crowell, D. (1985). Effects of caffeine ingestion on cardiorespiratory endurance in men and women. *Research Quarterly in Exercise and Sport, 56*, 301–305.

Cott, J. (1997, November). St. John's wort under study as antidepressant. *Clinical Psychiatry News,* P1.

Cowart, V. S. (1988). Human growth hormone: The latest ergogenic aid? *Physician and Sports Medicine, 16*(3), 175–185.

Duda, M. (1983). Drug testing challenges: College and pro athletes. *Physician and Sports Medicine, 11*(9), 64–67.

Ersler, A. J. (1991). Erythropoietin. *New England Journal of Medicine, 324*, 1339–1344.

Fuentes, R. J., Rosenberg, J. M., & Davis, A. (1994). *Athletic drug reference*. New York: Clean Data.

Green, G. A., & Puffer, J. C. (1997). Drugs and doping in athletes. In M. B. Mellion, W. M. Walsh, & G. L. Shelton (Eds.), *The team physician's handbook* (pp. 212–238). Philadelphia: Hanley & Belfus.

Ivy, J. L., Costill, D. L., Fink, W. J., & Lower, R. W. (1979). Influence of caffeine and carbohydrate feedings on endurance performance. *Medicine and Science in Sports and Exercise, 11*, 6–11.

Kiraly, C. L. (1987). Effect of testosterone and anabolic steroids on the size of sebaceous glands in power athletes. *American Journal of Dermatopathology, 96*, 515–519.

Linde, K., Ramirez, G., Mulrow, C. D., Pauls, A., Weidenhammer, W., & Melchart, D. (1996). St. John's wort for depression: An overview and meta-analysis of randomised clinical trials. *British Medical Journal, 313*, 253–258.

Lombardo, J. A. (1986). Stimulants and athletic performance: amphetamines and caffeine. *Physician and Sports Medicine, 14*(11), 128–139.

McIntyre, J. G. (1987). Growth hormone and athletes. *Sports Medicine, 4*, 129–142.

Marshall, E. (1988). The drug of champions. *Science, 242*, 183–184.

Mellion, M. B., Grandjean, A. C., & Ruud, J. S. (1999). *Sports medicine secrets*. Philadelphia: Hanley & Belfus, 117–119.

Narducci, W. A., Wagner, J. C., Hendrickson, T. P., & Jeffrey, T. P. (1990). Anabolic-androgenic steroids. *Journal of Clinical Toxicology, 28*(3), 287–310.

Pope, H. G., & Katz, D. L. (1988). Affective and psychotic symptoms associated with anabolic steroid use. *American Journal of Psychiatry, 145*, 487–490.

Puffer, J. C., & Green, G. A. (1990). Drugs and doping in athletes. In M. B. Mellion, W. M. Walsh, & G. L. Shelton, G. L. (Eds.), *The team physician's handbook* (pp. 111–127). Philadelphia: Hanley & Belfus.

Underwood, L. E. (1984). Report of the conference on uses and possible abuses of biosynthetic human growth hormone. *New England Journal of Medicine, 311*, 606–608.

Webster's New Collegiate Dictionary (10th ed.). (1996). Springfield, MA: Merriam-Webster.

Windsor, R. E., & Dumitru, D. (1988). Anabolic steroid use by athletes. *Postgraduate Medicine, 84*, 37–49.

III

THERAPEUTICS

9

The Sport Psychiatry Examination

Ronald L. Kamm

THE SPORT PSYCHIATRIST'S EXAMINATION of an athlete is based on a specialized interview (table 9.1). This interview is similar to the general psychiatric anamnesis, in that its main goals are to gather the information necessary to make a diagnosis and to construct a psychodynamic formulation that results in a treatment plan. Another important goal, of course, is the formation of a therapeutic relationship with the patient that is based on trust and rapport.

The sport psychiatry interview differs from its general psychiatric counterpart in that the patient being interviewed is an athlete, and sometimes an elite one. The most successful interview will therefore be one that takes into account the unique needs of the athlete, the specific demands of the sport setting, and the stresses of high-level athletic competition, stresses that are placed on both the athlete and his or her family.

It is also not unusual for the interview to take place outside of the traditional office setting, in, for example, the hospital, sports complex, or work place. When a sport psychiatrist has a consultant relationship with a football team, the history-taking occurs in such "exotic" settings as the team bus, the sidelines, or at a local diner—the consultant having been

TABLE 9.1
The Sport Psychiatry Examination

I. The initial phone contact
II. The initial office interview
    A. Identifying and demographic data
    B. Chief complaint
    C. History of the presenting problem
    D. Athletic history
    E. Goals
    F. Personal history—putting the athletic symptom in context
        1. Sexual history
        2. Alcohol and substance abuse history
        3. Work history
        4. Legal history
    G. Family history
        1. Siblings
        2. Perception of parental attitudes and parents' athletic history
    H. Surrogate family
    I. Relationship with the coach and history of relationship with past coaches
    J. Medical status
    K. Sport psychiatry mental status examination
    L. Confidentiality
    M. Sports parents interview
        1. Joining and empathy
        2. General parental coping patterns
        3. Involvement
    N. Transference
    O. Countertransference
    P. Formulation
    Q. Recommendations
        1. Diagnosis(es)
        2. Treatment plan
        3. Medication
        4. Third party payment

casually invited by the player to "have a cup of coffee." While each of these locales presents its own unique interviewing challenge, the interview format described below is tailored to the more typical situation encountered by the sport psychiatrist: that of the child or adolescent athlete referred for a private office consultation. The interview's sequence and areas of inquiry need not be rigidly adhered to, however, as each athlete, family, and athletic situation is different. Some professionals in other sport mental health or exercise disciplines rely heavily on detailed questionnaires for their initial assessment (Lesyk, 1998; Taylor & Schneider, 1992). The sport psychiatrist, in his or her interview, however, strives in ways that a paper and pencil questionnaire cannot, to get to know the athlete as a person and to be responsive to the uniqueness of each interviewee, coach, and family.

THE INITIAL PHONE CONTACT

As in all branches of psychiatry, the initial examination in sport psychiatry begins with the initial phone contact. Particularly if the athlete is a child or adolescent, it is important to note who makes the call, as this often reveals family dynamics and may give a first clue regarding whether a particular parent is over- or underinvolved. Occasionally, an independent-minded adolescent may place the call him- or herself.

Whoever the caller, the sport psychiatrist should first inquire about how his or her name was obtained. This will place the family in some sort of context and may reflect on the family's operating style. For example, a family who has obtained the therapist's name from a phonebook advertisement would appear to make important decisions in a different way than a family who has found the psychiatrist through a friend, coach, or physician. At times, the caller may reveal that he went to great lengths to obtain the therapist's name, suggesting that the caller, at least, is very motivated for treatment.

For example, the father of a nationally ranked female athlete did thorough research before determining that the therapist was "the right one to call" for his daughter. The athlete's mother was uninvolved in the process and, as it turned out, in her daughter's sport. As would later become apparent, this father viewed his daughter as an extension of himself, and was quite overinvolved in her training and life. He was calling the therapist because he urgently (much more than she) wanted her to learn mental techniques so that she could emerge from a recent slump and modify "tantrumy" behavior.

Having ascertained the source of the referral and the relationship of the caller to the athlete, a brief history may be taken over the phone. Athletes and their families are often geared to the "here and now," so an inquiry regarding what event prompted the family to seek out the therapist at this time will often yield a good description of the chief complaint and presenting problem. Previous attempts at treatment by a sports therapist or by a performance-enhancement specialist should be explored, as well as any past history of psychiatric treatment. This latter is particularly important, since a psychiatric disorder sometimes presents as an athletic complaint. A perceived lack of motivation and energy, for example, may be part of an underlying depression, and poor performance under pressure may be the result of an anxiety disorder.

The initial phone contact also affords the therapist the opportunity, before the first visit, to establish and model the principle of open family communication. In more than a few families, parents will often not inform their child of important decisions they have made for them. Therefore, if the athlete is not the caller, is he or she aware that the call is being made? If not, reasons for the athlete's exclusion from the process might be tentatively explored, and some advice might be given to the parent(s) on how to broach the topic. The preparatory time taken on the phone with parents, especially regarding this issue, is invariably well spent. In fact, the way the parents present the consultation to their adolescent often determines whether the athlete actually comes to the first session and whether they stay to complete treatment.

In order to further model to the family that he or she values the child's feelings, the sport psychiatrist might offer to answer, over the phone, any questions the athlete might have regarding the consultation. In fact, if the athlete already knows of the call, the therapist may, as unobtrusively as possible, ask to speak to the athlete then and there. This enables the psychiatrist to hear the problem in the athlete's own words, demonstrates that the therapist is very interested in the athlete's point of view, and establishes the beginning of a therapeutic relationship prior to the first visit.

Continuing with the call mentioned earlier, the therapist was able to speak to the athlete, who confirmed a close parental connection, stating in her chief complaint that she had been "embarrassing" herself and her father on the playing field. She also shared her concerns about confidentiality, stating that she did not want her peers at school to know that she was coming for sessions. In addition, despite her closeness with her father, the athlete asked that he not be informed of the content of sessions. The therapist assured the athlete that he understood her concerns, saw them as valid, and would honor them. He then made sure that no patient who was scheduled immediately before or after her initial consultation was likely to know her or her father, and reminded himself to stress to the father how important the confidentiality of his daughter's sessions would be to treatment outcome.

Since sport psychiatry is a relatively new field, it may be helpful, as the initial phone call comes to an end, for the sport psychiatrist to clearly define to the family the length, format, and fee of the initial session, and to offer to answer a parental question or two. One of the more common parental concerns is the overall length of time that therapy will take, and, depending on his or her treatment paradigm, each therapist will respond to this question differently. Magical expectations should be defused at the outset, with the therapist emphasizing that sport psychiatry is not a "quick fix," and that a detailed history, obtained over several meetings, provides the best cornerstone for diagnosis and treatment planning.

Despite these best-laid plans, however, the initial contact with the sport psychiatrist may come in the form of a desperate phone call, wherein a distraught parent beseeches the therapist to help their athlete overcome a debilitating performance problem on the virtual eve of an important athletic event. While agreeing to see the athlete under such circumstances, the therapist should nevertheless make it clear that one or two crisis sessions will not necessarily result in an immediate improvement in performance, and that it is more important to come to a full understanding of the problem and to give the athlete the tools to prevent its future occurrence than to provide a "quick fix."

I usually inform families that a comprehensive initial evaluation will take at least four sessions. Other therapists work differently, of course, and it is important to be flexible enough to tailor the evaluation process to the athlete's or parents' particular needs. In general, the four-session evaluation model proceeds as follows: (1) meet with the athlete alone for the first session; (2) the parents alone for the second; (3) the whole nuclear family (including siblings, if indicated) for the third session; and (4) at the fourth session, parents and athlete both separately and together to discuss diagnosis and treatment recommendations.

On a practical note, communication patterns in an elite athlete's family are frequently dysfunctional. It is therefore helpful to give information regarding location, date, and time of the first appointment directly to the driver (if not the athlete), thereby hopefully eliminating possible third-party communication mishaps.

In summary, the detailed initial phone interview can yield many benefits. The therapist hears the chief complaint from the parent and athlete and begins to conceptualize it within several diagnostic possibilities. The brief phone evaluation may also allow the therapist to formulate preliminary psychodynamic and family-dynamic hypotheses, consider possible performance-enhancement strategies, and, perhaps most importantly, it begins to establish a relationship with the athlete and family even before the first session begins. In addition, the phone interview helps lower athlete and family anxiety about what sport psychiatry (and the sport psychiatrist) is like, affording all parties the opportunity to make a preliminary determination as to whether they are a good "fit" for one another. With practice, the interview described above can actually be accomplished in about 15 minutes.

THE INITIAL OFFICE INTERVIEW

Identifying and Demographic Data

As mentioned previously, though the paper-and-pencil assessments used by other professionals can be useful as adjuncts, the sport psychiatrist relies mainly on his or her clinical skills as a physician and interviewer to obtain a history, establish a diagnosis, and devise a treatment plan.

For example, even while obtaining identifying data, the therapist observes and shows interest in the athlete's feelings. When inquiring which school the athlete attends, he pays attention to the tone with which the athlete responds and his or her body language and facial expressions. What grade is the athlete in (held back by parents or "red-shirted" in order to be older and more physically mature than classmate competitors)? How does she like school, and how is she doing academically? Is the school in her "district," or is she attending an out-of-district or private school? If so, was this by invitation of a coach or athletic director at the school, or was the special placement an athletically dictated parental decision? It is never too early in a sports interview to introduce the concept that having fun is important and that there is life beyond sports. The therapist may therefore ask what the athlete's favorite subject and after-school activity are (other than the current varsity sport), and what, outside of her sport, she does for fun. Has the athlete thought about what she wants to do when she graduates high school (attend college? where? major in what? go into what profession)? or is the athlete so narrowly focused on sports that she has not thought in terms of the bigger picture of her life?

Chief Complaint

Though the adolescent and one or both parents have now given their description of the problem (along with, perhaps, a causative theory), it is a good idea to specifically ask the athlete, "So what brings you here?" If the patient cannot clearly articulate the problem or chief complaint, another tack might be to ask the athlete, "What is your goal in coming today" (that is, what is he or she hoping will come from current—or future—sessions with you)?

As is usual in psychiatry, the therapist records the complaint verbatim:

"I've just lost my competitive desire and I don't know how to get it back."

"I let opponents beat me who I should be beating and I don't know why."

"I just lose it on the court. I've just been going crazy, throwing my racquet, and crying when a call goes against me."

History of the Presenting Problem

Having heard the chief complaint in the athlete's own words, the interviewer now attempts to flesh it out. The athlete is asked to go into more detail and to describe the last time he or she noted the problem happening (often the event that precipitated the initial phone call). The therapist then asks, "When did all this start (first onset)?" and "How frequently has it occurred since then?" The very first episode is then explored in detail, which often provides clues regarding the psychodynamic meaning of the symptom, possible precipitating events, and a picture of the athlete's coping capacity at that time.

A diver in her early teens had lost confidence in trying difficult dives from the high board after she landed flat on her back during a major competition two years previously. She recalled that her upper back and neck had turned bright red from the poor landing, and that she was in pain. The athlete could still vividly remember "turning red all over in embarrassment" as she got out of the pool. After some initial reluctance to try the dive again, the athlete seemed to have been able to put the poor landing behind her, but in the past year, since entering high school, she had become more and more fearful of attempting any difficult dives from the high board.

History revealed that, in the past year, the athlete's mother (a former competitive diver) had been putting great pressure on her both to improve her diving and to excel academically, "now that she was in high school." The athlete, however, had been feeling insecure since her entrance into ninth grade. Not as mature physically as the other girls in her class, she felt self-conscious about her body. In addition, an older sister, also a diver, had recently left for college and the athlete now felt that her mother's attention was "completely on me." She added that her mother had always urged her and her sister "to reach higher and higher" and had always "hated weaklings." Her father was described as being relatively distant, uninvolved, and, in a way, "weak." During difficult spinning dives off the high board, the athlete reported feeling "lost and not knowing where I am." Her goal in coming to therapy was to "try and get me to relax and understand why I have this fear." Interestingly, she had little trouble with dives off the lower board.

Table 9.2 provides an outline of factors to be examined when exploring the presenting problem, including the first episode. In obtaining the details of the presenting problem, the interviewer will probably vary his or her questioning style. Some inquiries may be very open-ended: "Describe the competitive scenario," while others need to be very specific: "What was the score at that point in the match?" The interviewer's main objective here is to gather sufficient details so that a clear, comprehensive picture of the problem scene emerges. Once visualized, the therapist might increase rapport with the adolescent by sharing a validating remark, such as: "Gee, this all must be very frustrating."

Athletic History

At this point in the interview, the athlete usually welcomes a shift away from the current problem area, and the therapist may oblige by transitioning to the athletic history.

As when taking the personal history in the traditional psychiatric exam, certain developmental milestones and issues should be touched on. The therapist might begin with the open-ended "How did you get started in sports?" This question in itself may provide corroborative data regarding

TABLE 9.2
Outline for Detailed Examination of the Presenting Problem

I. Environmental factors
  A. Competitive setting
    1. Performance level at the time of competition
    2. Stage of the season
    3. Level and importance of competition
    4. Opponents
    5. Familiarity and comfort with competitive site
  B. Physical status
    1. Quality and quantity of training
    2. Technique
    3. Current health: injury? illness? fatigue?
  C. Status of equipment
II. Precompetitive psychological factors
  A. Describe thoughts: obsessive? negative? focused? scattered?
  B. Describe feelings: anxious? confident? motivated? calm? lost?
  C. Describe behavior: pacing? meditating? superstitious habits? usual warm-up?
  D. Did you use mental skills training?
III. Competitive psychological factors
  A. Describe thoughts: obsessive? negative? focused? scattered?
  B. Describe feelings: anxious? fearful? confident? motivated? calm? lost? intimidated? determined? angry?
  C. Describe behavior: "just flowed"? assertive? aggressive? off balance? unsure? tentative? passive?
  D. Did you use mental skills training?
IV. Social influences
  A. Teammates, opponents, coaches, parents, others
  B. Any recent changes in relationships?
  C. Any recent changes in school? at work?
V. Consequences
  A. What happened after the problem occurred?
  B. How did significant others react?
  C. What kind of thoughts and feelings did you have?
  D. Did you blame yourself? others? who?

(*continued*)

TABLE 9.2
Continued

VI. Greater explorations
   A. Is there a consistent pattern?
   B. During what situation does the problem seem to be at its worst?
   C. Are there certain other situations where the problem rarely occurs at all?
   D. Any theory as to what's causing it?
   E. What have you tried in order to get over it?

Some data from Taylor & Schneider, 1992.

the degree of parental involvement and pressure. For example, was achievement by proxy disorder (Tofler, Knapp, & Drell, 1998), where parents display a pathological interest in their child's athletic activities, living vicariously through them, evident from the start? Or, conversely, did the athlete just happen to be a very "sports-minded" youngster with relatively uninvolved, unathletic parents? According to Weiss and Petlichkoff (1989), children most often get started in sports for "affiliation, fitness, and fun."

Whatever the athlete's reasons for getting involved in sports, table 9.3 highlights many of the areas of the athletic history about which the sport psychiatrist might inquire, but which would not usually be explored in the traditional psychiatric developmental history. As the positioning of question 3 illustrates, it is important to ask *early on* in the interview about some of the high points or "sunny spots" (Nideffer, 1981) in an athlete's career. The recitation of these accomplishments at this point in the interview often provides the athlete with a much-needed emotional "lift" and a reminder that he or she has been (and can again be) quite successful. When the athlete's presenting problem involves persistent displays of poor sportsmanship, frequent disqualification, a history of aggressive behavior with the intent to cause harm, or the use of illegal means to gain a competitive advantage, then particular attention might be given to an assessment of the athlete's exposure to, and level of, moral reasoning (question 20) (Shields & Bredemeier, 1995).

Certainly the amount of "trash-talking," and the use of performance-enhancing substances among athletes have increased dramatically in the past 30 years, and today's athletes have been raised in a society and a

TABLE 9.3
The Athletic History

1. How did you get involved in your sport, and at what age did you decide to intensively involve yourself?
2. How did you get yourself to the level you have now attained?
3. What have been some of the high points of your career?
4. What have been some of the low points?
5. Who have been the people most responsible for your continued interest and participation in your sport?
6. What is your earliest sports memory?
7. At what age were different sports played?
8. "Playground conditioning" (Begel, 1992): Describe your involvement in child-organized, spontaneous games.
9. Are you currently involved in more than one sport? If so, which sport do you enjoy most?
10. What has been your past level of enjoyment, and to what extent has the family been involved in each sport?
11. Role Models: Who is the athlete in your sport(s) who you most admire? What qualities of this athlete do you admire or respect most?
12. How many days and hours per week throughout the year do you practice?
13. When does your season begin and end?
14. Athlete's comfort level with aggression since infancy. Level of aggression in sports at the beginning, in latency, now.
15. How overtly competitive were you and how much did you enjoy competition when you were younger? now?
16. History of sports-related syndromes and how athlete handled them: choking, slumps, conflicts with teammates, conflicts with coaches, adapting to changes in events, positions, coaches, level of competition
17. Presence of other sport-specific syndromes: "prima donna syndrome," "achilles complex," loss of interest (Begel, 1992).
18. Relative primacy of athletics in person's life.
19. Athletic life cycle: At what stage of your athletic career do you now see yourself? beginning? peaking? "over the hill"? at the end?
20. Exposure to moral reasoning.
21. Detailed exploration of goals: short-term (regarding correction of the problem), intermediate-term, and long-term.

Some data from Lesyk, 1998; Stryer, Tofler, & Lapchick, 1998; Taylor & Schneider, 1992.

sports-media world that glamorize explosive responses to anger and an "in your face" mentality. Thus, when an athlete presents with boundary-violating behavior, it behooves the therapist to investigate the possible source. Has the athlete's physical prowess exempted him or her, over the years, from normal responsibility and accountability for his or her actions? Who have been the main granters of such exemptions: the family? which parent? the neighbors (who, for example, because of the adolescent's athletic prowess and celebrity, gave the athlete a break when he placed a cherry bomb in their mailbox)? teachers, counselors or administrators at school? law-enforcement officials? coaches? Who are and who have been the athlete's role models in sport and in life? How do these role models conduct themselves? Has the athlete been asked to reflect on the moral norms undergirding sport—fairness, compassion, sportsmanship, integrity (Shields & Bredemier, 1995)?

These are not trivial questions when one considers that "sports mirrors society," that there is now a youth violence epidemic sweeping the country, and that sports participation may, potentially, ameliorate or actually aggravate this problem. For example, players of contact sports seem to exhibit *less* restraint on their off-the-field aggression than nonplayers, and "moral reasoning maturity"—the ability to adhere to agreed-upon rules, even at personal cost—seems inversely proportional to the level of athletic achievement (Shields & Bredemier, 1995).

Personal History: Putting the Athletic Symptom in Context

After the athletic history has been taken, the parallel unfolding of the athlete as a person is then explored. The nature of the presenting problem and the amount of time available for the consultation (one session? several sessions?) dictate which areas of the personal history need to be explored first, and in what detail.

Divided into the usual major developmental periods, the personal history begins in infancy, where it is helpful to look for early clues regarding parental perceptions (and projections). For example, what adjectives were used to describe the athlete when he was an infant: active? passive? quiet? temperamental? When parents have reminisced about the athlete as a preschooler, what potentially prophetic phrases has the athlete heard: "not afraid of anything"? "a bull"? "a jock"?

An exploration of the grammar-school years might reveal whether, because of his or her athletic ability, same- or opposite-sexed peers conferred any special status upon the athlete.

Early signs of anxiety should be inquired about. Was the athlete "close friends" and "in tight" with members of his peer group or was he on the periphery? How did the athlete adjust to the changes and separations of childhood, such as leaving home for kindergarten, or grammar school for middle school? Was there performance anxiety regarding test-taking?

Sexual history. The sexual history is particularly important, as both male and female athletes are at relatively high risk for sexual exploitation by coaches (Nyad, 1998; Westhead, 1997). A world-class female endurance athlete was forcibly raped by her coach, beginning at the age of 13. The sexual abuse continued for several years and left the athlete feeling guilty, depressed, ashamed, and alone. She felt that because her parents valued the coach so much, she could not confide in them and if she did they would not believe her.

Alcohol and substance abuse history. Recent evidence indicates that high-school athletes, though they get better grades, are more likely to use drugs and alcohol than their nonathletic classmates (Eccles & Barber, 1998). The use of these substances should therefore be examined, as should the use of steroids and other performance-enhancing substances and techniques, such as rapid weight loss or yo-yo dieting (in wrestling and lightweight crew, for example). Such practices can be harmful, even fatal, yet may not be perceived negatively. Indeed, coach, parent, and athlete may view such practices positively and as perfectly acceptable, tied as they are to a "laudable" conformity to the sports ethic of "Win at all costs." Such performance-enhancement and "getting a competitive edge" practices have been referred to by sport sociologist Jay Coakley (1997) as "positive deviance," and they are on the rise. Ominously, a survey that recently appeared in *Pediatrics* revealed that 2.9 percent of middle-schoolers (fifth to eighth grade) were using steroids. That number increased to *9 percent* when serious gymnasts and weight-lifters in the same age group were polled (Faigenbaum, Zaichkowsky, Gardner & Micheli, 1998).

Work history. To what degree has the adolescent been exempted from all nonathletic responsibilities so that he or she can concentrate purely on his or her sport? Some families do not inform the athlete of the reality of high training and equipment costs, even when such expenses are causing the family financial hardship. By not asking the athlete to "help out" by working, parents may subtly be fostering an attitude of entitlement and lack of accountability, an attitude that can sometimes lead the athlete to believe that society's rules do not apply to him or her.

Legal history. In this vein, a legal history should also be taken, exploring whether the athlete has ever been charged with violent and/or sexual assault (Crosset, Benedict, & McDonald, 1995); underage alcohol use, drug possession or drug dealing, drunk driving (Nattiv & Puffer, 1991); or shoplifting, all of which seem to have a higher incidence among athletes. An inquiry should also be made regarding whether the athlete has ever been expelled from school or from an athletic facility for illegal or rule-breaking behavior. At times, adolescent athletes get into legal trouble not as part of an "entitlement" syndrome, but because they cannot directly express their feelings to their parents.

Family History

The family sport history's main focus is the athlete's perception of how supportive, involved (over- or under-), and/or pressuring the family is and how important his or her accomplishments are to parental status and identity. A male athlete, who was conflicted about whether to continue his sport past high school because of other interests, became angry at his parents every time they "bragged" about his athletic accomplishments and his future Olympic and professional destiny. He stated to the therapist that he often felt that his athletic achievements were more important to his parents than he himself was.

Siblings. Are there siblings also participating in sports? Are they of the same or opposite sex? How do their relative skill levels compare, and has one sibling been a role model for another? To what degree are the siblings friends or rivals?

Perception of parental attitudes and parents' athletic history. What does the athlete know of the parents' youthful athletic aspirations and accomplishments, and what sports, if any, did the parents play? An adolescent athlete did not understand why his mother was so angry when he missed important competitions. The mother, who had played an individual sport at the masters level, explained that she was frustrated by her son's stomachaches and headaches because she was determined that he realize his "full athletic potential." Though the mother had wanted to make her own father "proud," she felt that, because she was a woman and went to college in the early sixties, she had not been encouraged or "pushed hard enough" to make the most of her athletic ability. She considered her father, husband, and all men "weak" and could not stand any perception of this quality in her son.

How does the athlete view the marriage? Do the parents get along or is the athlete a substitute focus for problems in the relationship? What was the emotional and athletic relationship of the athlete's parents to their own parents? In chapter 11, Hellstedt discusses using such a "vertical" family analysis and approach when considering an athlete's problem, while other family therapists describe the "intergenerational transmission of unresolved tasks" (Begel, 1992) to partially explain an athlete's difficulties.

Finally, what does the athlete perceive that each parent does for fun and/or recreation? Are the parents involved in competitive sports, such as tennis, golf, bowling, basketball, volleyball, or relatively noncompetitive recreational activities such as aerobics, dance, or yoga (Begel, 1998)? Conversely, are one or both parents perceived as "workaholic" or "driven," having no source of gratification, athletic or otherwise, other than their child's performance and athletic career?

Surrogate Family

Hopefully, the athlete has been allowed (and has been able) to separate somewhat from their family of origin, and has begun to establish a support system outside of the home. Such a support system may consist of teammates, nonathletic friends, the parents of teammates and friends, and/or the coach.

The members of this system may vary from time to time in their perceived degree of supportiveness, being idealized and seen as "totally supportive" one day, then being perceived as "cut-throat" and "back-stabbing" the next.

Relationship with the Coach and History of Relationship with Past Coaches

What is the coach like and what does the athlete perceive the coach's main strengths and weaknesses to be? Transferential similarities to one or the other parent should be explored, as should the nature of the parents' relationship with the coach. Is there a "power struggle" going on between coach and parents for "control" of the athlete? Do coach and parents clearly communicate their expectations to each other, or is the athlete used as a "middleman" to relay messages back and forth or as a sounding board for the complaints of parents and coach about the other?

For example, a female athlete began an individual sport at 13, had a meteoric rise, and became her "coach's favorite." The athlete had a strong need to please adults, had great fun winning, and enjoyed seeing her coach's reaction. At 16, however, she began going to parties and socializing more with friends and with boys, missing one practice for social reasons, and actually going out the evening before a competition. The coach became enraged and complained to the parents. Though initially confused about what to do, the parents decided that their daughter should have a social life, and stood up to the coach, who reluctantly backed off. Unfortunately, in subtle ways he began making the girl feel guilty for not being "totally committed." Feeling torn, the athlete began to lose confidence, enjoyed her sport less, and experienced a performance decline. Though it was difficult to do so because of their long and close relationship, the parents eventually fired the coach.

Medical Status

The athlete's current health should be explored. Has the athlete recently been ill, or is he or she presently being treated for a medical problem? Does the athlete have allergies for which he or she is being treated, and do they affect the athlete's performance? Is the athlete currently taking medication for a medical or psychiatric condition, such as asthma (sympathomimetics), or ADHD (stimulants), and do the medications positively or negatively affect the athlete's performance?

Though an outstanding college prospect, a teenage basketball player was referred by his allergist because of asthmatic attacks and wheezing, which would occur when he was bringing the ball up court. The player would then have to be removed from the game, resulting in a loss of confidence and raising the concern of his coach, teammates, and family. Standard anti-asthma medications were not preventing the attacks, which the athlete subsequently came to understand were caused by emotional stresses, which he learned to control with mental skills techniques.

Past medical illnesses, particularly loss of consciousness, head trauma, or seizures, should be investigated, as should any history of injury, particularly injury sustained in the athletic arena. It is instructive to inquire in detail how an athlete has coped with a training or competitive injury, as many young athletes feel invincible until they are seriously injured. At that point, realizing that they are, indeed, "vulnerable," some athletes become depressed. Others, such as runners who are obsessed with running a certain number of miles each day in order to maintain a certain weight or to "insure" that they do not suffer another heart attack, may become anxious when not permitted to exercise. Yet another group of athletes may "milk" an injury, using it to "gracefully" avoid the stress of competition, perhaps out of fear of failure. The issue is complicated by the fact that a study of men referred to an outpatient psychiatric clinic showed that those who scored high on a scale of athleticism had more somatic symptons than nonathletic counterparts, and complained of more disorders precipitated by injury or physical illness (Little, 1969). Ominously, a history of repeated "overuse" injuries in latency and preadolescence may be an early warning sign of achievement by proxy disorder (Tofler, Knapp, & Drell, 1998), and may be due to relentless parental pressure to practice and train, even when the athlete is injured or "hurting."

Any past or current history of psychiatric illness should be thoroughly explored, and the interviewer must determine whether the athlete's sporting involvement may be one etiological factor in his or her illness (judging preferences in certain sports/anorexia nervosa) or whether an underlying psychiatric disorder is manifesting itself as a performance problem.

The athlete should be asked the date of his or her most recent physical examination and whether any medical problems or blood work abnormalities were noted. These and the pulse should be known before prescribing SSRIs, for example, as these compounds can alter certain liver function tests, and can slow the heart rate of an athlete, who is probably bradycardic to begin with.

In the female athlete, one would be interested in the age of menarche and whether periods are regular. It is also important to directly ask for the date of her last period, as cessation of menses may suggest a diagnosis of anorexia nervosa, overtraining syndrome, or pregnancy. An inquiry should also be made regarding the existence and degree of severity of premenstrual syndrome, a condition that can negatively impact training, performance, and relationships, yet may be quite amenable to current treatments.

In the male athlete, has there been onset of puberty, as indicated by body and facial hair, voice lowering, and nocturnal emissions? It is as important to be alert to the possibility of a hidden eating disorder in a male athlete as it would be if treating a female (Thiel, Gottfried, & Hesse, 1993). Certain "fad" diagnoses (ferritin-deficiency anemia or diffuse intravascular candidiasis), which the athlete may be using to explain tiredness or a decline in performance, should not necessarily be accepted at face value.

Before completing the medical review, one should be certain to have asked the athlete whether he or she is taking any alternative medicines, vitamins, or herbal supplements, as these may have side effects. Specifically, it is very important to determine whether the athlete is taking any over-the-counter or prescription medications that could be on the "banned substance" list for his or her particular sport.

Sport Psychiatry Mental Status Examination

As in all of psychiatry, it is important that a thorough history be supplemented by a careful mental status exam. Using the clinical and observational skills which have been acquired by virtue of his or her training as a psychiatrist and physician, the sport psychiatrist takes note of any physical, mental, and/or interactional signs of Axis I and II disorders. Such disorders may present themselves as athletic problems, exist independently, or be partially caused by the athlete's competitive experience, pressures, and milieu. In addition to screening for Axis I and II disorders, the sport psychiatrist also uses the mental status exam to identify or rule out the existence of common sports-related syndromes, such as anorexia athletica (Sundgot-Borgen, 1994), achievement by proxy disorder, or Achilles syndrome (Begel, 1992), which may cause, be caused by, or exist independently of the chief complaint.

As it is assumed that the reader is familiar with the general structure of the psychiatric mental status examination, this discussion will focus on those particular aspects of the *sport mental status* to which attention should be paid.

One caveat: When observing an athlete's behavior during the interview, and when inquiring about different areas of athletic and personal functioning, it is important to take the patient's unique social, cultural, and intellectual characteristics into account. When the therapist exhibits an understanding of the athlete's racial, ethnic, and socioeconomic realities, rapport will probably be enhanced and the interviewer will be able to couch questions appropriately. The sex and sexual orientation of the athlete and interviewer must also be taken into account, as these may similarly dictate the demeanor, phrasing, and areas of questioning appropriate to the initial interview.

To conduct a good sport mental status exam, the therapist need not have actually been an elite-level athlete, or even possess a working knowledge of the athlete's sport. However, having such experience and knowledge can be a great advantage, particularly when trying to establish a relationship (and credibility) with an adolescent patient.

Appearance. What, if anything, is striking? Does the athlete look physically younger and less mature than his or her stated age? If younger, is this a boy who feels at a competitive disadvantage with his more developed peers or a girl who is overtraining to the point of delaying her growth and menstruation? The skin should be observed for signs of steroid abuse: acne, folliculitis, sycosis (Goldstein & Odom, 1993), hairiness (females), and bruises. One should note whether the eyes exhibit reddened conjunctiva, possibly indicative of chronic marijuana use. The clothing worn by an adolescent athlete may give a clue regarding his or her identity struggle. For example, is he or she in street clothes or sports attire? Regarding autonomy, who chose the athlete's clothes for the interview, and who shops for and puts together the athlete's wardrobe?

An elite female athlete was having a difficult time deciding whether to accept a scholarship to a famous Division I school, where she would have to practice intensively, or a Division II college, where the program was more relaxed. Though she had visited both schools, she consistently wore the sweatshirt of the more nationally known school to sessions. When asked about this, the athlete acknowledged her true preference for the "big" school, but voiced, for the first time, a concern that the established starters on the Division I team would not be welcoming to her. Presumably threatened by her ability, the starters had been "cool and aloof" to the athlete at a recent campus visit.

Attitude, demeanor, and relationship to examiner. If the athlete is a child or adolescent, is there a marked reaction to separation from the parent in the waiting room, indicating a possible anxiety disorder, dependent personality, or parental overcontrol?

If the athlete's problem is violent or rule-breaking behavior, how does he or she relate to the interviewer? Is there overt aggression, defiance, or oppositionalism? Might the violence and rule-breaking be a symptom of parental emotional, physical, or sexual abuse? At times, the sport psychiatrist is the first professional to uncover abuse, and must report physical and sexual abuse to the appropriate agency (Carter-Lourensz & Johnson-Powell, 1995).

Regarding demeanor, does the athlete loosen up as the interview progresses (a good prognostic sign) or does he or she seem fixed, robotic, programmed, and joyless (achievement by proxy disorder)?

Motor behavior. If the athlete seems restless and in constant motion, could these problems be a manifestation of ADHD, stimulant abuse, or bipolar disorder? If there is obvious muscle tension, is the athlete suffering from anxiety disorder, PTSD, or barely controllable rage?

Speech and language. Athletes who are racially, ethnically, and/or socioeconomically different from the interviewer may use colloquialisms and slang expressions, which graphically describe their feelings or an athletic maneuver, but with which the examiner is not familiar. Depending on the fame and status of the athlete, the examiner might be hesitant to ask the meaning of such a phrase, wanting to appear "with it" and well acquainted with the athlete's culture and sport. Such hesitation can backfire when the interviewer later uses the phrase incorrectly. Genuine attempts by the therapist to understand the athlete and his or her world, no matter how "ignorant" the question may appear, will go much further toward establishing rapport than pretending to understand.

Thinking and perception. What does the athlete predominantly worry about? The next competition? Not getting a scholarship? What his or her father will think? Would the athlete characterize him- or herself as having been a worrier "since birth" (anxiety disorder)?

Is there a palpable, overriding fear of losing or failure, or a preoccupation with food and weight? Are there obsessions about body fat or miles swum? Following an injury, is there a phobia regarding getting beaned again (baseball) or paralyzed by a tackle (football)?

Does the athlete daydream or dream at night? Are there recurrent dreams or nightmares? If so, are any of these day or night dreams aggressive in nature, even for the athlete's sport? If so, does the athlete express the aggression or is the athlete on the receiving end? Further, what kind of aggression or violence is involved in the fantasy: verbal abuse? property destruction? homicide? suicide?

In the course of examining an athlete's thought processes, the interviewer may discover that the athlete has been pushed along in the educational process not because of academic merit, but because of his or her highly valued athletic prowess. Alan Page (1998), the Hall of Fame defensive lineman for the Minnesota Vikings and current associate justice of the Minnesota Supreme Court, related the following: Late in Page's career, the Vikings got a new defensive line coach. Though the players were part of one of the greatest units in NFL history, the coach insisted that each defensive line meeting consist of one player reading plays from the Vikings defensive playbook to the others. As the playbook was passed around the room, it became apparent to Page that four of the seven linemen in his unit could not read.

Like Page, the sport psychiatrist may uncover illiteracy during the mental status exam (though the athlete will most probably have been referred for another problem). Detecting this condition, and helping the athlete overcome it, whatever the stage of his or her education, can only enhance the player's self-esteem and lessen any anxiety about being "found out."

Mood. Is the athlete's predominant emotional state happy, sad, anxious, depressed? ashamed, embarrassed, fearful? tense, hostile, angry, apathetic? Do moods vary, even within a day, indicating possible drug, alcohol, or steroid abuse, bipolar disorder, or PMS? When in the day are the moods worse?

Affect. How expressive is the athlete of his or her emotions? Are they appropriate, and of what intensity? At times, children of achievement-by-proxy parents have a vacant, robotic look. Talented as they are, they are workers, fulfilling someone else's dream.

Object relations. Is the athlete's libido totally invested in him- or herself? Is there concern for others' rights or is there an apparent need to dominate others both within and outside of the athletic arena (narcissistic personality disorder, conduct disorder)?

Psychosexual history. If this has not already been discussed in the initial interview, what is the athlete's degree of sexual involvement? Does the athlete use birth control methods? What is his or her gender identity?

Symptoms. Especially if persistent rule violations or fighting are part of the chief complaint, the athlete should be asked about "over the line" aggressive behaviors, including sexual assault. Is the athlete currently using substances such as alcohol, drugs, nicotine, caffeine, stimulants, and "legal" or illegal performance-enhancing compounds?

What is the athlete's most prevalent emotional state: depression? euphoria? anxiety? panic? Is the athlete phobic or compulsive? Does he or she appear obsessed? What are the athlete's most prevalent personality traits? Could the athlete, from the interview behavior, best be characterized as egocentric, narcissistic, or "selfish"? Or, conversely, does he or she appear to be self-critical, isolated, and riddled with shame and guilt ("I let down my school, teammates, and family by dropping the ball")?

Is the athlete's self-esteem appropriate to his or her achievements and physical and characterological assets, or is it exaggeratedly high or low? How stable is the athlete's sense of self-esteem, and does it vary greatly depending on victory or defeat?

A sense of the athlete's coping capacity should also be gathered. How does the athlete cope with stress, for example? Does the athlete know and use mental-skills techniques and, if so, which ones and how regularly? In the past, how has the athlete adapted to change, as in training regime, competitive routine, coach, coaching philosophy, or level of competition?

Sleeping and eating are very important activities to most athletes, and both are sensitive barometers of underlying anxiety and depression. Disturbed sleep and eating habits can also have a devastating impact on performance. Athletes should therefore be asked directly how they have been sleeping. If there is a sleep problem, the athlete should be queried regarding its impact on training and competitive performances. Is the athlete having difficulty falling asleep, awaking frequently, or waking up earlier than necessary? The athlete's thoughts as he or she lies awake can be very revealing of current anxieties and conflicts, as can dreams, especially recurrent ones. Dreams are particularly important to explore since athletes, as a group, tend to be superstitious and more than a few believe that dreams can foretell their future. For example, before he fought Lou Del Valle in their July 1998 bout, light heavyweight champion Roy Jones dreamt that the soft-punching Del Valle would knock him down. Though Jones won the fight, Del Valle did, in fact, knock him down, the first time in his life that Jones had ever been off his feet (Eskenazi, 1998).

Eating and body image. Though highly publicized by the press, every athletic eating problem is not anorexia nervosa. Therefore, possible medical explanations for weight loss must be given at least as much consideration as psychological ones. One tends to view a star athlete as the epitome of fitness, almost immune to common ailments, yet in the past two years two major league superstars have been diagnosed with colon cancer.

Each athlete should therefore be asked not only how his or her appetite has been, but also whether eating and/or bowel habits have recently changed. Has his weight also changed, and how does he feel about how much he currently weighs? As with sleep, has the change in the athlete's eating habits or weight influenced his training or performance in competition? How does the athlete feel about his body build in general? Gymnasts with eating-disordered body images believe they are too fat, even when emaciated, whereas weight lifters with body dysmorphic disorder feel that their body is "too small," though they appear large and muscular to the observer (Pope, Gruber, Choi, Olivardia, & Phillips, 1997).

Moral development. Though moral reasoning has been explored to some extent in the athletic history section, the athlete's current level of moral development needs to be formally assessed, particularly if the athlete has shown signs or symptoms of competitive or societal "over the line" behavior. How "self-regulating" is the athlete, that is, how much in control is he or she of his or her sexual and aggressive impulses, and how capable is the athlete of taking and receiving criticism? Can it be said by those who know the athlete that he or she has "moral values"? What has been (or is) the athlete's involvement with the moral agencies of the community (church, synagogue, mosque, "young" political or environmental groups, scouts, other volunteer organizations)? What are the athlete's opinions, if any, about social conditions in the world today? If the athlete is high-profile, how much of his or her time (not money) is devoted to altruistic causes?

Insight. How much insight does the athlete have regarding his or her reason(s) for seeing the clinician, and regarding the causes and magnitude of his or her problem(s)? Is the athlete distressed by his difficulties, or unaware of the impact the problem is having on himself, his family, the team? Does the athlete show signs of denial? entitlement? narcissism? conduct disorder? How capable is the athlete of recognizing the connection between past events in his life and the current problem (psychodynamic approach)? How does the athlete understand the clinician's role in helping to solve the problems and how inherently optimistic, pessimistic, and/or realistic is the athlete regarding the degree to which his situation can improve?

Judgment. When assessing an athlete's judgment, one might begin with an examination of the athlete's history of on- and off-the-field accidents and injuries. Has there been thrill-seeking or "out of control" aggressive behavior that has led to injury? Does there also seem to be a lack of appreciation for the dangers associated with certain practices or activities (ADHD/depression/achievement by proxy)? Does the athlete seem to possess a reasonable respect for authority? Do the athlete's assumptions tend to be correct regarding the consequences of his or her actions?

Adaptive capacities, strengths, assets. Much of the sport psychiatry mental status exam is, like its general psychiatric counterpart, a search for pathology. Yet in treatment it will be necessary to call on the patient's strengths to effect change. Athletes especially may feel "weak" for not being able to solve their problems themselves, and it may be necessary for the therapist early on to acknowledge and validate the athlete's many strengths and accomplishments, strengths without which the athlete never could have achieved the elite level. Only then can many athletes, especially the more narcissistic personalities, face their weaknesses.

The sport psychiatrist's implied message as the mental status exam comes to a close should be that sports, wonderful as they are, are not the only fulfilling activity in the world, nor is the athlete's next performance the only way he or she will be measured as a person. High-profile athletes can be pointed to and used as role models to emphasize this point: superstars who pursue and enjoy very nonathletic hobbies or who have developed other admirable skills—artistic, musical, verbal. Some superstars may be exemplary for their community work, getting more from it than they give. Others may be quietly admired around the league (and among the media) for the strength and durability of their friendships, the "class" they show on and off the field, or, perhaps most importantly, for their qualities as a parent.

Confidentiality

Confidentiality is designed to ensure privacy and facilitate the development of trust between therapist and patient. Therefore, either during the initial phone contact or at the end of the first session, the issue of confidentiality and any limitations on it must be addressed by the sport psychiatrist.

Legally, ethically, and clinically, a patient's confidentiality must be respected. It is important, however, for the therapist to inform the patient that there may be some limits to absolute confidentiality, such as the psychiatrist's "duty to warn" if the athlete intends to violently harm another person, or the psychiatrist's duty to inform an athlete's parents or family of imminent suicidal behavior. It is also important that therapists advise parents from the beginning that, for the work to proceed fruitfully, the child's privacy must be honored and that it is not productive to query the athlete about what transpired during his or her session. This may be particularly difficult for some sport parents to accept, especially those who view the sport psychiatrist as just one more "coach" to whom they have taken their child for "stroke analysis," the essence of which they expect will be communicated to them. Therapists must define their role clearly from the outset, telling parents that the therapist's main job is to understand and help their son or daughter, not to give them the details of what goes on in therapy.

When parents do call the therapist, either for reassurance, direction, or to report on the athlete's latest misadventure, it must be with the understanding that the essence of any communication between them and the therapist will be relayed to the child. When the sport psychiatrist is employed by or is a paid consultant to a professional sports franchise, the issue of a player's right to absolute confidentiality becomes even more clouded. For more information on this topic, see chapter 12.

Sports Parents Interview

Having laid out the parameters of confidentiality described above, and having obtained the athlete's permission to meet with his or her parents, the sports parents interview begins with several purposes in mind. The first is to obtain more facts about the athlete's current problem than could be conveyed during the initial phone contact. Given an opportunity in their own private session, parents can share their impressions and concerns about the athlete more freely.

To begin, the parents should be asked for their chief complaint regarding the athlete and what they are hoping the athlete will get from the sessions. Their agenda may be different from the athlete's. Some parents, for example, may have long wanted their adolescent to come to therapy because of "attitude" problems, and only now, with the adolescent experiencing a performance decrement, have they found a "lever" with which to nudge the athlete in for a consultation.

After the parents' chief complaint (and each may have a different one) is explored, their version of the history of the athlete's presenting problem is then examined. When added to the athlete's account, a comprehensive picture of the course of symptom progression will hopefully emerge. Previous attempts at treatment should be detailed, and the parents' sense of the adolescent's current emotional and athletic status should be obtained.

The second purpose of the parental interview is to review the athlete's account of his or her athletic and developmental history. These need not be examined separately, as one is inextricably bound with the other. Parents can now describe firsthand how active or passive the infant was and how the child first became involved in sports.

When the index of suspicion has been raised in the athlete's initial interview, the presence of relatively common athletic syndromes, as well as those traditionally thought to be linked to family process, should be explored. Some of these may be outside the athlete's awareness or they may be "secrets" the athlete has not yet wanted to share with the therapist—an eating disorder, substance or steroid abuse, or promiscuity.

Other goals of the sport parents interview are to get to know the parents as both individuals and parents, to assess family dynamics, and to consider how much of the athlete's symptomatology might be related to the latter. A window into family dynamics may be gained by reviewing, once again, how the parents prepared their child for the initial consultation and what the parents asked the athlete following his or her initial interview. Since resistance to seeing a sport psychiatrist may have been high for both athlete and sport parent, the therapist might inquire how the athlete seemed to feel about the first consultation, how the parents felt about it, and what their feelings were about coming to their own separate session today.

Joining and empathy. A brief acknowledgment by the therapist of the special stresses faced by an elite athlete's family is usually well received at this point. Such families have, after all, been buffeted for years by the emotional, financial, and time demands of their adolescent's sport. In addition, sport parents have had to make difficult decisions for, and with, their child, often with little guidance and support. These decisions and how they were made are important parts of the sport parent interview. Important decisions may include how involved to be in the child's sports experience, how to relate to the child's coaches, and what degree of financial commitment to make.

Involvement. Though sport parents will frequently tell an interviewer that they "just want their athlete to have fun" and "don't care if their athlete plays sports or not," when the details of their involvement in their son's or daughter's athletic life are teased out, a different picture may emerge. It is crucial to the identity and status of some parents that their athlete be a high achiever. Tofler and colleagues (1998) have termed this phenomenon "achievement by proxy distortion," and signs of it should be inquired about.

1. Did the athlete have many overuse injuries in latency and preadolescence?
2. Have the parents ever been told that they might be pushing their child too hard?
3. How do the parents view each other's spectator and coaching decorum?
4. Has either parent ever been:
    (a) asked by child, spouse, coach, or league official not to attend a practice or game?
    (b) disciplined or suspended by the league for behavior at their child's athletic event?
    (c) accused of abusive behavior toward their own or someone else's child (verbal, emotional, physical, sexual)?
5. Has a coach ever been given inordinate power and "say" in the child's life?
6. Has there been an inordinate economic or geographic sacrifice made for the athlete (mortgaging house for special training, equip-

ment, or private coaching; moving, or allowing the athlete to move, to another city so that the athlete can train with a special coach)?

Certainly parental overinvolvement with the child athlete can be caused by parental intrapsychic, marital, or family systems issues, so each parent's personal history should be explored. How did each parent relate to the members of their own nuclear family, and how important were athletics to their nuclear family life? How close are the parents now to their family of origin, and do grandparents, uncles, and aunts follow the athlete's exploits as well? Are the parents rivalrous with one or more of their siblings, and are there athletic cousins to whom the patient is compared?

It is important to ask about and review any specific medical or psychological problems suffered by either parent or by their relatives. If there is or was a mental illness, what is the diagnosis, what has been the treatment, and has psychotropic medication been prescribed? Is there any family or parental history of alcoholism or drug or steroid abuse? Has either of the parents been involved, as perpetrator or victim, in verbal or emotional abuse or physical or sexual assault?

What was the role of athletics in the courtship, and how would each spouse characterize the marriage at this time? Are the parents themselves currently involved in competitive athletics (tennis, golf, bowling, other) and to what degree? Did they participate in sports in childhood? Do they now participate in relatively noncompetitive recreational pursuits such as yoga, dance, aerobics, jogging, nautilus, weight training? Are there family problems that are adding to the stress level in the household, such as difficulties with other children, previous marriages, in-laws, or finances? Finally, what is each parent's theory about what might be causing the athlete's problem, what solution have they imagined the therapist might propose, and how do they feel about certain modalities that the therapist might be considering (hypnosis, medication, etc.)?

When the sport parent and family interviews are completed, the main question that needs to be teased out and answered (if it can be) is: How much of the athlete's symptomatology is sports-related as opposed to being a manifestation of underlying psychiatric illness and/or family dynamics?

Transference

Throughout the consultation, the athlete's transference to the psychiatrist is noted. The transference may be quite positive, in that the athlete seems to relate to the therapist as if the latter were quite a valuable, able asset. Conversely, and not infrequently, the transference may be negative with the psychiatrist initially being viewed as an adult authority figure and a parental agent.

The therapist should not jump to the conclusion, however, that rejecting, hostile behavior on the athlete's part is negative transference. It may instead represent the athlete's defense against anxiety or it may be "testing behavior," designed to see how much the therapist is willing to "take."

Countertransference

If the adolescent is acting out (and particularly if the therapist has an adolescent child), the sport psychiatrist must be aware of, but resist, the temptation to "side with" the parents. The perception by the athlete of such an alliance would surely inhibit his or her openness during the evaluation and his or her willingness to remain in treatment. Conversely, couples who in their actions and manner remind the psychiatrist of his or her own parents may nudge the therapist in the direction of an alliance with the athlete. If this stance is too overt, it is the parents who will probably sabotage future treatment.

In working with particularly elite or famous athletes, the psychiatrist must guard against the dangers of "countertransference awe" and of "needing" the consultation and treatment to lead to improved performance so that the therapist can "take credit" for a great athlete's career. The more elite and famous the athlete, the more the therapist must guard against the temptations of overidentification, basking in reflected glory, and using the athlete in the service of narcissistic needs. In addition, because the athlete's world is so competitive, he or she may consciously or subconsciously try to draw the therapist into a competitive sparring contest (Begel, 1992), a stance which usually requires interpretation.

Formulation

There are certainly a wide variety of ways in which a sports clinician can conceptualize and formulate an athlete's problem. Sport psychiatrists, as the above format would suggest, follow the guidelines of the biopsychosocial model. Underlying medical and psychiatric conditions are considered in as much detail as psychodynamic factors and character issues. The athlete's social and athletic behavior and the impact on the athlete of the social and athletic milieu are also examined, as are parental and family dynamics. The basic question to be answered, if possible, is: How much of athlete's problem is "sports related" and perhaps amenable to brief therapy and/or mental skills training, and how much may be secondary to, or influenced by, underlying medical or psychiatric conditions?

Recommendations

Diagnosis. At the end of the fourth consultative session, a diagnosis of the problem and recommendations for treatment are made to the athlete and his or her parents. The athlete's and the family's strengths should be enumerated first, and then Axis I diagnoses, if present, should be frankly discussed. Alcohol, drug, and steroid abuse need to be handled in a special manner, and the athlete should be referred for a consultation with a specialist if underlying medical conditions are suspected.

At times, especially with families or adolescents who are wary of "labeling," a formal diagnosis need not be given. Rather, a general description of the problem ("She doesn't seem able to keep her focus in tense situations" or "He's feeling like he's under too much pressure") may suffice, along with any causative theories the therapist wishes to share.

Treatment plan. Treatment recommendations will vary. One possibility is that the consultative process will have been sufficiently therapeutic that no further treatment is necessary. More often, depending on the nature of the problem and the orientation of the psychiatrist, some combination of individual, family, and/or marital therapy, mental-skills training, hypnosis, coach-therapist communication, and/or psychopharmacology will be recommended. Such recommendations must be geared to the level of psychological sophistication and receptiveness of the athlete and family, their level of commitment, time availability, economic resources, and, if medication is indicated, their attitude toward it. "We'll shore up Suzie's strengths and strengthen any areas that aren't so strong" is one generic orientation that most athletes and their families can endorse.

Medication. If, as Beisser (1967) has suggested, athletes resist psychological explanations for their problems because "thought is an opponent against which no concrete action can be taken," one might assume that they (and their families) would be even more resistant to a sport psychiatrist's recommendation that psychotropic medication be taken to help the athlete with his or her problems or symptoms. This, in fact, does seem to be the case. Athletes and their families, coming from a "fitness orientation," often see taking psychotropic medication as "unhealthy," a sign of weakness, a stigma, and, unconsciously, a means by which the therapist wishes to "control" them.

Adolescent athletes seem to prefer "talk therapy" or mental-skills training to the taking of medication, though, ironically, they may concomitantly be using illegal drugs or alcohol for recreation and considering the use of, or may actively be using, over-the-counter preparations or illegally obtained steroids for the purpose of performance enhancement.

Athletes and their parents seem unusually wary of any medication's potential adverse effects. Therefore, should medication be recommended, the match between the specific demands of the athlete's sport and the drug's potential side effects must be seriously taken into account.

Female athletes, particularly, will stop a medication that seems associated with weight gain, and one must be particularly cognizant of the potential impact of a drug on an athlete's coordination, vision, cardiovascular system (pulse is often low to begin with) and any other autonomic effects (dry mouth). As Begel (1992) points out, there have been reports of negative inotropic responses to phenothiozines and tricyclics, so, with other alternatives available, one would probably avoid the use of these agents in weight lifters and endurance athletes.

Vigorous training and competition are often associated with profuse sweating and fluid loss. The interviewer is therefore well advised to remember that plasma levels of certain medications may increase, and that smaller than usual starting dosages of a particular medication may therefore be necessary.

If medication is prescribed, it may be important to ask the coach (with the family's permission) for his or her "informed support" (Popper, 1987) for the prescription of medication. This tends to prevent the sport psychiatrist's efforts from being competitively undermined by the coach's comments, prejudices, or pharmacologically unsophisticated concerns. Certainly when medication is initially prescribed, the demands placed on the athlete during practice and the coach's expectations of the athlete may have to be altered and additional safety precautions (e.g., in gymnastics) may need to be taken. Lastly, through communication with parents, coaches, and the governing body of the athlete's sport, the sport psychiatrist must become aware of, and avoid using (if possible), medication that would ban the athlete from competition (e.g., beta-blockers in archery, riflery).

Third party payment. Athletes or their families often will pay 100 percent of the sport psychiatrist's fee themselves. This particularly holds true when parents "don't want a record" of their athlete having been in treatment because of fear that such a record might adversely affect an athlete's future application to a college or for insurance coverage.

Many parents and athletes, however, inquire about whether the evaluation and treatment might be covered by their health insurance. Certainly, should the athlete be found to have an Axis I disorder, such as anorexia nervosa, or an Axis II disorder, such as narcissistic personality, billing under such a diagnosis is entirely proper. Sometimes a *DSM-IV* Axis I diagnosis of adjustment disorder is applicable (Sachs, 1993), if "the athlete's performance problem is causing 'significant impairments' in his social (including sports), academic, occupational, and/or family functioning" (American Psychiatric Association, 1994, p. 623). When the athlete has a medical condition that may worsen when the athlete is experiencing great competitive stress or performance problems, a diagnosis of psychological factors affecting medical condition would certainly seem warranted.

REFERENCES

American Psychiatric Association. (1994). *Diagnostic and statistical manual of mental disorders* (4th ed.). Washington, DC: Author.

Begel, D. (1992). An overview of sport psychiatry. *American Journal of Psychiatry, 149*(5), 606–614.

Begel, D. (1998). The psychotherapist and the adolescent athlete. In I. R. Tofler (Guest ed.), *Child and adolescent psychiatric clinics of North America: Sport psychiatry* (Vol. 7, No. 4, pp. 808–815). Philadelphia: Saunders.

Beisser, A. R. (1967). *The madness in sports*. New York: Appleton-Century-Crofts.

Carter-Lourensz, J., & Johnson-Powell, G. (1995). Physical abuse, sexual abuse and neglect of child. In H. Kaplan & B. Sadock, (Eds.), *Comprehensive textbook of psychiatry* (6th ed., p. 2458). Baltimore, MD. Williams & Wilkins.

Coakley, J. (1998). *Sport in society: Issues and controversies* (6th ed.). New York: McGraw-Hill.

Crosset, T. W., Benedict, J. R., & McDonald, M. A. (1995). Male student-athletes reported for sexual assault: Survey of campus police departments and judicial affairs offices. *Journal of Sport & Social Issues, 19*(2), 126–40.

Eccles, J., & Barber, B. (1999). The student council volunteering basketball or marching band: What kind of extracurricular involvement matters? *Journal of Adolescent Research, 14*(1), 10–43.

Eskenazi, G. (1998, July 20). First knockdown breaks the monotony for Jones. *The New York Times*, p. C3.

Faigenbaum, A. D., Zaichkowsky, I. D., Gardner, D. E., & Micheli, I. J. (1998). Anabolic steroid use by male and female middle school students. *Pediatrics, 101*(5), E6.

Goldstein, S., & Odom, R. (1993). Skin & appendages. In L. Tierney, S. McPhee, M. Papadakis, & S. Schroeder (Eds.), *Current medical diagnosis & treatment* (pp. 64–124). Norwalk, CT: Appleton & Lange.

Lesyk, J. (1998). *Developing sport psychology within your clinical practice: A practical guide for mental health professionals.* San Francisco: Jossey-Bass.

Little, J. C. (1969). The athlete's neurosis: A deprivation crisis. *Acta Psychiatrica Scandinavica, 45*, 187–197.

Nattiv, A., & Puffer, J. C. (1991). Lifestyles and health risks of collegiate athletes. *Journal of Family Practice, 33*(6), 585–590.

Nideffer, R. (1981). *The ethics and practice of applied sport psychology.* Ithaca, NY: Movement Publics.

Nyad, D. (1998, May 28). *Violence, agression, and unsporting behavior: Where to draw the line?* Presentation at The Summit: The International Conference on Ethical Issues in Sport, The Ethics Center, University of South Florida.

Page, A. (1998, May 28). Keynote address at The Summit: The International Conference on Ethical Issues in Sport, The Ethics Center, University of South Florida.

Pope, H., Gruber, A., Choi, P., Olivardia R., & Phillips, K. A. (1997). Muscle dysmorphia: An underrecognized form of body dysmorphic disorder. *Psychosomatics, 38*, 548–557.

Popper, C. (1987). (Ed.). *Psychiatric pharmacosciences of children and adolescents.* Washington, DC: American Psychiatric Press.

Sachs, M. (1993). Professional ethics in sport psychology. In R. Singer, M. Murphy, & L. Tennant (Eds.), *Handbook of research on sport psychology* (p. 929). New York: Macmillan.

Shields, D., & Bredemeier, B. (1995). *Character development and physical activity.* Champaign, IL: Human Kinetics.

Stryer, B., Tofler, I., & Lapchick, R. (1998). A developmental overview of child and youth sports in society. In I. R. Tofler (Guest Ed.), *Child and adolescent psychiatric clinics of North America: Sport psychiatry* (Vol. 7, No. 4, pp. 697–724). Philadelphia: Saunders.

Sundgot-Borgen, J. (1994). Risk and trigger factors for the development of eating disorders in female elite athletes. *Medicine and Science in Sports and Exercise, 26*, 414–419.

Taylor, J., & Schneider, B. (1992). The sport-clinical intake protocol: A comprehensive interviewing instrument for applied sport psychology. *Professional Psychology: Research and Practice, 23*(4), 318–325.

Thiel, A., Gottfried, H., & Hesse, F. W. (1993). Subclinical eating disorders in male athletes: A study of low weight category rowers and wrestlers. *Acta Psychiatrica Scandinavica, 88*, 259–265.

Tofler, I., Knapp, P., & Drell, M. (1998). The achievement by proxy spectrum in youth sports: Historical perspective and clinical approach to pressured and high-achieving children and adolescents. In I. R. Tofler (Guest Ed.), *Child and adolescent psychiatric clinics of North America: Sport psychology* (Vol. 7, No. 4, pp. 803–820). Philadelphia: Saunders.

Weiss, M., & Petlichkoff, L. (1989). Children's motivation for participating in and withdrawal from sport: Identifying the missing links. *Pediatric Exercise Science, 1*, 195–211.

Westhead, R. (1997, January 9). Canadian police widen junior hockey sexual assault probe. *The New York Times*, p. B13.

10

Psychotherapy with the Performing Athlete

Daniel Begel

CLINICIANS WORKING WITH ATHLETES have used a variety of psychotherapeutic methods. Some of those methods emphasize the benefits of fully understanding oneself, while others aim to quickly modify behavior and correct habitual errors of thought. Some therapies are brief; others are lengthy. Therapy may be interpretive or instructive, and may either exploit or ignore the power of the relationship between athlete and therapist. Regardless of focus, type, or emphasis, all psychotherapies use symbolic strategies consisting primarily of meaningful conversation. With athletes, they all focus attention to some degree on both personal issues and issues of athletic performance, though they may differ greatly in the relative weight assigned to each of these realms.

Although Beisser (1967) was of the impression that athletes are inclined to consider psychotherapy "of dubious value," that is not necessarily the experience of sport psychiatrists in recent years. In part, the difference is a result of psychiatry's maturing perspective on the athlete, so that the athlete's training and performance is no longer regarded either as trivial recreation or exotic magnificence. Fostering our patient's capacity for "loving and working," to paraphrase Freud, means that we now give athletic life the same careful and dispassionate respect applied to every other realm of work and pleasure. Another factor that promotes receptivity to psychotherapy is the solicitous attention that a psychotherapist pays to the nuances of an athlete's thinking. This attention may appeal to the athlete's narcissism and mirror the exquisite interest taken by the athlete in every aspect of his or her own physical and mental functioning.

In an informal survey of 127 athletes in one professional baseball organization, Garfield Creitz and I found that 85 percent of the athletes polled perceived a positive role for mental health professionals. Some of the notions of these athletes were quite subtle, such as the belief that a therapist "yields to the patient's opinions" in order to "gather ideas about them and increase their awareness of the barriers to success." A preventive role in "limiting the peaks and valleys" and a supportive role in "helping to restore confidence" were also noted. Most of the criticisms of mental health professionals elicited in this survey were fair ones, such as, therapists "analyze too much" or their work is overly subjective. There were very few responses like that of the person who said, "They charge outrageous prices for little service. I'd rather talk to a bartender."

BRIEF THERAPIES

The willingness of athletes to open up to a therapist is not always followed by a willingness to continue to do so. The requirements of performance and the great sensitivity of performance to even mild psychological disturbances often invest therapeutic encounters with a sense of urgency. Although the therapist may caution the athlete not to expect immediate results, such cautions often fall on deaf ears. Many athletes want results now or never, and so it is not uncommon for their psychotherapies to consist of a single session.

A psychiatrist was asked by the employee assistance consultant to a professional basketball team to see a player who had been shooting poorly for several months. The consultant was impressed by how irritable and withdrawn the athlete had become, and suspected that behind it was the fact of the athlete's father having recently been diagnosed with a recurrence and metastasis of a colon cancer that had been thought to be in remission. The athlete was not any more interested in talking to the psychiatrist than in talking to anyone else, but agreed to do so "one time."

The athlete initiated the meeting by pouring out his frustration over his slump. He described his efforts to change certain technical flaws with the help of a shooting consultant the team had brought in, and he railed at what he perceived to be unfair public criticism for not living up to the standard set implicitly by his rather lucrative contract. He knew, he said, that some people blamed his slump on his father's illness and this troubled him especially. He described a close relationship with his father, "a disciplinarian" and his first coach, who was now an avid follower of his son's career. His father would want him to be "strong" in the face of the bad medical news, and the athlete felt that by playing poorly he was letting his father down.

In an intuitive interpretive observation, the psychiatrist remarked that the athlete seemed to feel as if he were being "punished" for something. The athlete then became tearful. When his father was first diagnosed with cancer, he said, both athlete and father had minimized the potential dangers. Surgery was performed in the father's small town hospital, followed by chemotherapy, and the disease went into remission. Follow-up visits were carried out according to a schedule determined by the father's managed care organization, which also required that he see physicians on their panel of providers. Without ever saying so, the athlete suspected that his father was getting inadequate care, and when the diagnosis of a recurrence was made, he furiously berated himself for not hiring "the best doctors," as he could well have afforded to do. Before each game, during the playing of the National Anthem, the athlete thought of his father, and of his failure to take care of him. "I've killed him," he said.

Toward the end of the meeting the psychiatrist responded with a cognitively oriented comment. It seemed "truly irrational," he remarked, for the athlete to punish himself in this way, since his athletic achievements clearly brought his father enormous pleasure. As the conversation drew to a close, the psychiatrist offered further meetings, which he felt would be necessary, but the athlete declined, stating that his slump was his own problem to solve.

As a result of this meeting the athlete's mood lightened considerably. On the way out of the meeting room, which was in the suite of team offices, the athlete joked with one of the secretaries. The employee assistance consultant was impressed later by his joking and bantering with his teammates in the locker room. He said, "I've never seen him like that."

Although a shooting slump is not usually thought of as a clinical emergency, this intervention resembled other crisis intervention interviews in its rapid identification of a central dynamic issue and timely offer of a healing perspective. In sports, these brief and crisis-driven psychotherapeutic encounters may occur anywhere: in the locker room, on the team bus, in the landing pit, and in the dugout. They often bring immediate relief and a rapid improvement of performance. Frequently, however, the improvement is not lasting. In the case of the basketball player mentioned above, his shooting improved quickly and remained adequate for the rest of the season, but deteriorated again the following year.

Brief therapies that respond to an athlete's sense of urgency and at the same time provide an opportunity for more thorough look at the clinical issues tend to have more lasting effect than these single encounters. Ogilvie (1997) sometimes takes the interesting approach of inviting athletes to visit him at his home for several days, during which time they engage in intensive exploration of whatever issues may be of concern. A more traditional approach involves a series of meetings scheduled around the athlete's training and competition over a relatively short period of time.

A downhill skier who had choked in a previous Olympic trials visited a psychiatrist several months before the subsequent ones. He had not suffered a second episode in the intervening world championships, but was concerned because of a strong family history of panic attacks that he thought might "bite me in the ass." Panic disorder with agoraphobia afflicted two of his siblings as well as his father, who had once successfully demanded to be let off of a passenger train between stops. In addition to his anxiety about an untimely episode of anxiety, he expressed some concerns about his girlfriend, who appeared to be more distant of late, as well as some irritation with his coach. He mocked his coach's old-world habit of ordering food for the entire team when they traveled, and of requesting the restaurants to serve this food in common trays, "family style."

Skier and psychiatrist met six times in the course of three weeks, during which the athlete aired his concerns. There was some discussion of the family's tendency toward enmeshment, and that it was okay for the athlete to loosen the ties a bit, especially in the face of an increasing demand to focus on training as the trials neared. The psychiatrist learned of several unusual and untimely previous illnesses and the fear of another unexpected one. It seemed important for this athlete to understand that although a great deal may happen that would be out of his control, the basic bond between himself and his family would be remain secure. The athlete did well at the trials, qualifying for the team, and returned for several more meetings about a year later to quell some residual doubts.

PSYCHODYNAMIC PERFORMANCE ENHANCEMENT

Both the crisis intervention therapy of the basketball player and the brief therapy of the downhill skier straddled the boundary of performance and personal life, as many therapies with athletes understandably do. It is almost an axiom of sport psychiatry, illustrated many times over in these pages, that performance parallels the overall mental well-being of the athlete. Although better athletes are not necessarily healthier individuals than worse athletes, any given athlete plays better healthy than sick. Thus, a therapy that attends to the entire inventory of a person's concerns is "performance-enhancing," even though it may not use the signature techniques of performance-enhancement therapy, such as imaging, meditation, and self-talk.

At times, the psychiatrist may initiate a therapy that specifically incorporates some of the relaxation and imaging techniques developed by sport psychologists. Prior to initiating an imaging exercise, the athlete will be taught diaphragmatic breathing, unless he or she is already familiar with it. Diaphragmatic or "yoga" breathing seems to induce a state of relaxation sufficiently deep to fully connect mental images with kinesthetic ones, especially when such breathing is combined with simple meditation methods. In the fully relaxed state, rehearsal scripts are mentally enacted. These may be oriented not only toward perfecting performance, but also toward discovering hidden roadblocks and untapped potentials. When applied in a context that takes into account the psychodynamics of the athlete and the ambiguities of the therapeutic relationship, performance-enhancement techniques become a part of "psychodynamic performance enhancement" (Begel, 1994), a hybrid of interpretive and instructive therapeutic methods.

An adolescent gymnast, for example, became inhibited about performing routines that required her to go backwards. It began with an inability to do a back handspring on the balance beam without her coach spotting her and progressed to the point where she was unable to perform a back handspring on the floor, a trick she had known since she was little. A conscientious person, this athlete tended to do well in situations in which adult expectations were clear, but had become uncertain about situations that required her to trust her own instincts. She was troubled by the question of "how far to go" with her boyfriend, and school situations in which she was required to respond extemporaneously were extremely anxiety-provoking, unlike those situations for which she could prepare.

The therapy that was initiated for this athlete involved a mixture of performance-enhancement and insight-oriented procedures. The therapist's basic posture was one of active listener, enabling the patient to discuss her desire for freedom and intimacy, her fear of losing parental love, and her dread of letting go. At times, however, the therapist became prescriptive, instructing the athlete on relaxation techniques and constructing scripts for mental rehearsal that were designed to ease the athlete into developing confidence in autonomous actions. The scripts that were developed involved themes that were based on the athlete's dependency struggles, in which the degree of participation of the "spotter" was varied from excessively involved to totally remote, and the identity of the spotter was similarly varied, including not only the coach, but also the athlete's parents, boyfriend, therapist, and the athlete herself.

A combination therapy of this type carries certain risks, and some sport psychiatrists avoid it altogether. One of the risks is that the athlete, the therapist, or both, will turn their attention to sport when personal issues that are coming to the fore may be likely to cause discomfort. A related risk is that therapist and patient will recreate a relationship that is problematic in the athlete's life or act out an issue that is better explored. In the therapy just mentioned, for example, the therapist, in prescribing performance-enhancement exercises, was unconsciously reinforcing the athlete's dependence on a parental figure. The therapist attempted to alleviate this problem as much as possible by enlisting the athlete's creativity in creating and utilizing rehearsal scripts. When the therapist sensed that the patient was depending on the prescriptions of the therapist as a defense against trusting her own capacities, an effort was made to discuss this possibility.

Not all therapies that address performance issues give equal weight to personal ones. Even when personal issues are at stake, it may be that they are sufficiently well-managed to be left alone. A young golfer who was recently awarded a scholarship to a college with an excellent golf team suffered a string of puzzling blunders in the spring of his last year of high school. There seemed to be a number of possible separation issues that could have been contributory, including the facts that he was the last child of his family to leave home and that in leaving home he would also be leaving his girlfriend of two years. These topics were explored willingly by the patient, and he seemed to have a balanced emotional perspective on them.

A therapy oriented toward performance, in which rehearsal techniques were used as a method of discovering possible performance problems, revealed a relatively slight holding back of aggression when called upon to use his fairway woods. This was dealt with in a quite straightforward manner with breathing and imaging techniques oriented toward the swing itself and designed to restore an attitude of easy attack.

In embarking on a therapy for sports-related problems, it is important to keep in mind the possibility that athletic problems may be part of a developing mental illness. An athlete who chokes may be suffering from other anxiety and phobic symptoms. An athlete who is in conflict with a coach may have a more generalized conduct disorder. Somatization disorder may appear first as excessive hypochondriasis, greater than that which is based on the importance for an athlete of paying especially close attention to bodily sensations.

When the extent of a problem is not known and the problem is mistakenly thought to reside primarily in the realm of sports, reassurance that the situation is a normal one for athletes may be given prematurely. If the athlete and clinician continue to meet, it will usually become apparent that reassurance has been insufficient, since it will result in little beneficial effect. Although it may be apparent to the therapist that significant personal or family issues are unresolved, it can be difficult to address them if the patient, as well as the family, expect that attention will be paid exclusively to performance. A therapist who advertises as a specialist in sports is especially likely to step into this predicament.

A therapist received a phone message from a mother who wished to have a sport psychiatrist help her daughter with her swimming. When the therapist returned the call he was greeted by the patient's father with a response that was characterized in the therapist's notes as "sarcastic and ugly." Mother and daughter insisted, at their first appointment, that theirs was just "a typical American family," and explained away father's unpleasant style as a result of his "weird sense of humor." They met any attempt on the part of the therapist to explore nonathletic issues with a blunt air of puzzled unresponsiveness, in spite of explanations on the relevance of such matters to athletic performance. Although they mentioned that another sister received extensive therapy for an eating disorder, they considered this to be an extraneous event in the swimmer's life and, on the whole, gave an impression of people with something to hide. Yielding to the insistence that the only troubles were athletic ones, the therapist embarked on a treatment geared solely to athletic performance while looking, where possible, for openings that might evolve into a broadened discussion. It was not surprising that this treatment failed quickly.

TRANSFERENCE IN BRIEF THERAPY

Although most brief therapies depend upon the establishment of a comfortable and trusting therapeutic relationship for their effect, this relationship is often not explicitly addressed. Brief psychotherapies in which manifestations of transference become important vehicles, however, may also result in beneficial effects on performance. Although some of the links between performance and personal history may be apparent to the therapist at the time of assessment, others may emerge in the course of attempting to understand the athlete's reactions to the therapist. Transference reactions may provide a vehicle for exploring the links between performance and personal life and in rendering these links meaningful for the patient.

For example, a tennis player who was in the process of sabotaging his likely election to captain by verbally abusing his coach was referred to a sport psychiatrist. In addition to his problem of controlling his anger at his coach, his play suffered from a recent inability to "put away" his opponents when the opportunity presented itself on the court. In school, he also experienced some difficulty with academic deadlines.

The athlete's mother, a wealthy descendent of a scion of the industrial revolution, had divorced the athlete's father several years earlier when he had contracted a fatal disease, from which he subsequently died. After the divorce, the athlete had lived with his mother, and split loyalties interfered with his mourning his father's death. The therapist suspected some connection between his problematic expression of aggression and his unresolved mourning.

One day the athlete happened to witness the therapist at the tennis court, and at the next session complimented the therapist on what he generously termed a "pretty good game." The athlete's suppressed smile, however, indicated that he had some other reactions to his therapist's performance, and in response to his being asked about this, proceeded to playfully mock the therapist's abilities, which the therapist took good-naturedly. Suddenly the patient stopped and reported a memory in which his father, as a result of his illness, had fallen on the driveway of his mother's house after a visit, and the patient had suppressed his laughter. When the therapist gently stated that laughing would no longer hurt his father, the patient appeared greatly relieved, and began to mourn his father's death, and the circumstances of it.

THERAPY AS A TRAINING TOOL

Sometimes an athlete and therapist will embark on a brief psychotherapy and discover, several brief therapies later, that it has become long-term. This may happen as a result of the therapy uncovering a vexing personal issue, as when, for example, an accomplished archer who sought help for a tremor discovered the complex ramifications of childhood sexual experiences that he thought had been resolved. A long-term therapy can also develop when an athlete uses therapy as an element of training.

Used as a training tool, psychotherapy visits acquire a character that resembles, to a certain degree, the course of the athletic season. Preseason visits focus on the psychological foundation, the doubts, hopes, and tasks for the coming season, as well as the stability of the athlete's personal life. Early and mid-season visits focus more on the sport, and especially on the psychology of specific techniques. Mid- and peak-season visits are oriented almost exclusively toward competition. With mature athletes, psychotherapy for the purposes of training can proceed, with breaks, for the duration of a competitive career and beyond.

An adult polo player visited a sport psychiatrist, seeking to improve his own riding and the record of his team. Among other issues, he mentioned that while he thrived on competition he occasionally lost his enthusiasm at inopportune times. He was an experienced rider, and although his business obligations prevented him from training full-time like his competitors among "the pros," he felt he had the knowledge and ability to lead his team to victory over anyone. At times he played aggressively, riding "up the ass and out the nose" of the other riders' horses, as he put it. But he was frequently unable to put together a series of good matches in the course of a major tournament. He found various ways to lose, by fouling, for example, or he would suddenly find that his enthusiasm disappeared, especially during a slow game. His aim was not only to win the two major national competitions that had eluded his team, but to become "dominant."

This athlete had been riding since the age of 12, when his father, a grocer, had reached a point in his business where he was able to move his family from the immigrant neighborhood where they lived to a home in an affluent community. The move resulted in a significant change in the socioeconomic class of the boy's environment, and he adapted to the change happily, but perhaps not entirely easily. He wanted to learn to ride horses like some of his new friends, and although riding frightened him at first, he quickly became, with his father's encouragement, one of the better young polo players, first in his club, and then in the Midwestern states.

When the father retired, the athlete took over the business with his brother, two years his junior. With this change, the business rapidly grew to include flower shops, bakeries, and restaurants, along with grocery stores. This growth was primarily due to the efforts of the athlete, who was always more aggressive and competent than his younger brother, who was asthmatic, shy, and not very athletic. "Carrying" his brother in the business did not seem to disconcert the athlete in any way, however, and he seemed to simply accept it as a filial responsibility.

The athlete and psychiatrist met a half dozen or so times a year over the course of many years. Meetings tended to be clustered in the preseason and around particular competitions. In the course of time many issues were discussed. Technical issues needed to be explained to the psychiatrist, who could not ride a horse, much less play polo. Family issues were discussed, including the athlete's relationship with his brother, father, and son. Generic issues of athletic training, diet, nutrition, and management of time spent on business, family, and athletic needs were part of the conversation. Precompetition preparations and protocols were addressed, and imaging techniques were developed.

The athlete put slightly more weight on technical errors as the cause of defeats than the psychiatrist, who tended to look for mental factors, and in the course of discussion both points of view were explored. It appeared at times that the athlete's caring attitude and bonding with others might be interfering with his free expression of competitive drives. He was very careful and thoughtful about removing an old and close friend, who was also a skilled and knowledgeable player, from his team when it became important to do so. He had felt for some time that this friend's moodiness interfered with their communication on the field, but his sympathy for his friend's troubles temporarily overrode his interest in winning. On one occasion, his collegial attitude led him to spearhead a protest by several teams of an official's ruling to suspend play on account of the weather, and this same attitude required him to make deliberate efforts to disassociate himself until the competition was over from those nocturnal recreational activities that could interfere with the next day's matches. This dissociation was symbolized, perhaps, by his choosing to carry out his precompetition imaging in the john.

It may be fair to say this athlete came to grant himself a kind of "permission" to give full rein to his abundant competitive drives in the course of his therapy, without feeling he was in any way relinquishing his bonds or betraying his brother, his father, or his colleagues in competition. At some point his team was ranked first nationally in their competitive class, which brought less satisfaction than his eventual victories at the two national events that were most important to him. This improvement was so gradual and steady that the psychiatrist wondered at times if there was any improvement at all. The athlete felt that the therapy was helpful, both to help him organize his training plans and to tap his motivation. On more than one occasion he left their meetings "pumped," feeling like he could "tame a bull." Eventually, he bought out his brother in their business and laid plans to compete internationally, to the chagrin of his board of directors.

PSYCHOTHERAPY AND FAMILY THERAPY

Any of the kinds of individual psychotherapies, brief or long-term, behavioral or insight-oriented, performance- or personally-focused, can be carried out in conjunction with other therapeutic modalities. An athlete may simultaneously be treated with medications, as described by Baum in chapter 13, or with family therapy, as described by Hellstedt in chapter 11. Collateral family therapy and individual therapy make particular sense in the case of those adolescent athletes whose families have been overly invested in their training.

In some families, a child's athletic activities have evolved into the most important source of satisfaction and interest for the family unit. Father or mother may be the child's coach, significant financial resources may be diverted to the child's career, and the family may move to a particular city or state in order to provide their child with optimal athletic opportunity. There may be an asymmetrical interest in the child's participation, with one parent providing transportation to practices and games, scheduling family business around the requirements of the season, and having significant emotional investment in the child's success, while the other parent becomes increasingly detached from the ever-tightening dyad.

Sometimes one parent, usually the father, will have a reputation within the family as having had a successful athletic career, and the children's careers will be measured against that reputation, whatever its accuracy. One high-school runner, for example, believing her father to have been a great distance runner because he won a national competition as a high-school student, was unaware of the fact that he failed to improve on his time in four years of college. To the extent that she was unconsciously competing with her father, her lack of complete information placed her at a disadvantage.

Overinvolvement of the family may result in the premature imposition on young athletes of training that is excessively intense, systematic, result-oriented, and exclusive to a single sport. Because this training is thought to be motivated by the needs of parents and coaches to solve some other life problem of their own, either consciously or unconsciously, this circumstance has been described as an "achievement by proxy" distortion (Tofler, Knapp, & Drell, 1998, and chapter 6).

Prior to adolescence, children who are either pushed in their sport by parents, or whose parents derive an unnatural degree of satisfaction from the athletic exploits of their children, do not often protest. In middle childhood, the primary symptoms of the achievement by proxy syndrome seem to be overuse injuries and subclincial performance anxiety that does not come to the attention of the psychiatrist. In adolescence, however, we see a wide variety of symptoms developing as the person struggles to achieve some degree of emancipation from emotionally overinvolved parents. Although the achievement by proxy dynamics may contribute to such symptoms as eating disorders, drug use, sexual acting out, participation in groups that incur parental disapproval, and any other sort of behavior that defies parental expectations, it frequently appears as a simple desire to quit the sport.

Since the desire to quit originates in a family obsession that the athlete has had an active hand in creating, the athlete will find it easier to complain, "It's not fun anymore" or "I don't like my new coach," than to say, "My parents spoiled it for me." Family therapy by itself is often effective in these circumstances, as Hellstedt describes in chapter 11, but sometimes it is useful to see the athlete in individual therapy as well, after first meeting with the family as a group for several sessions.

In the preliminary family sessions, the athlete's ambivalence may be on display, as he or she pokes fun at the parents' behavior during competition and at practice while at the same time protecting the parents from suggestions by the therapist that the parents are overly involved. After a few sessions, it becomes plausible to schedule separate meetings for parents and athlete. In the meetings with parents, issues may come up that had been dropped long ago as the family's attention became diverted toward sport, and the parents may obtain partial relief from the need to be obsessively involved with the athletic accomplishments of their offspring. In the athlete's individual therapy, ambivalence toward athletic participation may become differentiated from ambivalence about parental ambitions. Self-esteem, in other words, may become disentangled from athletic performance.

The formal separation of therapies provides a structure for the loosening of rigid emotional bonds and the differentiation of boundaries. A meeting with the entire family at the end of treatment may provide an opportunity for everyone to confirm that the family has survived this loosening and differentiating intact. Usually the athlete will modify his or her attitude toward the sport without quitting altogether, although the severely dysfunctional "level 3" families described by Hellstedt in chapter 11 may require a complex and multifaceted therapy with many twists and turns.

COUNTERTRANSFERENCE

In any therapy, it is inevitable that therapist and patient will have feelings about each other and about their work. Although the therapist may not choose to explore transference and countertransference feelings, they will nevertheless exist. Frequently, countertransference feelings toward athletes will lead to uncustomary violations of confidentiality. It is not unusual for even well-trained psychiatrists to discuss their famous athletic patients in public and mention them by name in articles in professional journals. A Freudian analyst once mentioned the case of a swimmer he was treating to a colleague who was interested in sport psychiatry. Although the analyst did not mention the athlete's name, he claimed that as a result of the analysis the athlete went "from third to first in the Olympics." When the colleague expressed interest in hearing more details, the analyst declined to provide them in the interest of "confidentiality," even though the most distinguishing feature by which the analysand could be identified had already been revealed.

There are a number of generic sources of countertransference excitement in treating athletes. Both the therapist's personal pleasure in playing sports and the aura of reverence that often surrounds athletes may encourage excessive admiration. This admiration may be enhanced by the perception that athletic competition is especially fair and pure, and that the athlete has succeeded on the basis of performance alone, without recourse to tricks, special favors, or legal maneuvering. The occasional loosening of boundaries of place and time that may accompany the psychotherapy of an athlete encourage the psychiatrist to inappropriately step out of a clinical role. Taking credit for an athlete's performance, playing "coach," and even putting on a uniform in order to "get closer" to the players are manifestations of countertransference that have been seen. Another manifestation involves advocacy for one's particular therapeutic approach, trying to convince the athlete that it "really works." It is also common for therapists to attempt to draw a similarity between their athlete patients and themselves, and inadvertently offend their patients in the process. An Olympic discus thrower, for example, soured on his therapy when his psychiatrist compared the athlete's concerns with "bending and blocking," *termes d'arte* in the discus, with his—the psychiatrist's—own problems "bending" to field ground balls in his recreational softball games.

Unrecognized countertransference feelings may be compounded by an athletically oriented transference created by the athletic patient. In this type of transference, the therapist is chosen to play one of two roles. He may be cast as someone who is extremely knowledgeable about sports, and in this role become tempted to offer observations on athletic techniques, the emotional characteristics of "winners," and other subjects beyond his expertise. Or, the therapist may be subjected to subtle putdowns and provocations, teasing about the obvious shortcomings of his physique, and testing of his memory, ability to take a joke, and knowledge of sports. The therapist may try to protect himself from these attacks by closing off, building himself up, or privately putting down the athlete in return.

All of these countertransference manifestations interfere with honest talk and should be mastered for that reason. Athletes are often bombarded by the emotional and material needs of persons around them, including fans, administrators, coaches, and family. In their environment, communication readily becomes exploitative and deceitful, and the extent to which an athlete perceives any communication in competitive terms may add an extra measure of suspicion to even ordinary discourse. It thus becomes especially important for the therapist to ensure the opportunity for truthful discussion, without the discussion being distorted by the needs of another for vicarious satisfaction. Schafer (1976) has suggested that the efficacy of psychotherapy is based on the internalization of the therapeutic process. Nothing is more important for an athlete's therapy than the opportunity to internalize truthful dialogue.

REFERENCES

Begel, D. (1994, May). *Psychodynamic performance enhancement.* Presentation at the annual meeting of the International Society for Sport Psychiatry, Washington, D.C.

Beisser, A. R. (1967). *The madness in sports.* New York: Appleton-Century-Crofts.

Ogilvie, B. (1997, May). *My life in sports.* Presentation at the annual meeting of the International Society for Sport Psychiatry, San Diego, CA.

Schafer, R. (1976). *A new language for psychoanalysis.* New Haven: Yale University.

Tofler, I. R., Knapp, P. K., & Drell, M. J. (1998). The achievement by proxy spectrum in youth sports: Historical perspective and clinical approach to pressured and high-achieving children and adolescents. In I. R. Tofler (Guest Ed.), *Child and adolescent clinics of North America: Sport psychiatry* (Vol. 7, No. 4, pp. 803–820). Philadelphia: Saunders.

11

Family Systems–Based Treatment of the Athlete Family

Jon C. Hellstedt

HOOP DREAMS IS AN AWARD-WINNING FILM that documents the athletic and emotional development of two inner-city basketball players and their families as they progress through adolescence and into young adulthood (Gilbert, James, & Marx, 1994). The film presents a striking case study of the impact of intensive athletic involvement on the family system. Family members project many of their own unfulfilled dreams, hopes, and wishes for a better life onto the two young boys.

Curtis Gates, William's older brother and the parental child in the Gates family, comments on how important William's gaining a Division I scholarship is to him. He states, "This means everything to me. This is the fulfillment of my own dream for myself." This statement illustrates the projection process and family emotional entrapment of a talented young athlete.

But it is not just Curtis who is overinvolved in William's success. His mother, estranged father, extended family, coaches, and his sports medicine team conspire in seeing his basketball success as dream fulfillment and the elixer for urban poverty. These powerful forces result in William losing his spontaneous love of basketball and developing an extrinsic reward system which slowly erodes his performance on the court. The strong emotional forces of family and coach also support a premature return to competition from knee surgery which has disabling long-term effects.

Hoop Dreams vividly portrays how our culture's obsession with sports has penetrated to the deepest level of American family life. Like the broader culture, family cultures sometimes become obsessed with the sport future of their sons and daughters. In these families, powerful emotional forces are at work which have a profound effect on children and family life. These forces result in excessive pressure on developing athletes as well as anxiety and depression, or in developmental delays which prevent the athlete from separating from the family of origin. Finally, conflicts that develop around the degree of sport involvement of the children can result in irreconcilable or poorly managed conflict between the spouses or intense sibling rivalry in the sibling subsystem.

In previous writings (Hellstedt, 1995), I have defined an "athletic family" as a family system that involves parents and their children or adult offspring who are involved in intensive youth sports, collegiate athletics, or professional sports. Many of these families keep a proper perspective and balance athletic and nonathletic family activities. Sport involvement in well-balanced families results in strong familial bonds, excitement, and a shared value system. However, in many athletic families, conflict and dysfunction result from an imbalance in which the energies of the family are too narrowly and intensely focused on the athletic participation of one or more members of the family.

Sadly, as the professionalism and economic power of sports has grown, so have many excesses within American families. The most noticeable is the overinvolved, narcissistic parent who invests excessive psychic energy in the athletic successes of his or her children. The "little league parent" syndrome can be easily observed at soccer games, high-school basketball games, and hockey tournaments in every town and city across America. It has also penetrated the clinical practices of psychologists and psychiatrists. Many of the families who present for treatment have some involvement in youth sports; some are casual soccer or T-ball families, but others are overinvolved emotionally and financially in their children's athletic development. It is also becoming more commonplace for elite athletes and/or their families to present for treatment, either with complaints of intrapsychic genesis or with family conflict that results from the stresses of intense athletic involvement.

A well-functioning and supportive family is an essential social support for athletes. Many studies document that the family is the source of support that affirms the young athlete's sense of self (Kesend, 1991). Social support is also of great importance in giving an athlete a proper set of tools for dealing with injury, excessive stress, and the pressures of competition (Smith, Smoll, & Ptacek, 1990).

It seems, therefore, that understanding the family system of the athlete provides a rich resource for predicting and optimizing both the athlete's performance and sense of self-competence. It provides a useful way of understanding the process of individuation that underlies personal development. Whether treatment focuses on the whole family, subgroups of the family, or work with an individual athlete using a family-focused framework, a family systems approach is of great value to the sports therapist.

This chapter will first describe a model for athlete-family interaction and development, and then some various treatment approaches based on this model. Clinical examples from these families will be used throughout the chapter as case examples.

A FAMILY SYSTEMS MODEL

There are many different perspectives and emphases among family theorists. There is basic agreement, however, that the family is an interacting social system in which the component parts affect one another and that symptom formation in an individual is embedded in developmental impasses or structural problems within the individual's family.

There are three major influences within the family therapy movement that are useful in working with athlete families. First, the structural model of family functioning developed by Minuchin (1974) maintains that the basic structural components of the family are the power hierarchy, that is, the rules that guide the behavior of family members, interactional communication styles, and the nature of emotional boundaries between the subsystems. Second, the developmental perspective of Bowen (1978) elaborated upon by Carter and McGoldrick (1999) provides normative task-based markers for individuation of the family member from the family system. Third, Rolland (1994) developed a model for how families deal with excessive stresses of chronic illness and disability. Many of Rolland's observations can be applied to work with families where similar stressors from intensive athletic involvement are present.

TYPOLOGY OF ATHLETE FAMILIES

Generally, there are three types of families that present for treatment. These families lie on a continuum from reasonably healthy to highly dysfunctional. Because the presenting problems and therapeutic needs of these three groups are so vastly different, it is necessary to define the differences between the family types. Genograms for each description appear at the end of the discussion (page 212) to further illustrate these differences. Therapeutic goals will be discussed later in the chapter.

Level 1 Families

In terms of degree of dysfunction, level 1 families form a system that generally functions well, but the parents feel the athlete or the family is experiencing conflict, which affects others within the family. These families usually consult a therapist to help them maintain a proper perspective and resolve minor conflicts within the family and self-esteem issues with the developing athlete

Mr. and Mrs. Whitehead have two children, Melissa, 17, and Caroline 15. The two daughters have been involved in figure skating since they were 10 years old, and are now competing with one another for the top spot at various competitions. Melissa achieved early success in her competitions but now Caroline is passing her by in recent finishes. Melissa has developed an adjustment disorder characterized by low self-esteem, loss of a sense of personal competence, discouragement, and high precompetition anxiety. Mr. and Mrs. Whitehead ask for a consultation to learn how to manage Melissa's difficulties.

Level 2 Families

This second group of families is engaged in patterns that strain time and financial resources, resulting in a stressful family environment which negatively affects both the children and adults. Unhealthy or dysfunctional triangles develop, marital conflict emerges, and the family system occasionally reaches an emotional impasse. This is the largest group of families that are referred or who self-refer for treatment.

The main focus of the Greenfield family is a recent conflict involving Cheryl Anne, a 20-year-old Division I basketball player at a large university. Her sister, Angela, is 18, several months away from high-school graduation, and a two-sport athlete. She plans to attend another university but not continue with athletics. Because of Cheryl Anne's talents and successes as a high-school and collegiate athlete, the family has focused much of its time and energy on her career, and has somewhat neglected Angela. During her summer vacation, Cheryl Anne is home training and announces to her parents that she is in love with another woman. Her "coming out" throws the family into a crisis, which brings up intense conflict.

Level 3 Families

A third group of families are those who are headed by at least one, but sometimes two, overzealous or narcissistic parents who create a family system that becomes severely dysfunctional, with high levels of conflict becoming chronic or intensifying over time. The differing levels of intensity and emotional involvement of the parents in the child's sport career often result in severe marital schism and, in some cases, high-conflict divorce. As these families move through the developmental stages of family life, they become increasingly dysfunctional. The projections and power manipulations of one or both of the parents influence the entire system. Children get trapped in emotional binds. In families where one or more of the children are involved in athletics, this projection process can have a crippling effect. Severe systemic pathology or dysfunction can result, which takes the form of extreme marital conflict, divorce, or child abuse.

The Blackburn family consists of divorced parents Myrone and Wilma and their two sons, Ryan, 15, and Toby, 13. Ryan is a nonathlete but a very bright and talented student. Toby is a talented athlete and is on the verge of becoming a highly sought-after soccer goalie. The crisis that precipitated treatment was a restraining order taken out by Mrs. Blackburn to protect Toby from verbal and physical abuse during recent visits with his father. Toby complains of longstanding verbal and physical abuse related to his lack of effort as a goalie on an elite youth soccer club team.

Joe and Patricia Altona sought marital therapy to salvage their relationship. They presented with severe marital discord, sexual inactivity, and a threat on Patricia's part that they either fix the problems in their relationship or head to the divorce court. In the initial interview, it becomes apparent that they have been in open conflict since the departure of their son James, a nationally ranked diver. After solid finishes at the nationals, James made a decision to attend a prestigious university and take an educational moratorium from his athletic career. James's father, Joe, was the primary parent in his sport career and hid many of the costs of his training from Patricia. He ran up large debts, which resulted in the refinancing of the house in order to pay for James's athletic expenses.

In the initial interview it became clear that James is a fulfillment of many of Joe's unfulfilled wishes for himself. Only modestly successful in his career, James's success became wish fulfillment for Joe. Patricia, who was the oldest daughter in a high-conflict alcoholic family, is a conflict avoider and ignored many of the deceptions involving Joe and James. When James left for college, Joe and Patricia felt a huge loss. The son in whom they could bury their conflict is gone and now they have to face each other.

In all of these cases a family systems–based method of treatment was utilized. This approach is based on systemic concepts such as boundary formation, triangulation, and a task-based stage theory of family development.

COMPONENTS OF FAMILY FUNCTIONING IN ATHLETE FAMILIES

Four systemic components are present in all families, and are useful theoretical constructs when working with athlete families. These components are the level of cohesion in the family, the nature of emotional boundaries between family members, patterns of triangulation in the family, and developmental impasses in the family life cycle. The components described below are the author's adaptation of constructs described by Rolland (1994) and the developmental framework of Carter and McGoldrick (1999).

Cohesion

To the outside observer, many athlete families often appear to be highly cohesive, well-functioning family units. Athlete families are highly organized systems with clear rules and expectations. The parents are success-

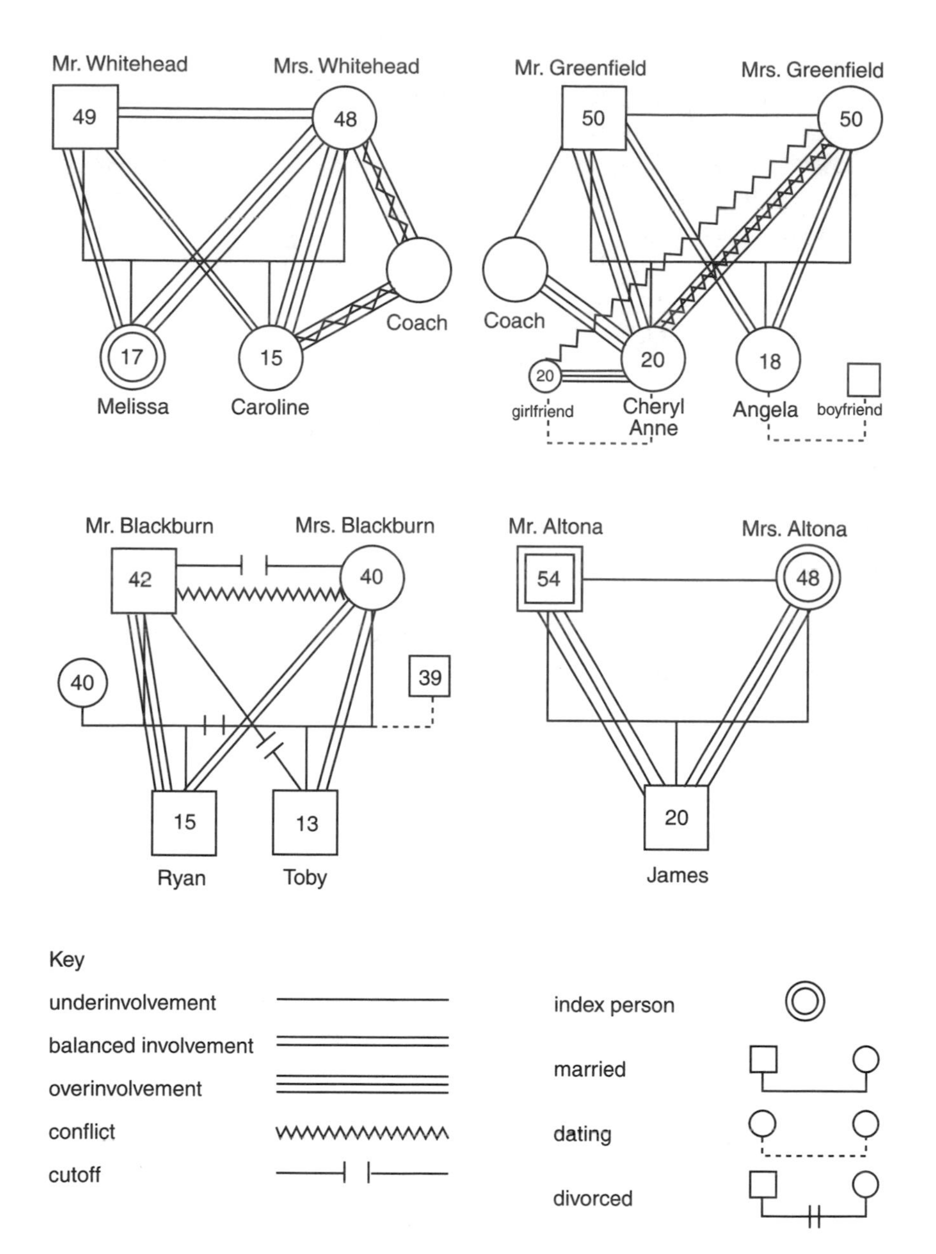

Figure 11.1 Genograms depicting the typology of athlete families.

ful and have high expectations for their children. The family spends considerable time together traveling to events and competitions. Once there, parents and youth engage in many pre- and postevent interactive rituals. While this closeness has some very positive qualities, it also can be a cover-up for latent conflict and unexpressed anger.

The Greenfield family looks like the ideal family: two parents who appear to get along well, an athletically gifted daughter who has a full scholarship at a prestigious university, and another daughter who has very clear career goals and firm educational plans. The parents organize around the expectations they have for their children. However, the cohesion in the family hides some tensions around individuation. Mr. and Mrs. Greenfield are enmeshed parents who have become overinvolved in their children's development; they have lost the enjoyment of their own marital relationship and are having difficulty letting their young-adult daughters make their own decisions. There is a system imbalance in the direction of the commitment to their young athlete's sport involvement.

Boundaries

A boundary is the space, or lack of space, that separates the cognitive and psychic systems of individual family members from one another. Rolland (1994) describes interpersonal boundaries within the family as rules that define the relationship and the degree of separation between family members. Boundaries also refer to the degree of overlap or separation between subsystems within the family (such as the parental or sibling subsystem) and between the family and the outside world (external family boundary). Family boundaries are on a continuum from enmeshment to disengagement. Enmeshed boundaries are characterized by considerable overlap of one family member in the cognitive, affective, or behavioral sphere of other members. Disengaged boundaries are characterized by a lack of involvement of members in one another's affective or behavioral sphere. While athlete families can fall anywhere along this continuum, the families that present for treatment often occur at the enmeshed end. Both parents may have permeable boundaries or there may be one parent who is enmeshed with the athlete offspring, and another who is more disengaged.

Even though they are divorced, Mr. and Mrs. Blackburn attend all of Toby's soccer games. Mrs. Blackburn looks upon Toby's soccer as a fun activity and a chance for him to meet friends. Mr. Blackburn is more intense. He is convinced that his 13-year-old son is going to be an outstanding soccer goalie. He constantly attempts to motivate him with harsh performance demands and motivational pep talks. After a game in which his son played poorly, Mr. Blackburn took his son aside and within earshot of the other players, coaches, and parents, berated him for his poor performance. Later that evening, Toby and his father had an argument about his play earlier in the day and Mr. Blackburn hit his son several times. Mrs. Blackburn was very angry at her ex-husband's behavior and went to court and obtained a restraining order to prohibit continued visitations between Toby and his father.

Cheryl Anne Greenfield is home for the summer vacation. She is in her second year of college and is struggling to keep a starting position on the team. She has some nagging injuries and is involved in a daily workout routine. She is also working on the staff of a summer sport camp. Toward the end of the summer she announces to her parents that she developed a lesbian relationship during the past year. Her parents, especially her mother, are thrown into a major crisis. Her mother becomes depressed and is not able to eat or sleep. She also begins to talk of suicide because she feels she has been "a complete failure as a mother." A family consultation with mother, father, and Cheryl Anne shows a previously cohesive family with enmeshed boundaries. Both parents have been emotionally involved in Cheryl Anne's life but mother was the emotional "center" of the family. Mr. Greenfield and the two daughters protected her and worked hard not to upset her. Cheryl Anne's decision to be involved in a lesbian relationship throws the family into a state of crisis. Mr. Greenfield plays the role of the rescuer and mediator, supporting his wife and telling her that she has been a good mother; at the same time he tries to support his daughter's decision. He finds himself caught in a bind between his wife and Cheryl Anne.

The boundary systems in these families are enmeshed and the parents are overinvolved in the life of their children. However, the degree of enmeshment varies between the parents, resulting in an imbalance with one parent being more emotionally involved than the other in the athletic activities of the child. The family organizes its time around the athletic activity of the child and as the child approaches adolescence, the parents want to continue to control the child and the transition from dependence to autonomy is difficult and conflictual. The athlete is often confronted with two choices—conform to parental wishes to the detriment of his or her sense of self or rebel and abandon athletics entirely.

Toby Blackburn has quit playing soccer. Though a very talented player, he cannot tolerate his father's emotional intensity and lack of control. He refuses to visit with his father and to play on his club team. He is giving up something that he enjoys because of his need to establish some boundaries in his relationship with his father.

Triangulation

Triangulation occurs when two people, often the husband and wife, avoid dealing with the conflict between them by focusing their attention on a third member of the family, often the athletic adolescent or young adult. The most common form of triangulation is between an overinvolved father, his athlete son or daughter, and a somewhat excluded mother.

In the Altona family, father and son conspired in a relationship that excluded mother. Father and son would travel together to practice and competitions. Father would also clandestinely keep the costs from mother, until she found out he was about to refinance their house to pay for the son's coaching.

Another type of triangle is found in Cheryl Anne's family. The parents formed an alliance in which they buried their relationship conflict, put all their energies into the daughter's development, and neglected their own relationship. When this type of triangle occurs, the result is an athlete-centered family. Unfortunately, many athlete families become athlete-centered rather than family-centered. The young athlete and his or her world of coaches, training, traveling, and competing become the emotional center of the family. Triangles often involve nonfamily members as well. The most common form of external triangle involves the coach or, in some cases, the whole sport organization (Hellstedt, 1987). External triangles often occur in enmeshed families when the parents are not able to make room for another authority figure in the life of their son or daughter. When the coach begins to preempt the parent's influence, conflict develops between the parents and the coach. When there is a coalition, the coach (as is the case in the Altona family) becomes part of the triangle that excludes the other parent. In some cases the coach actually becomes a family member and allies with, or is in opposition to, the parental subsystem. In extreme cases, coaches become the parental subsystem of the family and the parents lose power and authority and become part of the child subsystem.

Melissa Whitehead's coach is a very authoritarian and controlling figure. He sets up many of the rules that the two competitive girls have to follow. Training is daily; mental skills training is weekly. Mrs. Whitehead volunteers to be the manager of the team, a position in which she has to contact other parents in the club to arrange transportation, collect fees, and organize workers at the competitions. Mr. Whitehead is very busy at his job and gets left out of the triangle. When asked if the coach was aware of the conflict between the girls and that the family had sought psychological consultation to deal with low self-esteem in the oldest daughter, Mrs. Whitehead indicates she does not want the coach to know about this. They fear it might form a negative impression in the coach's mind about the oldest daughter.

Another familiar pattern in triangulation with coaches is when the coach meets resistance when he or she attempts to influence the athlete in ways that are incompatible with one or both of the parents. There are many examples in the sport of tennis or golf when the parents are overinvolved with the athlete and prevent an alliance between the athlete and the coach. Coaches get fired because they do not view the athlete's talents or training emphasis in the same way the parents do.

Developmental Impasses

Analogous to the stages of individual personality development, a family undergoes a constantly changing developmental process. A useful perspective on this process of change and the connections between generations as the family develops is provided by Bowen (1978). Bowen's insights have been enhanced by Carter and McGoldrick's (1999) developmental framework. This framework is basic to the model developed in this chapter. Carter and McGoldrick state that the family is a social system that passes through a life cycle. Similar to the individual life cycle (Erikson, 1950), the family life cycle is a series of stages with certain tasks that need to be accomplished before the next stage of development can be successfully mastered. If these tasks are not completed in the early stages, there will be problems in later stages of development. The transitions from one stage to the next are particularly stressful for families and are often when symptoms appear in individual family members or in the family system as a whole.

The demands of athletic competition and training often present unique circumstances to families that are deviations from the "normal" family life cycle. For example, a young gymnast and her family may experience premature separation brought on by her leaving home for specialized coaching. A swimmer or figure skater must train many hours a day, absorbing family resources, which affects the entire family. In order to accomplish these daily demands, parents have to take an active role, often delaying the adolescent's progress toward independence. Such developmental delays, barriers, or impasses can negatively affect the young athlete. In the typical developmental delay, the family becomes so focused on the athletic career of the young adult that he or she is not allowed to work outside the home, finish his or her education, or emotionally separate from the family system. This developmental delay in the family life cycle is analogous to the identity foreclosure phase in the individual life cycle (Pearson & Petitpas, 1990).

The developmental stages and tasks of families are presented in table 11.1. There are constant stresses in the family system as the family passes through these stages. In athlete families, the normal stresses of family life are compounded by the sport-related stress brought on by financial pressures (the high cost of training, travel, and equipment), time management (blending training schedules and academic demands), and competition-based performance anxiety for both the athlete and the athlete's parents.

The two stages of family development that are particularly problematic for athlete families are the "family with adolescent children" and the "launching children and moving on." As indicated in column 2 of table 11.1, the major task of the adolescent family is to increase flexibility of family boundaries to allow for gradual independence of the child. Column 4 indicates that boundary flexibility requires parents to support independent decision-making, encourage nonsport social and intellectual development, and to maintain a spousal relationship apart from the activities of the child athlete. As is indicated throughout this chapter, powerful forces work against the development of this boundary flexibility. The resolution of adolescent identity issues can be easily delayed by the financial and functional demands of sport specialization.

Likewise, the launching stage is difficult for athlete families to negotiate. Accepting their children as adults and allowing entries and exits from the family is difficult for parents who engage in the family projection

TABLE 11.1
Stages and Major Tasks of Athletic Family Development

*STAGE OF FAMILY DEVELOPMENT**	*MAJOR TRANSITIONAL TASKS**	*GENERAL CHANGES NEEDED TO PROCEED DEVELOPMENTALLY**	*ATHLETIC FAMILY CHANGES NEEDED TO PROCEED DEVELOPMENTALLY*
Single young adult	Differentiation of self from parents and family of origin	a. Become emotionally and financially independent from family b. Develop intimate peer relationships c. Establish work and career identity	a. Attain psychological peace with athletic successes, failures, and unfulfilled dreams b. Resolve unfulfilled expectations from their parents c. View present and future athletic involvement as a mode of self-fulfillment and physical well-being
New married couple	Commitment and bonding in a new relationship	a. Develop internal relationship patterns in areas of commitment, caring, communication, and conflict resolution b. Perform external relationship tasks such as work and recreation to allow adequate space for marital relationship c. Realign family-of-origin and peer relationships to include spouse	a. Maintain boundary around athletic involvement to allow space for spousal relationship b. Join together with spouse in developing mutually fulfilling athletic and exercise activities

*Data from Carter & McGoldrick (1989)

Family with young children (children ages 4–12)	Accepting children into the family system	a. Adjust career and marital relationships to make space for children b. Share parenting and household management tasks with spouse c. Realign relationships with parents to include grandparental roles.	a. Introduce children to a variety of individual and team sport environments b. Provide or secure quality coaching and safe sport environment for proper skill development c. Emphasize fun and skill development and minimize competitive success d. Maintain permeable boundaries to allow for nonathletic individual and family experiences e. Demonstrate family value of hard work and goal attainment by parental example and role modeling rather than verbal persuasion
Family with adolescent children (children ages 13–18)	Increase flexibility of family boundaries to allow for gradual independence of children	a. Allow for gradual shift from parent to adolescent child in decision-making b. Develop permeable external family boundary to permit entrances and exits of adolescent and peers to and from family system c. Maintain strength of spousal subsystem within the family d. Refocus spouses on midlife identity, marital, and career issues	a. Encourage and support commitment of child-athlete to sport generalization or specialization depending on child's skills and desires b. Provide financial and emotional support without straining family financial and emotional resources c. Encourage permeable family and self boundaries to allow for nonsport social and intellectual involvement d. Allow for increasing independence of child-athlete in decision-making e. Secure safe and productive coaching environment for child-athlete

(continued)

Table 11.1
Continued

*STAGE OF FAMILY DEVELOPMENT**	*MAJOR TRANSITIONAL TASKS**	*GENERAL CHANGES NEEDED TO PROCEED DEVELOPMENTALLY**	*ATHLETIC FAMILY CHANGES NEEDED TO PROCEED DEVELOPMENTALLY*
			f. Allow for shift of influence on child-athlete from parents to teacher/coach g. Encourage and support goal attainment and work ethic through both role modeling and verbal teaching h. Maintain spousal identity and relationship apart from athletic activites of child-athlete
Launching children and moving on (children ages 18–late 20s)	Accept children as adults and allow entries and exits from family system	a. Refocus on spousal system as a dyad b. Develop adult-to-adult relationships with grown children c. Realign relationships with adult children to include spouses, in-laws, and grandchildren d. Accept disabilities and death in grandparental generation	a. Allow athlete to gain financial and emotional independence from parents b. Continue emotional support and crisis intervention if necessary c. Identify family as a "refuge" from the pressures and rigors of competition d. Accept authority of coach and accept lesser role in coach/parent/athlete triangle e. Reestablish spousal relationship in absence of direct involvment in athletic activity of children

			f. Continue participation in recreational sport for personal fulfillment and health maintenance g. Assist grown child athlete's retirement from competition and the transition from competitive athletics to career and work life
Family in later life (adult offspring ages late 20s to middle age)	Accept shift of generational roles	a. Maintain spousal relationship in face of decline in physical strength b. Support a central role in the family system of middle generation c. Enjoy grandparental role with youngest generation d. Engage in life review and integration e. Prepare for and enjoy a fulfilling retirement f. Prepare for loss of spouse, friends, and, eventually, one's own death	a. Complete unresolved issues over athletic accomplishments of grown children b. Assist adult athlete in retirement from competition and emotional resolution of the end of career c. Focus on nonathletic activities with spouse and grown children d. Participate in recreational sport and exercise for personal fulfillment and health maintenance

process and who have strong narcissistic needs that result in continued control over their athletic children. This is also the developmental stage when many conflicts with coaches emerge as parents refuse to let go of their children and trust their athletic development to the coach. It is often the transition from the adolescent stage to the launching stage that is most stressful for athlete families.

Cheryl Anne Greenfield is struggling with the launching phase in her family. Mom and Dad have always been overprotective. They have indulged her by taking care of her meal preparation, clothing, and some of her decision-making. They encouraged her to pick a university (she was recruited by several) near home so they could see her frequently and attend games. They become friendly with her coach and very involved in the activities of the team. They encouraged Cheryl Anne to spend summers at home and didn't demand that she work outside the home, partly to allow her time for extensive off-season training. When away at school Cheryl Anne calls home several times a week for long conversations with her mother. Her parents are continually trying to get her to date a boy that she had a brief relationship with in high school.

The stress that families face as they struggle to meet these developmental tasks is referred to as horizontal stress (Carter & McGoldrick, 1999). Stress is greatest in families during times of transition from one stage to the next. A common example is of an overinvolved or enmeshed father being unable to tolerate his son's normal drive toward independence. The father believes that he must continue to monitor and motivate the son to ensure that he will not deviate from training and competition. This father will overstructure the son with special coaching, summer camps, club teams, and equipment in order to keep him focused on his development as an athlete. This control inhibits the son from developing autonomy and meaningful peer relationships and produces a developmental delay. The son's life is controlled by the father. When the son begins to make the transition to young adulthood and wants to make his own decisions, the father is threatened with loss of control.

There is another type of stress, however, that often intersects with horizontal stress. Vertical stressors (Carter & McGoldrick, 1999) are the psychological issues that are passed down in families between generations. These can be major emotional conflicts involving losses or unresolved grief, family secrets, or components of the family projection process.

Joe Altona's father was an abusive alcoholic. Joe grew up feeling alone and both fearful of and abandoned by his father. He made up stories about his father to his friends in an attempt to convince himself and others that he had a real family. This abandonment as a child resulted in Joe developing an enmeshed relationship with his son, James.

When horizontal and vertical stressors intersect, there is a large increase in the intensity of conflict within the family. For example, when a father who feels abandoned by his own father and is in search of a replacement for that lost relationship (vertical stressor) is confronted by a situation in which his late adolescent son or daughter is developing a close attachment to an influential coach (horizontal stressor), an alarm of gigantic psychic proportions goes off. He attempts to hang onto his son or daughter by whatever means are available. Horizontal and vertical stressors intersected for the Altona family when James reached 10 years of age. In one of the conjoint therapy sessions, Patricia said, "I feel that when James was 10, Joe became obsessed with his diving. He wouldn't let him go to any practices or competitions alone. He had to be there to guide James." Investigation of family-of-origin issues discovered that Mr. Altona felt he lost his own father to alcohol at about the same age.

TREATMENT APPROACHES

Assessment and Treatment Goals

What makes family-based treatment different from more individual forms of sport therapeutic interventions is that the goal is to establish systemic change within the family rather than address the coping mechanisms of the individual members. This systemic change will in turn promote the affective growth and athletic development of the adolescent or young adult. In general, therapy seeks the following general goals:

- Work with families to identify sources of stress, especially those affecting the young athlete.
- Promote individuation within the family.
- Help families negotiate developmental transitions.
- improve communication patterns and problem-solving abilities.
- Seek to change the family from a source of stress for the young athlete to a refuge from the pressures of athletic involvement.

Assessment of family dysfunction is based on a structural analysis, the identification of unmet developmental tasks (horizontal stresses), and intergenerational conflicts (vertical stresses) that might be present in the family. This aspect of the assessment will identify the subsystems in the family, the types of boundaries, and any obvious triangulations. In the first session, taking a family history using the genogram (Hellstedt, 1995; McGoldrick, Gerson, & Shellenberger, 1999) will also help identify vertical stressors. Horizontal stress can be identified based on the developmental tasks identified in table 11.1. A three- or four-session format is useful for completing a family system assessment. When possible, sessions with the parental dyad, the sibling subsystem, and the whole family should be conducted. At the final assessment session, the therapist should present some observations to the family based on system analysis and identification of developmental tasks, as well as a treatment plan.

Treatment

Based on the assessment, the specific goals of family treatment vary depending on the presenting problem, the sources of stress, and the level of family dysfunction. The modality of treatment with these families usually involves the following: individual therapy with a family systems focus, therapy with subsystems of the family, or treatment with all family members present.

Level 1 Families

Because level 1 families are usually meeting the needs of their individual members, extensive therapy is usually not necessary. The intervention goals involve changes in activities, schedules, routines, and opening up new channels of communication. With these families a preventive-educative approach, where the family therapist serves as a consultant to the parents and the family, is often adequate. The family system is only slightly off track, there are no significant vertical stressors, and the index person in the family is in need of only minor intervention.

In the case of the Whitehead family, two consultations were held initially with Mr. and Mrs. Whitehead. During these sessions, a history was taken and a genogram completed. Neither parent presented significant family-of-origin issues. The focus of their concern was Melissa, who seemed to be having a crisis of competence and self-esteem. The therapist discussed with the parents the stressful task of parenting in an athletic family and the importance of Melissa's setting improved-performance rather than outcome goals. It was suggested that the parents structure nonathletic times together as a family and set aside times for all their children where they don't have to train intensively. The overtraining syndrome (McCann, 1995) was discussed, as was the danger of burnout if the children did not have some periodic breaks from the training regime. It was also suggested that Melissa compete in venues that did not involve her younger sister.

Three individual sessions were held with Melissa. The therapist helped her focus on the areas of her own performance that she wished to improve rather than focusing on how she finished relative to her sister. She had two upcoming competitions during the time she was being seen, so for each event the therapist helped her formulate some self-improvement goals. Relaxation methods were introduced and some positive cognitive cues were substituted for the negative precompetition thoughts she had been having. After three sessions, Melissa said she was doing much better and didn't feel the need to continue therapy.

Level 2 Families

Level 2 families require greater focus on both structural change within the family system and the completion of developmental tasks where there is a developmental delay. The emphasis in treating these families is on making modifications in triangles, boundaries, and the degree of individuation allowed for individual members. In most cases, the goal of therapy is to promote individuation of the young athlete so that he or she can think, act, and feel independently of the family belief system. Therapy with these families often involves sessions with the whole family present, as well as sessions with subsystems, particularly the parental dyad.

The main focus of the treatment for the Greenfield family was on boundary change and the re-establishment of the dyadic relationship between the parents. The extensive enmeshment in the boundaries between Mr. and Mrs. Greenfield in Cheryl Anne's life was identified early in treatment. The parents were able to see this as a problem and the therapist worked with them to spend less time worrying about Cheryl Anne or talking with her on the phone when she was away at school. Two sessions with all family members present were held at which Cheryl Anne discussed her lesbian relationship and how important it was to her. Mrs. Greenfield was very open about her distaste for that choice and encouraged her daughter to pursue heterosexual relationships. Mr. Greenfield expressed his sadness over her choice but was more accepting of Cheryl Anne's decision than was Mrs. Greenfield. Angela expressed her support for Cheryl Anne and her desire that her parents focus more on their own relationship rather than worrying about the children. Angela also expressed her fears of what would happen when both she and Cheryl Anne were away at school during the coming school year.

After Cheryl Anne and Angela returned to school in the fall, four conjoint marital therapy sessions were held with Mr. and Mrs. Greenfield. These sessions focused on rediscovering connections in their own relationship that had been overlooked for most of the past decade. They were encouraged to find new activities that they both enjoyed and to communicate more about their own relationship than about their two daughters. They were also encouraged to visit Cheryl Anne less during the school year and to attend fewer of her games. This was hard for them, but they saw the value of lessening their connections. Visits to Angela at her university helped them to balance the emotional energy they invested in their two daughters.

After a total of six sessions, some structural change had taken place within the family. The intense triangles were detoxified and the need for less permeable boundaries was established. The impact on individual family members was noticeable. Cheryl Anne was happy that she had "come out" to her parents and established her own space within the family. Although Mrs. Greenfield stated she will "never accept" Cheryl Anne's sexual object choice, she reported no suicidal ideation, less depression, and more ability to openly communicate her feelings with both her husband and her daughters.

Level 3 Families

Therapy with these families is difficult, often longer-term, and sometimes involves a team of therapists, interaction with the court system, and therapeutic interventions at many different levels. The conflict level is high and frequently feels unresolvable. The goal with these families is system redefinition. Serious and deep family wounds exist. Often there is a disengaged or divorced family structure, with spouses engaged in chronic warfare. A new family system has to be defined.

Therapy with the Altona family involved conjoint marital sessions to help Mr. and Mrs. Altona redefine their relationship. When they presented for therapy, lawyers had already been consulted regarding a divorce. The therapist began therapy by asking them to suspend judgment on pursuing a divorce until some therapeutic work could be done. Conjoint sessions helped them explore the reasons why they had developed such a dysfunctional triangle involving themselves and James. The therapist helped them to see that the intensive sport involvement with James had set up a collusive relationship between James and his father that excluded Mrs. Altona. It was also pointed out to them that James's temporary leave of absence from his diving was a way to break the triangulation and get them to resolve their differences with one another. The therapist asked Mr. and Mrs. Altona to confront their own family-of-origin issues and to see how the breakdown in their relationship resulted from problems with their own parents. Both were able to see how they used their relationship with James as an attempt to heal the many wounds from their pasts. A year of therapy was needed to heal their wounds, achieve a commitment to stay together, and develop appropriate boundaries with James so that he could make his own decisions as to whether he would return to competitive diving.

Because of the deep schisms within the family, therapy with the Blackburn family involved a team approach. During a custody dispute that followed the restraining order, a guardian ad litem was appointed to assess the family. The recommendation was for Mr. Blackburn to receive therapy for anger management, Toby and Ryan to receive therapy to deal with the impact of the high-conflict divorce on their own lives, and another therapist to serve as a parental coordinator to meet with Mr. and Mrs. Blackburn to help them work collaboratively as coparents. The treatment team's goals were to help Toby and Ryan deal with the stress in the family, bring the parents together around decision-making, and heal the deep wounds in the relationship between Toby and his father. Because of the author's background as a sports psychologist/family therapist, he was designated as the therapist to work with both boys, but more intensely with Toby. Individual sessions with Toby are ongoing and often focused on his ambivalence toward soccer and his anger toward his father. After a year of individual therapy, Toby still refuses to visit with his father. He has taken up another sport and has decided that he will resume visitation with his father when he is ready. He has set new boundaries for himself in the family system.

CONCLUSION

Family systems–based therapy is an exciting and fruitful area of therapeutic work for the sports therapist. It requires a thorough understanding of both family systems theory, sport science, and an appreciation of the stress level that constantly confronts athletically involved families. Therapy with these families is often exciting, and sometimes difficult. Developing an alliance with various family members requires great skill and the family sports therapist must constantly deal with the resistance of both family members and the family system to the prospect of change. Working with families requires flexibility of approach and time, and willingness to have evening and extended session appointments and to be part of a treatment team. The sports family therapist needs to be an active therapist, structuring sessions and constantly fighting against the family's unwritten rules about avoiding or enjoying conflict, "allergies" around closeness, and an unwillingness to engage in joint problem-solving. While family-centered approaches to sports psychiatry and psychology are in their infancy and more theoretical approaches and clinical guidelines are needed, it is an exciting clinical subspecialty.

REFERENCES

Bowen, M. (1978). *Family therapy in clinical practice*. New York: Jason Aronson.

Carter, B., & McGoldrick, M. (Eds). (1989). *The changing family life cycle: A framework for family therapy* (2nd ed.). Boston: Allyn & Bacon.

Carter, B., & McGoldrick, M. (Eds.). (1999). *The expanded family life cycle: Individual, family, and social perspectives* (3rd ed.). Boston: Allyn & Bacon.

Erikson, E. (1950). *Childhood and society*. New York: Norton.

Gilbert, P., James, S., & Marx, F. (1994) *Hoop Dreams* [film]. Kartemquin Educational Films. (Available from Turner Publishing Inc., 1050 Techwood Drive, NW, Atlanta, GA 30318)

Hellstedt, J. (1987). The coach/parent/athlete relationship. *The Sport Psychologist*, *1*, 151–160.

Hellstedt, J. (1995). Invisible players: A family systems model. In S. Murphy (Ed.), *Sport psychology interventions* (pp. 117–146). Champaign, IL: Human Kinetics.

Kesend, O. (1991). *The elite athlete's sources of encouragement and discouragement affecting their motivation to participate in sport: A qualitative study from a development perspective*. Unpublished doctoral dissertation, The Union Institute, Cincinnati, OH.

McCann, S. (1995). Overtraining and burnout. In S. Murphy (Ed.), *Sport psychology interventions*. Champaign, IL: Human Kinetics.

McGoldrick, M., Gerson, R., & Shellenberger, S. (1999). *Genograms: Assessment and intervention*. New York: Norton.

Minuchin, S. (1974). *Families and family therapy*. Cambridge, MA: Harvard University.

Pearson, R., & Petitpas, A. (1990). Transitions of athletes: Developmental and prevention perspective. *Journal of Counseling and Development*, *69*, 7–10.

Rolland, J. (1994) *Families, Illness, and Disability*. New York: Basic.

Smith, R., Smoll, F., & Ptacek, J. (1990). Conjunctive moderator variables in vulnerability and resiliency research: Life stress, social support and coping skills, and adolescent sport injuries. *Journal of Personality and Social Psychology*, *58*, 360–370.

12

Psychiatric Consultation to Athletic Teams

Robert W. Burton

PSYCHIATRISTS ARE WELL EQUIPPED to serve as consultants to athletic teams. Armed with knowledge of the human psyche and soma and organized by the biopsychosocial model that applies so well to sport performance, a psychiatrist can make a real difference. A psychiatric perspective is helpful at all levels of competition, from youth sports to the big leagues. Since psychological attitudes rather than physical attributes are most of what separates the more elite athletes from each other, the impact of a psychiatrist may be most apparent at this level. When one considers the span of an athlete's career, however, the opportunity to have the greatest positive influence is clearly with the younger athletes. The sport psychiatrist, like the psychiatrist in more purely clinical settings, is in a position to limit impairment and to optimize functioning and satisfaction.

Just as psychotherapists are most effective when they have a specific theoretical framework to work from, psychiatrists consulting to a team will similarly benefit from having an organized theoretical understanding and approach to their work with a team. Fortunately, psychiatrists are familiar with an excellent model from their training experience in consultation/liaison (C/L) psychiatry. The application of a C/L psychiatry model to consulting to athletic teams is a extremely useful for approaching the challenge and offers a way to effectively meet the conflicting needs of players, coaches, management, other team members, and staff. It also offers sufficient flexibility that allows for the intervention to be tailored to the particular characteristics of the team while maintaining an athlete-centered focus. The exact role of the consultant and the area or areas of focus can be modified over time as the team evolves.

THE STAGES OF CONSULTATION/LIAISON PSYCHIATRY AND ITS APPLICATION TO THE SPORT TEAM

Consultation/liaison psychiatry developed within the health care system where there was a commitment to the fact that patients' well-being was the primary objective. It grew out of recognition that there were people in the hospital setting that were in need of psychiatric and other medical services and yet were not receiving them (Lipowski, 1974). The office consultation practice model was not meeting these patients' or the health care institutions' needs, and a new one was necessary. The new model brought the consultant to the hospital or clinic setting. It made services more accessible to patients and allowed patients that had either limited resources or greater resistance to be seen by a psychiatrist. If the patient still refused to meet with the consultant, staff members could access the psychiatrist's knowledge base and work with him or her to learn how best to deal with the patient who presented an obstacle to their medical treatment.

Preintervention and Planning

In any C/L psychiatry activity there is a beginning phase, prior to the psychiatrist's involvement, where there is no psychiatrist available (McKegney, 1985). The very end of this stage is when the psychiatric intervention is being planned. The extent of planning and the length of time before a consultant actually appears to work with a team will vary. Ideally, a reasonable amount of time and a thoughtful process will have taken place during which the people in positions of responsibility and power will have clarified their reasons for wanting to involve a psychiatrist in the team's endeavors. Unfortunately, this is not always the case. Such decisions and the ones to hire and fire consultants are often made quickly and with insufficient forethought. On the other hand, some consultants have held long and protracted discussions about possible involvement with a team, sometimes for years before the opportunity is realized. Thus, it is the consultant's first task to determine the reasons his or her services have been retained. This preintervention part of the process is extremely important. It is when first impressions are formed and where the expectations of the consultant are born. If expectations are not adequately articulated and managed at this stage, it will become an obstacle to the success of the intervention. Realistic and unrealistic expectations should be explored and identified.

The biggest potential problem during this planning stage is that it actually begins during the interview process when the consultant is trying to sell the fact that he or she can do what is asked of them. The consultant's desire to get the job may influence the consultant to oversell and create or agree to unrealistic expectations. Once the consultant is hired, there may be little time devoted to covering this territory again with the people that matter. If the consultant feels that he or she is operating under unrealistic expectations at any point in time, these feelings should be addressed and the issues clarified as quickly as possible.

Active Consultation and Liaison

The stage of preintervention and planning is followed by the presence and availability of psychiatric consultation, during which there are increasingly intense liaison activities that build upon the consultation work. The fact that the intervention involves both consultation and liaison bears emphasis. A consultation mode alone without at least some liaison activity as part of the plan is not recommended. There will be so many different responses and reactions to the fact that a psychiatrist has become involved with a team that a forum must exist where these feelings can be expressed and addressed. Explaining the rationale for and process of the intervention during these meetings is extremely useful. Without the liaison activity, the organization's support of the consultant is in question. If the team is to take the psychiatrist seriously, it must make the statement that it is important enough to set aside time for it on a regular basis.

During this phase of active consultation and liaison, the consultant performs individual consultations at the request of the staff and works with the staff to understand the nuances of the process. Who gets seen by the consultant and for what reasons, how the transfer of knowledge concerning the outcome of that evaluation takes place, what information is conveyed, and in what way it will be useful to the team are the salient features. Again, it is essential that there be regular, preferably weekly, meetings with the team. These meetings can be used to discuss a wide range of topics that might be of interest and value to athletes. Examples of these would be psychological aspects of individual and team performance, coping with injury, dealing with the potentially divisive nature of the media, the elements of team building, issues of substance use and abuse, balancing sport with one's personal life, and the role of aggression in sport, among others. These meetings are not only useful for conveying important content and setting an educational tone for those who are receptive to it, they are also forums where the psychiatrist can become known to the players and staff and can in turn get to know them. The relationship that develops will form the foundation for the work that will be done together. Subsequent work may then be done individually, in small groups, or with the team at large.

There is a developmental process and life cycle to the intervention itself. Not only does the staff get to know the consultant and learn basic psychiatric and psychological concepts, there is also a process that takes place that is more indirect, subtle, and to some extent unconscious. The process of the intervention itself inculcates the values and components of effective teamwork, and ideally the consultant and other staff will model these for the players and other team members. These effects will be realized even more when the psychiatrist is a member of a consulting team, ideally one that is multidisciplinary and culturally diverse. For example, one such team consisted of a psychiatrist and two social workers, with one member an African-American and another a woman. When the team observes another, albeit smaller, team functioning well, it can be a powerful lesson.

The Mature Consultation/Liaison Relationship

Ultimately, there can be a stage of primarily liaison work in which the C/L psychiatrist works more or less exclusively with the people who work with the players on a day-to-day basis. This stage may be considered the mature C/L relationship, with an autonomously functioning staff capable of managing the routine situations that arise with players on their own, working together with minimal direct input from the consultant. Depending on the overall developmental stage and personality of the team, the consultant ideally would then have more involvement with leadership, and at times work more directly with them. In the sport setting, as in the hospital, this should be the goal, where the team can function well on its own, and the impetus for initiating the intervention has largely been resolved. The psychiatric consultant may then have little or no direct involvement with the team, except on an as-needed basis. It should be noted that it may take years for a consultant to be fully effective in the active consultation and liaison phase, only after which will the team become less dependent upon him or her and enter this mature phase.

OTHER CONSIDERATIONS IN THE SPORT TEAM SETTING

It is instructive to consider additional parallels and discrepancies between the health care setting and the situation on a sports team where a psychiatric consultant is being brought in. In general, a psychiatrist will be brought in when some need for psychological services is recognized. Usually the focus is on the players, but not necessarily on their health. The sport team's primary objective is successful competition. Only to the extent that a team subscribes to the philosophy that the team's primary goal is served by the players' personal health, growth, and development will a team have an investment in the players' mental health.

In sport, as one advances in age and ability there is a mounting emphasis on winning. Teams at early levels of sport participation, designed for younger and less accomplished athletes, are more likely to be interested in promoting health. It is important for the consultant to understand to what extent developmental objectives coexist with the competitive demands on a given team. It is also crucial for him or her to realize that nonplayer members of the team are in positions of authority over the players and typically determine these objectives. As an example, youth "traveling teams" are adults' creations in order to have more competitive experiences available than are typically found in school, neighborhood, or community organizations. Similarly, professional team owners and managers dictate how far their organizations are willing to go to offer programs for players to develop emotionally and intellectually. They determine the atmosphere and the concrete plans for such programs to be provided to the athletes. Players' unions have won some concessions from owners in these areas, but the fact that they were the result of an adversarial process indicates how the connection between mind and body is being overlooked.

A highly competitive team that is outwardly and consciously motivated toward winning as its primary goal may be forced to acknowledge the relationship between mental health and athletic performance, however. An example is the occasion where a psychiatric problem, often substance related, threatens an important player's ability to continue to perform athletically. In such a case it is arguably the performance concerns that ultimately lead the team to consider psychiatric intervention. Nonetheless, even without these more dramatic examples, the incompatibility between psychiatric problems and optimal sport performance is undeniable. Unfortunately, once a crisis has been averted or resolved, denial, avoidance, and resistance will often return. That mentally healthy athletes will perform better and for longer periods of time is a conclusion that is simple conceptually, but becomes complex in practice.

Most of the psychiatrists who have had the opportunity to work with a team have done so as a result of a psychiatric problem that affected a high-profile and valuable player (Feldman, 1991, Nicholi, 1987), creating an immediate performance concern for the team. Successful resolution of the problem led to the chance to become more broadly involved with the team. In most of these instances, however, the consultant typically has not had specialized training in sport, sports medicine, or athletic performance.

In whatever way it initially comes about, a psychiatrist may be invited to assist the team. There is, at that point, some underlying belief that the psychiatrist can help the team as a whole to play better. The way in which the team thinks the psychiatric consultant can help is important for both parties to attempt to understand from the outset. Chances are the intervention will evolve in a manner that parallels the development of a C/L psychiatry service in a general hospital. Someone in a position of authority will perceive that there is some kind of psychological problem hindering the team with which a psychiatrist might be able to help. This situation parallels the hospital administrator who realizes the overall value of a consulting psychiatrist in a given clinical setting. The consultant will then be interviewed and hired and begin to meet with people involved with the team, many of whom will have suspicions of or various misconceptions about how or why the consultant has been retained. Concerns about confidentiality are commonly expressed around this time. As a consultant to the individual players, the psychiatrist can only be effective if he or she has their trust, and that requires some specific assurances regarding their confidentiality. As in any setting, absolute confidentiality can never be guaranteed; it can only be an ideal that is aspired toward.

Unless the rationale for the hiring of the consultant has been explained to the team, the suspicions and misconceptions that are there will undermine the effectiveness of the consultant. In practice it is an ongoing process of educating and re-educating in this area. Determining various people's understanding and assessing their need to know in depth and in detail what is going on is one of the many challenges of the consultant. Obviously not everyone will need to have the same level of knowledge or involvement with the consultation process.

There are three fairly common reasons that a team will consider the addition of a sport psychiatrist. First and foremost is that there is a recent team performance problem. Typically it is believed to be the result of "problem players." These are players who are perceived as having considerable athletic talent but have not yet lived up to their potential. The natural conclusion is that they have a psychological problem that is holding them back, and that they in turn are holding the team back. Chances are good that such is the case and, further, that the athlete's "macho" attitude has gotten in the way of him or her getting help. By the time the psychiatrist is called in, many other people probably have tried to engage the athlete to try to work on whatever the problem might be, but to no avail. The psychiatrist is thus faced with "treatment-resistant" cases right off the bat. He or she must have a strategy to try to engage these individuals and not expect to find only willing and receptive athletes as clients. Gathering as much information as possible before actually meeting with the athlete is helpful, but the most important thing is to approach the player as a human being apart from his or her athletic talents.

The second common reason for a psychiatrist to become involved with a sports team parallels the typical presenting complaint of married couples for marital psychotherapy: poor communication. As with married couples, such a complaint may in fact indicate any number of causes. A clash in the styles of communication between team members may be the problem. It may also reflect the fact that the relationship between team members has deteriorated to the point where communication is strained or impaired. Sometimes both may be true. Only by directly observing the communication in question and gathering some history can the consultant begin to assess which is the more salient issue. In sport teams where the communication problem is between player and coach, direct observation may in fact be problematic. A psychiatric consultant will not be quickly invited into player-coach meetings, especially those involving a single player and coach. More likely, the consultant will be given one side of the story by the player, who has been identified as "a problem," and the other side by the coach, who is describing the "problem player" in hopes of enlisting the consultant to "fix" that player. A family therapy model of meeting with each party, observing their interactions, and working with the two of them conjointly, if possible, offers a good model and a place to start in the process of improving communications between the disparate parties. If the conflict is on a large team and involves more than a few people, then a decision will have to be made about how large the group to be worked with should be.

The third common reason for a psychiatrist to be invited to join or consult to a team is a prolonged or persistent performance problem, one that may even predate many of the players' being a part of the team (Nicholi, 1987). Teams that develop histories and patterns of losing when there is so much pressure to win will search for explanations and solutions in the less obvious places. Again, this is quite a bit like the treatment-resistant patient, where everything else has been tried and failed. The good news in this situation is that if the other things have not worked, by a process of elimination—or a diagnosis of exclusion—it very well may be a psychological problem, in good part, that is holding the team back. Obviously, there may be some overlapping of reasons why the consultant is initially being contacted.

The consultation/liaison model immediately sets up all kinds of power relationships and potential problems. The player identified as having a problem—or by inference, *being* one—may display various forms of resistance to meeting with a psychiatrist. He or she may be angry and resent the implication that there is anything wrong with him or her. Further, the psychiatrist will be perceived as having influence with coaches or management, even to the point of being accused of being a conduit of information—or a "spy"—of the coaching staff. In fact, it should be an openly agreed-upon function that the consultant will supply some general information and observations with the coaching staff and management, with the explanation that it is part of his or her job. Players will need to be convinced, however, that specific, detailed, and personal information will not be shared without their informed consent. Nonetheless, only with experience will the players trust the psychiatrist.

In certain instances, just as in the hospital setting, a person's resistance may be so high as to render the consultant powerless to work with the individual. The consultant can still improve the team's ability to deal with the identified "patient," however, by working with the staff and other team members. This work involves educating them in general terms about what appears to be the nature of the problem and by discussing the issues that it raises and helping them figure out effective ways of dealing with the athlete. For example, a broad discussion of personality types, coping mechanisms, or the different manifestations of anxiety or depression and how different people might respond to different interpersonal approaches would be a natural part of the liaison work, without betraying any confidentiality.

One remaining drawback is that, as readily applicable as this model is, it must be "sold" to the team. As a performance-driven organization, the team, or those in charge of the team, must be convinced that paying attention to the principals of mental health and human relationships will improve an individual's ability to perform athletically and that this will in turn help the team's performance. An alternative approach, and one that is favored by many sport psychologists, is convincing the same people in power that the consultant possesses special knowledge concerning human athletic performance that he or she can impart to the team in a uniquely effective manner. Ironically, the special knowledge of applied sport psychology tends to be quite generic in appearance and routinized, especially to the clinician used to working clinically with individuals or groups in psychodynamically informed ways.

TEAM-BUILDING

Chances are, the psychiatrist will be asked to assist in some fashion with team-building. Whether it is a stated objective from the outset or an issue that comes up later, the players may need to be convinced that team cohesion will be improved by taking care of the basics of human interaction and relationships. Things like establishing and maintaining trust, treating each other with respect and dignity, encouraging honest and open communication, and paying attention to boundaries, role definitions, and hierarchical structure will help the team reach toward its goals (Yalom, 1985). Just as most patients would love a magic pill that offers a quick fix to all their emotional problems, so teams would love a couple of "gimmicks" or group activities that would provide instant team-building and cohesiveness. For better or worse, teamwork, like other relationships, involves significant effort. Ingredients like the acknowledgment of common and opposing values, resolving differences while showing mutual respect, and a willingness to put aside individual differences for the good of the group do not just happen. As with most psychic events, they happen for a reason—or rather, for a number of reasons—and begin with a conscious and explicitly stated intention to do these things.

A group of children, adolescents, or young adults cannot simply be told to become a team. They need to be challenged, coerced, and cajoled into it—and shown how. They need to share more than the rigors of athletic training; they need to share something of themselves. Obviously, in many situations it simply does not happen. The group never becomes a team and never functions in a coordinated manner in the pursuit of any common goal. The relationships between team members never develop to the point where they cohere. Accordingly, effective coaches and other team leaders are those who can get people to come together.

Interestingly, groups that have developed this quality of actually being a good team and of working well together may not appreciate what they have or have done in order to achieve their success. Successful teams of all kinds can lose their edge over the competition quickly and easily—at times abruptly—as a result of a seemingly insignificant act or event. Other times, individual egos take precedence over team goals, and the team quickly disintegrates before people's watchful eyes.

As an example, one quite successful youth baseball team made up of an assortment of talents, personalities, and social backgrounds, had been playing together for a number of years. By the time they reached the high-school level they were comfortable with each other and had clearly established roles, positions, and identities. Their individual differences, while significant, were well known to each other and tolerated. They played hard and well together and often beat more talented teams. During one season, they became attached to and identified with a coach who appreciated them, accepted their differences, and had fun with them. When school authorities gave the varsity-coaching job to someone else on the basis of better credentials instead of moving the coach up with this group of ballplayers, the team failed miserably. Captains and other leading players quit, morale sank, and the team never came close to realizing its potential. This breakdown was the result of an administrative failure to recognize the dynamics of the team, the near-term detrimental effects on the current players, and the strength of conviction and power of the players to determine their own performance and fate. Limited attempts were made at counseling the disappointed players to remain with the team and to give the chosen coach a chance, but these were unsuccessful. In essence, the school administration sacrificed the present team for what they perceived as a more promising future with the new coach. Unfortunately for the affected players, as is typically the case, there was no second chance for their team.

The success of a team of individuals is typically a fragile and tenuous thing that comes under attack from a multitude of directions. It may appear impressively strong and easy to the casual observer, but for those who have participated on teams that have been asked to perform at the highest level it is clear that it is a difficult undertaking. If it were easy, more teams would be performing well. In contrast, it is easy to find poorly performing teams and to point out potential reasons for their lack of success. As a result, many people involved with teams will be inclined to take team-building lightly and not give it the attention it deserves. As one consultant put it, "If you are serious about team-building, treat it seriously." In other words, allocate time for it and put it on the agenda and in people's minds.

MANAGING TEAM TRANSITIONS

Team maintenance is particularly important during periods of transition, which may also threaten or obstruct the liaison. The psychiatrist can identify problems in the areas of team cohesion, communication, and collaboration and should be able to suggest various ways of maintaining team functioning. Regularly scheduled and crisis-generated group meetings, where feelings and ideas can be shared and where problems facing the team are reviewed and plans are made to address them, are two important approaches.

As mentioned previously, a major drawback to the application of the C/L psychiatry model is that the primary goal of the sports team is not to promote the health and fitness of the athletes. Instead, its priority is to win and to promote the well-being of the sports organization whose motives may be at odds with the athletes who are performing and competing. A multitude of competing interests may come into play. While it is feasible that the two will go together, at times the well-being of the organization may not be based primarily on winning. Financial concerns and power relationships may take center stage in the organizational concerns, a situation that is extremely difficult for players and others on the team and outside of it to understand and accept. It is in these instances in particular that a psychiatrist's services can be most useful. By facilitating discussion and the expression of different viewpoints while managing the process to keep it constructive, the psychiatrist can be very helpful in transitional periods. Such problems are especially frustrating because for most of the people involved there is often such limited control over them. The psychiatrist can help to direct people's efforts toward coming up with solutions to problems and to accept the decisions that are beyond their ability to change.

With some forethought a psychiatrist can become involved with the team before a crisis situation develops, and with a little more forethought a consultant can become known to the team members well in advance of the transitional process. In all cases, having a pre-existing relationship with team members will greatly enhance the consultant's effectiveness.

Of course, the consultant is also vulnerable, as are the other team members, players, and staff, during these transitions. With shifts in power the psychiatrist is in a position where he can easily become the scapegoat or be eliminated or replaced. One consultant, who had been working effectively with a team for some time, found himself blamed for the team's lack of aggressiveness when it encountered an uncharacteristic losing streak. He was unceremoniously terminated, even though there were numerous other factors in the team's performance decline. The move clearly reflected the coach's own personal bias against psychiatry. With this added factor—the generalized bias against psychiatry—there are probably few positions anywhere on the team that are as vulnerable as the team psychiatrist. The consultant must then be prepared for the worst, be secure in his or her beliefs and approach, and see these situations as opportunities to model appropriate coping behavior. In many ways the psychiatrist is placed in the same situation as the players, and coaches for that matter, all of whose jobs are on the line based on the team's performance and in any evaluation process little else may matter. They can be cut or released after a disappointing half-season. Sport, especially at the more elite and professional levels, can be cutthroat and ruthless in this way and individuals are often in need of support and therapeutic contact.

ENGAGING THE TEAM

How does a consultant engage a team? How does one individual develop that relationship? These are the challenges to any psychiatrist interested in attempting such work. While there is no singular answer, no specific prescribed or preferred approach, there are some important and helpful guidelines. The first ones to consider are those of professional conduct and ethical behavior. Responsible ethical behavior kept within the confines of the consultant's defined role, along with accountability and availability are essential. These are the same qualities that are desired in C/L psychiatrists in other settings.

Trust is especially important in working with athletes and it is enhanced by either having been a player in the sport or by demonstrating an intimate knowledge of the game. It is possible to engage a team without a strong working knowledge of the game, but it is considerably more difficult and will require the consultant's willingness to learn from the team, and quickly. There are many former players who have become successful coaches, as well as failed coaches who never played the game. Knowledge of the game or a lack thereof can determine whether or not an individual will be able to engage the team. Beyond demonstrating sufficient knowledge of the game, the psychiatrist and other team members will have to convey their trustworthiness to each other over time. Between players, this process of developing trust can take place interpersonally, athletically, or both. Some athletes will only be able to express their trustworthiness to their teammates within the athletic arena. In other words, they can be trusted to perform their roles on the field and to do what they are supposed to do athletically. There are innumerable opportunities for athletes to display that they can be trusted on the playing field. In some instances, it may be enough for them to be where they are supposed to be and do what they are supposed to do during games. More often, these behaviors will need to be supplemented by interpersonal actions and communications that reinforce trust around other issues. The consultant does not have the option of showing that he or she is trustworthy in the athletic realm. A consistent personality and approach displayed by a consultant, or any other team member for that matter, which leads to a predictability of behavior along with clarity of vision, will also promote trust. The same is true for the team leaders. If trust can be developed on a personal level, it is easier to extend it to the playing field, rather than the other way around.

Communication is another major challenge to teams and the ability to communicate effectively is invaluable. Since it is impossible to communicate with all members of the team perfectly and achieve uniform understanding, it is safest to assume that communication has been imperfect and insufficient at any given time. This assumption creates the routine task of trying to determine and correct misunderstandings or misinformation. Even in the relatively rare instance when the consultant may be able to address the entire team at one time, individuals' attention to and understanding of what the consultant may say will vary greatly. On top of the cognitive or intellectual differences, more active distortion will also occur with the listener hearing what he or she wants to hear. Athletes are prone to subtly altering what has been said in a way that will benefit the listener or reinforce his or her view of the world. Many times these distortions go undetected for quite some time before they are discovered, and only then can they be corrected. These are thoughts that athletes will tend to keep to themselves and only reveal under duress or in stressful circumstances when conflict may arise, sometimes for unclear reasons. To combat this natural process the consultant must make the communication of his or her role, knowledge base, and philosophical orientation a priority.

As mentioned previously, communication or the failure thereof within an organization is a common reason for a consultant to be hired in the first place. The failure of leadership to effectively communicate the vision for the organization and keep people on task can render the group as a whole ineffective. Leaders who perceive themselves as great communicators are not always. Ideally there will be built-in mechanisms and set times for two-way communication between team members and team leaders. Whether the majority of the time spent on communication is in the form of regularly scheduled meetings or informal, impromptu gatherings is more a matter of personal style and preference. If left to a more spontaneous or casual approach, however, the risk is letting it go, especially under the stressful conditions of a season of competition, or neglecting it for some reason and never spending as much time as intended or as is needed. In most instances, then, specific meeting times dedicated to team interaction will serve the team the best. Canceling these scheduled meetings during the heat of a competitive season will severely undermine their purpose, sending the message that they are not really that important. In fact, this is when they are most important and will have the most impact.

Leadership sets the tone for the communication within the group. If group leaders are open, encouraging communication, then chances are great that the team will behave in this manner also. On the other hand, if leaders are not, and they directly or indirectly discourage verbalization, self-disclosure, and the sharing of knowledge and emotions, then others on the team will be much less likely to do so. The psychiatric consultant can be a role model in this regard, modeling appropriate types or reasonable amounts of communication. The consultant will also have the opportunity to observe the coaches' styles of communication, and if an adequate relationship has been established with them, he or she may be able to offer constructive criticism.

At the more competitive levels of team play, a more authoritarian type of communication between coaches and players may have its advantages because of the nature of working with stronger, more firmly established personalities. In general, however, people in all teams need to feel that they can talk to each other, both to their peers and to their superiors.

They will benefit from an organizational structure with the lines of authority and communication clearly drawn and reinforced by the interactions that take place. Any functional group also needs the essential provision for feedback or two-way communication. In other words, individuals on the lower end of the totem pole must have a way to communicate to those higher up. By having access to leadership or management, and if treated with respect and dignity in the process, all members of the team can feel that they are a significant part of the organization and that they have an influence over their own destiny and that of the group. They are empowered and feel a sense of control that they would not otherwise. The days of blind obedience and deference to elders and authority figures appear to be long gone in sport, as elsewhere.

At all levels of competition and for a variety of different reasons, a more process-oriented, humanistic approach has its advantages. For youth and beginner sports, for example, an approach that encourages participation and enjoyment over winning, rewards effort over skill, and takes into account what the players' goals are is more likely to keep athletes involved and participating and will allow for their maximal motor skill development. As time goes on and with advancing skill level, more critical input is probably optimal with detailed and specific technical instruction required to progress. Efforts to keep the tone of the instruction constructive and positive will also allow it to be better received.

It is important to remember that team members' motivations are complex and change at the different levels of competition. While a benign presence is required to keep younger and less adept players involved long enough to develop a love for the game and to raise their basic skill levels, a more challenging coach will be necessary to help an athlete transcend his or her current ability. Obviously, different people are motivated differently, but the psychiatrist who realizes this and who can put these principles into practice and educate others involved with the team will be very helpful. In other words, the psychiatrist who can help discern what motivates individual athletes or groups of athletes on a team and explain these things to those running the team will be adding value and will have a much better chance of being successful.

OBSTACLES TO SUCCESSFUL CONSULTATION

The C/L psychiatry model is ultimately based on the shared goal of promoting patients' health within a multidisciplinary treatment setting. If sport teams do not share that fundamental goal or at least consider it to be a primary value, there will be resistance to the model. Presumably, there will be some agreement with the basic tenet that a healthier athlete is going to perform better for the team and forward the organization's image. At the very least, the psychiatrist consulting to a team will do well to realize that the team's commitment to health matters may be quite tenuous, and even quite weak at times, competing with other priorities such as winning, profitability, or other political issues.

Other obstacles include the various forms of bias against psychiatry. Some teams will say that they are not in the "baby-sitting" or "hand-holding" business, which can be another way of denigrating the people who suffer from mental disorders and the professionals who take care of them. Psychiatrists may be viewed with ignorance, indifference, or antipathy. Their work may be viewed as worthless or of limited value. Worse yet, there may be outright opposition, suspicion, and fear. The important thing for the consultant to remain cognizant of is that ultimately these attitudes are defensive and based upon individuals' fears about their own mental health. With this in mind he or she can listen to the concerns that are raised with empathy and try to dispel them without taking them personally or becoming defensive.

On the other end of the spectrum, expectations of what the consultant can do may be excessive or overly ambitious. Just as the failure of any staff member to define reasonable expectations can lead to staff morale problems, if the expectations of what the consultant can do are not properly formulated and managed, disappointment and frustration can ensue and threaten the survival of the relationship. While each consultant may have his or her own ideas about what is reasonable, basic conditions such as hours and pay and availability outside of normal working hours are best made explicit and negotiated at the outset (Calhoun, Ogilvie, Hendrickson, & Fritz, 1998). As mentioned previously, the better formulated the consultant's approach and intervention are, the greater the chances of success. Again, the team may not know exactly why they need the consultant or what they want him or her to do. Helping the team articulate their needs and objectives and coordinating them with the skills and abilities of the consultant will help to minimize this obstacle.

More generally, setting the expectation of specific performance gains of either the team as a whole or of individual players are probably best avoided. While it would be undesirable to completely separate the consultant's performance from that of the team, the factors involved in improving performance are so varied and complicated that it, in itself, becomes very difficult to predict. The area of "performance enhancement," as coined by sport psychologists, is probably the most problematic. Teams may have a difficult time grasping the concept that as psychiatrists, performance enhancement is something that we practice with each and every one of our patients. In our psychotherapy and other work, we are constantly striving to help our patients reach their potential. In team sports, the situations are somewhat different but not totally unique. Team performance requires individuals to know and perform their individual roles or positions well. In addition, the team's performance will be enhanced by teamwork based on high levels of commitment, trust, self-sacrifice, and free communication. Identifying these factors is not the difficult part. The challenge is convincing people to do them when they are otherwise not so inclined. Actually, this task involves engaging them in the group process and facilitating some internal change, which psychiatrists are well qualified to do.

In most instances, the effectiveness of the consultant will be best evaluated along several dimensions. The first dimension would be the fundamentals, as defined by parameters such as timeliness, responsiveness, conscientiousness, and overall handling of responsibility. The second aspect would be professional behavior within the context of the sport and the team. Working with the team will at times be considerably less formal than in a hospital or office setting (Begel, 1992). The consultant should, nonetheless, follow standards of professional and ethical behavior. The third dimension to be kept in mind is the quality of the relationships established with the team and the individual players and staff. It is these relationships that ultimately "work" or "do not work" and may matter more than any concrete information provided by the consultant.

Finally, an obstacle to the psychiatric consultant is the fact that he or she will be forced, at times, to identify closely with the athletes. A good example of this is during contract negotiations. The consultant may quickly learn how it feels to be in a position of limited power. The emotional impact of the negotiating process on players is extremely important for the consultant, and ultimately for the team, to understand. Relationships are made secure or undermined at these times. It is during this process that the player learns how much, or how little, he or she is valued by the people in charge of the team. It is a relative valuation, with only a minor connection to the usual value of money. The player learns how he or she compares to his or her peers, teammates, and opponents. In addition, he or she is inevitably subjected to the denigrating effect of learning that winning games is ultimately more important to a team than trying to make people feel better or furthering their education, growth, or development as a person. And when, once again, compared to the medical setting, winning is more important than limiting human suffering. These are the realities of being a professional athlete, but the same applies to many other elite athletes as well. There is a regular cycle of evaluation, with concrete evidence of one's worth offered at intervals of contract length. In addition, there are more subtle communications about one's worth that eventually give rise to the commonly heard comments that the sport in question is "a business" and that athletes feel that they are just "meat" or "hired help." These also form the basis for the animosity displayed during the labor disputes in professional leagues and subsequent player strikes or boycotts and owner lockouts.

These are aspects that most fans of the games do not appreciate because they are so removed from the world of being an elite athlete. Fans cannot see beyond the fact that the players, coaches, and owners all make a lot of money. Because of that, they feel that they should have no complaints about their working conditions. But every occupation has its own methods of determining relative value and these things are well known to athletes. Awards and nonpecuniary means of recognition account for something, more to some athletes than others, but the money one is paid makes it simple and straightforward. And the process of determining compensation is often dehumanizing. Both sides in a negotiation process are usually guilty of overstating their cases, with the athlete getting caught in the middle, not knowing who to believe, and ultimately concluding that he or she cannot believe either. It takes an extremely stable individual to go through such a process without being changed in some way.

In spite of these times when the consultant will be forced to identify with players, it is important for him or her to keep a neutral stance that allows for objectivity and to maintain an alliance with all parties. If the consultant can remain mindful of all of these potential pitfalls, keep one eye on his or her own performance and the other on the lookout for pathology, and be effective as a teacher and communicator, then he or she has a chance to help the team.

CONCLUSION

While psychiatrists are trained and educated in areas that prepare them to be effective consultants to sport teams, they are not often asked to do so. Only on occasion has this occurred. The reasons for the infrequency of this type of work being available to psychiatrists are many-faceted. From the societal bias against psychiatry in general to the athletes' tendency not to ask for psychological help, formidable resistance exists. In addition, there are a number of other obstacles to overcome in order to be effective doing this type of work. Only after a number of psychiatrists have successfully consulted to athletic teams, shared their experiences, learned from each other, and communicated among themselves and with other disciplines about their experiences will it become a more common practice.

Interestingly, psychiatrists as a group frequently work in multidisciplinary settings and find themselves members of a team. As such, they are often charged with the responsibility of understanding and maintaining the group dynamics of that team just as they would in the sport setting. Perhaps because as physicians they are frequently given status as the leader of the teams in these other settings they are not as inclined to consult to a sports team. There they would not necessarily be the leader or one of the leaders. In fact, for some time the consultant will actually be an outsider, and only become accepted as a team member after establishing a working relationship with the team.

An additional reason for the relative absence of psychiatrists in this type of work may be that psychiatrists have not typically been very organized or vocal about their interest in working with sports teams. Only recently has there been a specialized society (The International Society for Sport Psychiatry) in existence to study and share psychiatrists' experience working with athletes. While the American Psychological Association established a division of its organization for sport psychologists, the American Psychiatric Association has no comparable entity or avenue to support the study and practice of sport psychiatry. Apparently, the rationale has been that athletes are too narrow of a subgroup to dedicate the resources to, or that there has not been justification for a separate area of inquiry and practice. Hopefully with the publication of this volume and the ever-expanding world of sport and athletics there will soon be sufficient cause to do so. It would greatly benefit the field if there were a comparable entity within the structure of the psychiatric association.

REFERENCES

Begel, D. (1992). An overview of sport psychiatry. *American Journal of Psychiatry, 149*, 606–614.

Calhoun, J. W., Ogilvie, B. C., Hendrickson, T. P., & Fritz, G. K. (1998). The psychiatric consultant in professional team sports. In I. Tofler (Guest Ed.), *Child and adolescent psychiatric clinics of North America: Sports psychiatry* (Vol. 7, No. 4). Philadelphia: Saunders.

Feldman, L. (1991, July 7). Strikeouts and psych-outs. *The New York Times Magazine*, pp.10–13, 27, 30, 33.

Lipowski, Z. J. (1974). Consultation-liaison psychiatry: An overview. *American Journal of Psychiatry*, *131*, 623–630.

McKegney, F. P. (1985). Consultation-liaison psychiatry. In H. I. Kaplan & B. J. Sadock (Eds.), *Comprehensive textbook of psychiatry* (4th ed., pp. 1219–1223). Baltimore, MD: Williams & Wilkins.

Nicholi, A. M. (1987). Occasional notes: Psychiatric consultation in professional football. *New England Journal of Medicine*, *316*, 1095–1100.

Yalom, I. D. (1985). *The theory and practice of group psychotherapy* (3rd ed., pp. 299–311). New York: Basic.

13

Psychopharmacology in Athletes

Antonia L. Baum

THE USE OF PSYCHOTROPIC DRUGS in athletes is a largely unexamined area. On occasion, the prescription of medication becomes necessary. When prescribing medications for athletes, it is important to consider the physiological changes that take place during physical effort. Exercise is associated with increases in plasma adrenaline and noradrenaline, and an increase in heart rate of up to 180 beats/minute (Taggart, Parkinson, & Carruthers, 1972). Athletes may metabolize drugs differently during exertion than at rest. The increase in cardiac output and VO_2 max during exercise may affect the metabolism of certain medications. Fluid loss associated with exercise can also influence drug levels.

A number of substances, some of them prescription drugs, are banned at various levels of athletic competition. This is a factor that needs to be taken into consideration when choosing a medication for an athlete. Nearly all psychotropic medications—along with skeletal muscle relaxants, antiemetics, and sedating antihistamines—are banned by the United States Olympic Committee (USOC) for the two sports involving riflery, the modern pentathlon and the biathlon. Still others are also banned by the National Collegiate Athletic Association (NCAA) (Fuentes, Rosenberg, & Davis, 1995). This creates an ethical dilemma when a drug deemed necessary by a physician is not allowable in the athletic arena. Although this is a potentially discriminatory practice that merits attention, athletes are making a choice to compete and must conform to regulations designed to preserve fair competition. A great deal more work needs to be done to further our understanding of any potential ergogenic aspects of psychotropic drugs.

ATHLETES AND PSYCHIATRIC ILLNESS

There are many indications for psychotropic drug use in athletes. Contrary to the mythic ideal that athletes are not only of sound body, but also of sound mind, athletes are susceptible to psychiatric illness. (For a more in-depth discussion of psychiatric illness in athletes, see chapter 4.) Some sports may engender psychiatric problems. Eating disorders are particularly prevalent in aesthetic sports (dance, gymnastics), sports in which low body fat is advantageous (running, swimming), and sports in which the athlete is required to "make weight" for competition (wrestling, horse racing). Antidepressants may be used for either the comorbid depression so frequently encountered in patients with eating disorders, or to decrease the frequency of bingeing and purging episodes in bulimics. Neuroleptics are occasionally used in patients with eating disorders who may have either psychotic thought processes or significant anxiety.

Muscle dysmorphia, a variant of body dysmorphic disorder, recently described by Pope, Gruber, Choi, Olivardia, and Philips (1997) is an unhealthy preoccupation with being muscular. This disorder is most often seen in body-builders and weight-lifters, and can be treated with serotonergic antidepressants, in antiobsessional dosages. This patient population is susceptible to anabolic steroid abuse. Athletes from a number of sports (e.g., football, weight-lifting) who do not necessarily meet criteria for muscle dysmorphia, may also have a tendency to abuse anabolic steroids. The psychiatric sequelae of anabolic steroid abuse (depression, psychosis) may require treatment with antidepressants or antipsychotics.

Depression is not uncommon in the general population, and athletes are not immune to this illness. Some aspects of life in the athletic arena may actually contribute to the development of depression. When a childhood characterized by sacrifice does not result in stardom, depression may follow. The vagaries of injury—postponing or ending an athlete's career—can also cause substantial mood disturbances. The usually short-lived careers of professional athletes, with little preparation for retirement, can result in depression. When the symptoms of depression are marked, antidepressant medication or possibly a mood stabilizer may be required.

Other uses for antidepressant medications in athletes have been identified. A review article on the treatment of headaches in athletes concluded that for the prophylaxis of chronic, recurrent tension headaches in athletes, the preferred treatment is a tricyclic antidepressant like nortriptyline, or a serotonin specific reuptake inhibitor (SSRI), and that for the prophylaxis of migraines in athletes, optimal treatment might include either an antidepressant or valproic acid (VPA) (Swain & Kaplan, 1997).

Anxiety disorders are not unknown to athletes, so anxiolytics also need to be considered in the psychopharmacotherapeutic armamentarium for care of the athlete. Some of the pressures unique to athletes, particularly those for whom athletics is a career, may increase an athlete's susceptibility to anxiety. The enormous financial stakes and "win at all costs" mentality in today's elite athletic competitions are significant stressors. Posttraumatic stress disorder can result from the physical attacks that have occurred on athletes in an effort to eliminate the competition. The pressure of being thrust into the public eye can also create anxiety.

There may be psychiatric disorders that predispose one to involvement in athletics. In these cases, psychotropic medications may be indicated. Patients with attention-deficit/hyperactivity disorder often have difficulty with academic pursuits. The disorder may not interfere with athletics, so a child with ADHD may choose to spend time in sports. Success in this area may provide the positive reinforcement so often lacking in an academic setting. Among professional athletes, one might find a larger than expected number of players with adult ADHD. Psychostimulants may be very helpful to the athlete with ADHD. This may present an ethical problem for coaches, psychiatrists, and athletic administrators. Because it is considered a drug with the potential for performance enhancement, methylphenidate is banned by both the USOC and the NCAA (Fuentes et al., 1995).

PSYCHOTROPIC DRUGS IN ATHLETES

There are no double-blind studies exploring the pharmacologic treatment of athletes with psychiatric problems, much less sound epidemiologic studies of the incidence of psychopathology in this patient population.

The following is a brief overview of what is currently being prescribed for the psychiatric treatment of athletes. Although limited in its scope, the discussion—and the study (Baum, 1999) on which it is based—open the door to further exploration of this field.

To learn more about the prescribing practices of psychiatrists who treat athletes, the members of the International Society for Sport Psychiatry (ISSP) were surveyed. There was a 25% response rate to the questionnaires, which were sent out in two mailings approximately six months apart. The results were based on a total of 19 responses, with the geographic distribution of participants being 84% from the continental United States, and 5% from each of Puerto Rico, Egypt, and Croatia.

A caveat in the interpretation of these results needs first to address the low total number of respondents, as well as the relatively low response rate. Though all psychiatrists who are a part of the ISSP are interested in the psychiatric treatment of athletes, not all members have necessarily had the opportunity to treat this population. This owes in part to the difficulty in identifying this select group of patients, both because of a lack of recognition of psychopathology in athletes, and because of substantial resistance. This resistance comes not only from the athletes themselves, but also from their coaches, families, sports organizations, business managers, and the media.

Athletes in treatment covered the gamut of sports (figure 13.1). Just 11% of the respondents specified that they were treating elite athletes, consisting of professional baseball and football players. These two sports were also the most heavily represented in general, with 47% reporting that they have treated baseball and football players. Other sports represented included gymnastics (26%), basketball and swimming (each 21%), running or track and field (16%), marathon racing, golf, soccer, handball, weightlifting, tennis, and volleyball (each 11%), and ski jumping, sailing, fencing, boxing, ice skating, and cross-country running (each 5%).

Side Effects

The first survey question addressed the side effects each psychiatrist was most likely to try to avoid when using psychotropic drugs with patient athletes (figure 13.2). Sedation was the side effect most widely avoided; it was cited by 84% of respondents. Clearly, sedation during an athletic contest is contraindicated, both for safety and efficacy. Logically, extrapyramidal side effects (EPS) were viewed as undesirable by 68%, with tremor following closely behind at 58%. Any movement disorder is going

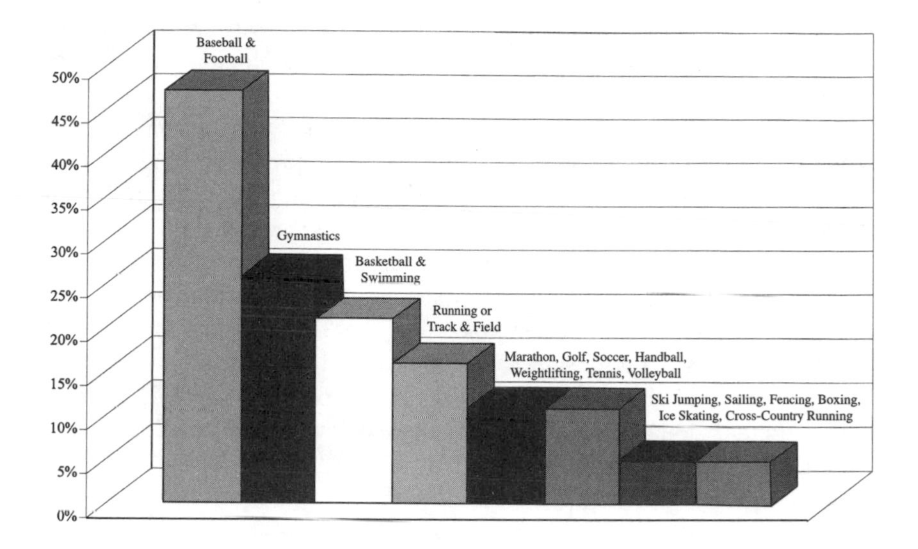

Figure 13.1 Sports.

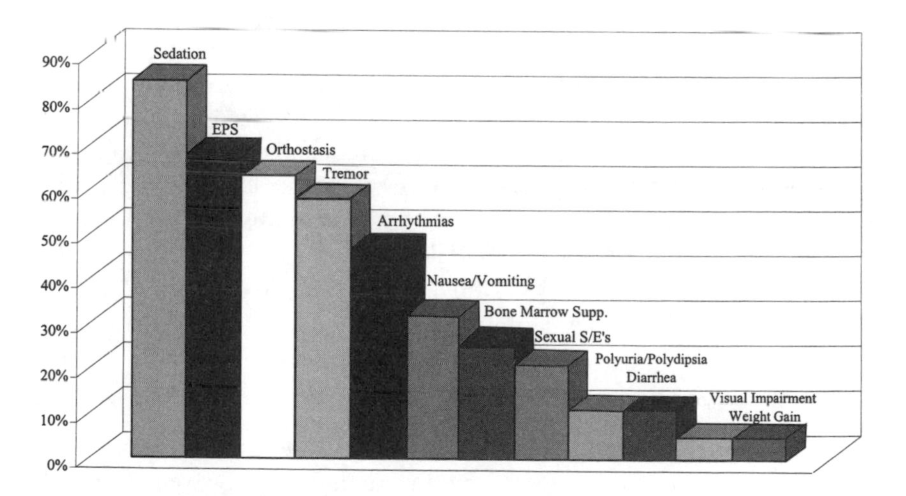

Figure 13.2 Side effects.

to interfere with athletic prowess. Arrythmias were felt to be a concern by 47% of those surveyed. Cardiac side effects while using medication in athletes are perhaps the most acute clinical factors to be considered, and ones about which we know remarkably little, particularly with respect to psychotropic medications.

Other side effects that sport psychiatrists avoid included nausea and vomiting (32% of respondents), bone marrow suppression (26%), sexual side effects (21%), diarrhea and polyuria/polydipsia (each 11%), followed by visual impairment and weight gain (each 5%). Sexual side effects are likely a significant side effect to be avoided in athletes. Athletes are generally physically healthy and possibly somewhat younger than nonathletes on psychotropic medications, and they may therefore be more vocal about these symptoms. That a side effect like visual impairment is cited so infrequently is likely a reflection of the fact that psychotropic drugs with this particular side effect are probably not extensively used in this patient population.

Antidepressants

According to the survey, the most widely used antidepressant in athletes is fluoxetine (63%) (figure 13.3). A fairly distant second is sertraline (37%), followed by venlafaxine (21%), SSRIs in general (16%), bupropion (11%), nefazodone, fluvoxamine, paroxetine, and clomipramine (each 5%). Fluoxetine was favored because it is nonsedating, and is in fact activating, because it does not cause weight gain, and because it is an effective and generally well-tolerated antidepressant. It is likely, too, that the more familiar and experienced a clinician is with a particular medication, the more likely he or she is to use it in a specialized population.

The tricyclic antidepressants are the most frequently avoided in athletes (63% of respondents), with reasons cited as sedation, anticholinergic side effects, cardiac side effects, tremor, weight gain and orthostasis. Monoamine oxidase inhibitors are also less desirable in athletes (21%) because of the dietary constraints and sedation. The SSRIs are avoided by 5% of respondents because of anorgasmia.

Mood Stabilizers

Among the mood stabilizers in the treatment of athletes, valproic acid (VPA) is used most often (58%) because it is generally well tolerated (figure 13.4). Specifically, VPA does not raise the concern of alteration

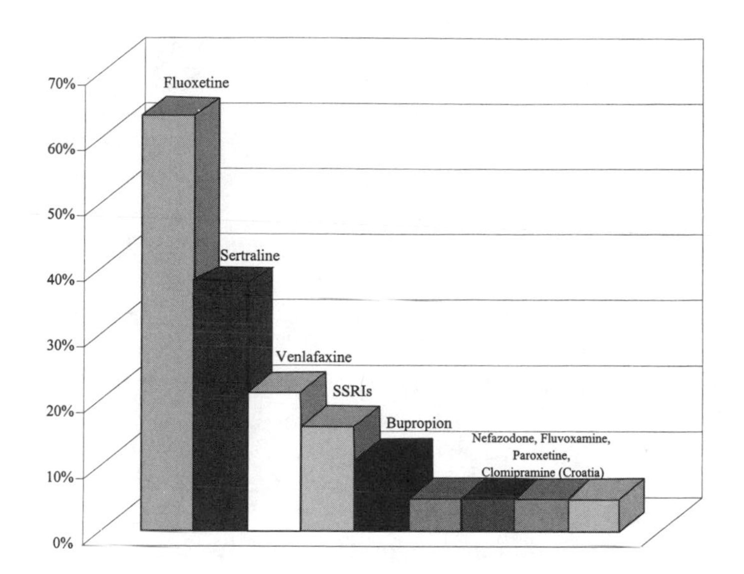

Figure 13.3 Antidepressants.

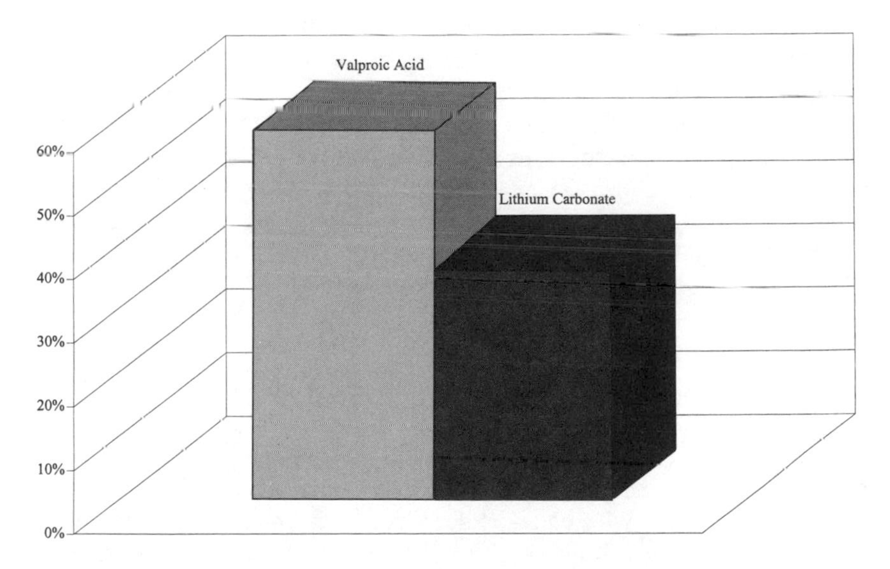

Figure 13.4 Mood stabilizers.

in drug levels with dehydration, and it is less sedating, less likely to cause tremor and weight gain, and requires less laboratory work than lithium carbonate. Lithium was avoided by 53% of psychiatrists in the treatment of athletes, because of additional concerns including electrolyte imbalance, polyuria/polydipsia, and cardiac, renal, and gastrointestinal side effects. Also cited was the relative contraindication of concomitant use of nonsteroidal antiinflammatories, a factor that can be particularly problematic in an athlete with frequent musculoskeletal injuries. Twenty-one percent of respondents also avoided the use of carbamazepine in athletes due to concerns with ataxia and hepatic impairment.

In one case, a marathon runner taking lithium was experiencing difficulty with polyuria, a symptom that was bothersome during his training runs and frankly detrimental to his races. Having taken his lithium in divided doses, the patient consolidated his daily lithium to one bedtime dose. This change in dose schedule reduced the polyuria. In addition, this patient opted to hold his lithium on the eve of the race, to good effect. It has been demonstrated that once-daily dosing of lithium and/or a reduction in the total dose will result in lower urine volumes (Bowen, Grof, & Grof, 1991).

A common misconception is that the dehydration associated with strenuous exercise will result in an increase in lithium levels with the risk of lithium toxicity. However, one study of four healthy volunteer subjects (Jefferson et al., 1982) and a subsequent case report of a bipolar subject (Norman, Mathews, & Yohe, 1987) revealed the opposite finding, a lowering of the lithium level. The quantity of lithium excreted in sweat appears to be signicant; the sweat-to-serum ratio of lithium was greater than that for sodium by a factor of four, hypothesized to be due to the selective conservation of sodium. Strenuous exercise may therefore be associated with a decrease in serum lithium levels, possibly necessitating an increase in lithium dose during periods of exertion.

Anxiolytics

Because of significant concerns about the sedative qualities of benzodiazepines, as well as the risk of dependence, 37% of sport psychiatrists favor the use of buspirone (figure 13.5). Other reasons cited for the general avoidance of benzodiazepines in athletes include impaired reflexes/performance, problems with balance, decreased concentration, and memory impairment. However, because of the rapid onset of action and short half-life of alprazolam, this benzodiazepine is used by 32% of those surveyed,

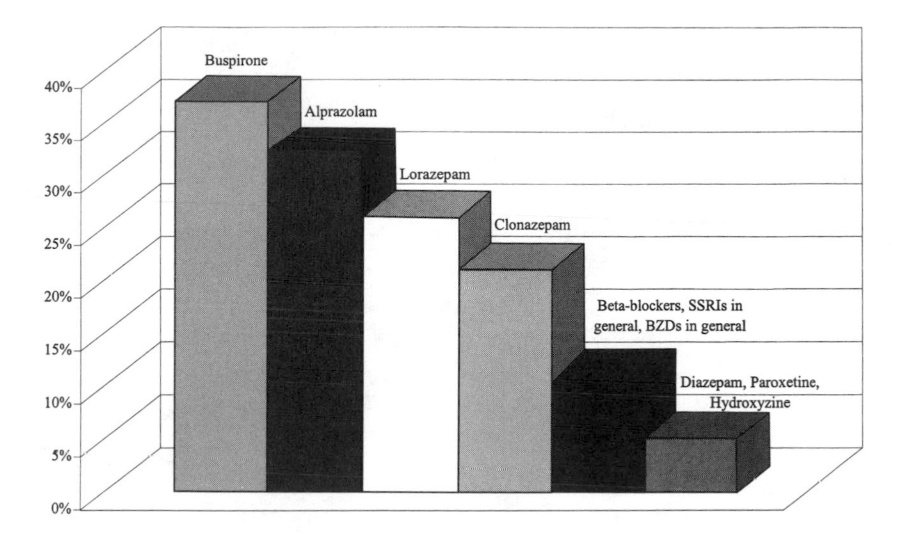

Figure 13.5 Anxiolytics.

followed by 26% using lorazepam for similar qualities. Conversely, 21% use clonazepam because it is long-acting and does not tend to induce euphoria. Eleven percent favor the use of beta blockers, although these are banned by the USOC and NCAA in particular sports, including riflery, archery, the biathlon, skijumping, and luge because of their potential for performance enhancement (Fuentes et al., 1995).

Neuroleptics

The atypical antipsychotics are the most widely used by sport psychiatrists in the treatment of athletes (figure 13.6). Forty-two percent of respondents to the survey use risperidone; 32% use olanzapine. It is, however, noteworthy that when the initial questionnaires were sent to ISSP members, olanzapine was not yet on the market. Both of these atypical neuroleptics are used because they are nonsedating and because of their decreased tendency to cause extrapyramidal side effects. Sixteen percent of those responding to the survey reported use of atypical neuroleptics in general, in an athletic patient population. Haloperidol and trifluoperazine are used by fewer practitioners (each 11%), and in each case are chosen by virtue of the prescriber's familiarity with these drugs.

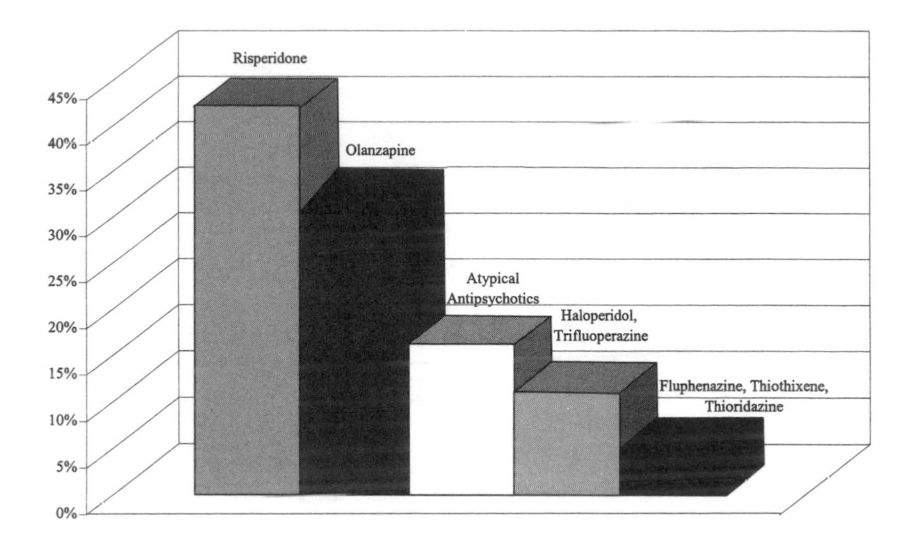

Figure 13.6 Neuroleptics.

Twenty-one percent of those surveyed identified low-potency neuroleptics in general, and another 21% identified chlorpromazine in particular, as antipsychotics to avoid in the treatment of athletes. The clinical concerns are sedation, anticholinergic and antihistaminic effects, orthostasis, and impaired coordination. Another 21% choose not to use haloperidol because of extrapyramidal side effects and the possibility of weight gain.

One patient with a new diagnosis of bipolar affective illness had been prescribed valproic acid and a low-dose neuroleptic, both for mood stabilization. She was a young woman for whom daily exercise and weight training were central to her sense of herself. This medication combination resulted in such significant fatigue, as well as a rapid 10-pound weight gain, that she was unable to sustain her daily exercise routine. This was highly distressing to the patient. Discontinuation of her neuroleptic resulted in improved energy and weight loss, enabling her to return to her workouts.

FUTURE RESEARCH

There is a need to establish sound psychopharmacological practices for treating athletes. This requires a psychoeducational effort to promote awareness of psychiatric problems in the athletic arena so that more effective research can be carried out. Such research must include:

- psychopharmacological drug trials on athletes
- a study of drug metabolism using athletes and nonathlete controls during exercise and rest
- exploration of the side effects relevant to athletes

The design of drugs, taking into account their pharmacokinetics and side-effect profiles, can be undertaken with use by athletes in mind. This endeavor might ultimately lead to an improved product.

A review of currently banned drugs in athletic competition is also in order. These potentially discriminatory practices should be reconsidered. It will be important to be aware of special cases and maintain an open mind. Ideally, there should be the possibility of an individual review of cases, rendering it possible for athletes with any conceivable diagnosis, on medication, to be considered for participation.

REFERENCES

Baum, A. L. (1999). *The psychopharmacologic treatment of athletes*. Manuscript in preparation.

Bowen, R. C., Grof, P., & Grof, E. (1991). Less frequent lithium administration and lower urine volume. *American Journal of Psychiatry, 148,* 189–192.

Fuentes, R. J., Rosenberg, J. M., & Davis, A. (Eds.). (1995). *Athletic drug reference '95*. Research Triangle Park, NC: Clean Data.

Jefferson, J. W., Greist, J. H., Clagnaz, P. J., Eischens, R. R., Marten, W. C., & Evenson, M. A. (1982). Effect of strenuous exercise on serum lithium levels in man. *American Journal of Psychiatry, 139*, 1593–1595.

Norman, T. C., Mathews, W., & Yohe, C. D. (1987). A case study on the effects of strenuous exercise on serum lithium levels. *Nebraska Medical Journal, 72,* 224–225.

Pope, H. G., Jr., Gruber, A. J., Choi, P., Olivardia, R., & Philips, T. E. (1987). Muscle dysmorphia: An underrecognized form of body dysmorphic disorder. *Psychosomatics, 38,* 548–557.

Swain, R. A., & Kaplan, B. (1997). Diagnosis, prophylaxis, and treatment of headaches in the athlete. *Southern Medical Journal, 90,* 878–888.

Taggart, P., Parkinson, P., & Carruthers, M. (1972). Cardiac responses to thermal, physical, and emotional stress. *British Medical Journal, 71,* 71–76.

Index